Business Model Innovation in Creative and Cultural Industries

Business model innovation occurs when an organization discovers a new way of creating revenues or profits via its products or services. This book examines the concept as it applies across the creative and cultural industries in practice.

This book examines market, social, and political environments which impact creative and cultural organizations' business models, such as sustainability, new forms of competition, digitalization and data management, emerging technologies like AI, and shifting social trends and lifestyles. This book not only analyses these influences but also presents best practices, key success factors, and compelling case studies. Employing a case study format, a range of creative or cultural sectors are analysed, including fashion, architecture, and gaming.

The result is a book which delivers value for researchers, advanced students, and reflective practitioners involved in the creative economy around the world.

Pierre Roy is Associate Professor of Strategy and Management at the University of Montpellier, France.

Estelle Pellegrin-Boucher is Associate Professor of Strategy and Management at the University of Montpellier, France.

Routledge Research in the Creative and Cultural Industries
Series Editor: Ruth Rentschler

This series brings together book-length original research in cultural and creative industries from a range of perspectives. Charting developments in contemporary cultural and creative industries thinking around the world, the series aims to shape the research agenda to reflect the expanding significance of the creative sector in a globalised world.

NFTs, Creativity and the Law
Within and Beyond Copyright
Edited by Enrico Bonadio and Caterina Sganga

Craft as a Creative Industry
Karen Patel

Researching the Creative and Cultural Industries
A Guide to Qualitative Research
Simone Wesner

Gender Equality and the Cultural Economy
Comparative Perspectives
Helmut K. Anheier and Darinka Markovic, with Sofia Todd-Tombini

Cultural Politics of the Creative Industries
Phil Graham

Business Model Innovation in Creative and Cultural Industries
Edited by Pierre Roy and Estelle Pellegrin-Boucher

For more information about this series, please visit: www.routledge.com/Routledge-Research-in-the-Creative-and-Cultural-Industries/book-series/RRCCI

Business Model Innovation in Creative and Cultural Industries

Edited by
Pierre Roy and Estelle Pellegrin-Boucher

Routledge
Taylor & Francis Group
LONDON AND NEW YORK

First published 2025
by Routledge
4 Park Square, Milton Park, Abingdon, Oxon OX14 4RN

and by Routledge
605 Third Avenue, New York, NY 10158

Routledge is an imprint of the Taylor & Francis Group, an informa business

British Library Cataloguing-in-Publication Data
A catalogue record for this book is available from the British Library

Library of Congress Cataloging-in-Publication Data
Names: Roy, Pierre, 1979– editor. | Pellegrin-Boucher, Estelle, editor.
Title: Business model innovation in creative and cultural industries / edited by Pierre Roy and Estelle Pellegrin-Boucher.
Description: Abingdon, Oxon ; New York, NY : Routledge, 2025. | Series: Routledge research in the creative and cultural industries | Includes bibliographical references and index.
Identifiers: LCCN 2024028701 (print) | LCCN 2024028702 (ebook) | ISBN 9781032714424 (hardback) | ISBN 9781032714479 (paperback) | ISBN 9781032714462 (ebook)
Subjects: LCSH: Cultural industries—Technological innovations. | Business planning.
Classification: LCC HD9999.C9472 B87 2025 (print) | LCC HD9999.C9472 (ebook) | DDC 338.4/77—dc23/eng/20240712
LC record available at https://lccn.loc.gov/2024028701
LC ebook record available at https://lccn.loc.gov/2024028702

ISBN: 9781032714424 (hbk)
ISBN: 9781032714479 (pbk)
ISBN: 9781032714462 (ebk)

DOI: 10.4324/9781032714462

Typeset in Sabon
by codeMantra

Contents

Figures

Tables

About the contributors

Federica Antonaglia is Associate Professor and Head of the Marketing Department at Excelia Business School. With a PhD in management, her research deals with the professionalization processes of cultural and creative industries. She does so from a marketing perspective—the museum visitor's experience—and from the entrepreneurial perspective of orientation and business model innovation.

Arthur Caré-Famchon is Associate Professor in Management Sciences at the IAE Tours Val de Loire (University of Tours) and researcher in the VALLOREM (Val de Loire Recherche En Management) laboratory. His research focuses on innovation and sustainable business models, with a particular focus on the scaling-up of these sustainable innovations within specific industries and markets such as fashion and apparel and cinema.

Arnaud Fernandez is MSc student at Excelia Business School. His final dissertation, under the supervision of Prof. Antonaglia, is about the artification process in the wine and spirits sector. As a work-student, he is currently working for Hennessy's Marketing Division in the Visual Identity, Design, and Artistic Collaboration Department.

Romain Gandia is Associate Professor at the University Savoie Mont-Blanc. His research and teaching focus on innovation management and digital business models in cultural and creative industries. At IREGE laboratory, he co-heads a Chair in open innovation and 4.0 management.

Gaël Gueguen is Professor of Strategy and Entrepreneurship at TBS Business School (France). He holds a PhD in management and his research focuses on ecosystems. For the past 25 years, he has been studying business ecosystems as well as entrepreneurial ecosystems.

Paulina Knobloch is Media Scientist based in Sweden. She holds a BA in Media and Communication Studies from the University of Bonn and a MSc in Media Management from KTH Royal Institute of Technology in Stockholm. She currently works as a producer at a Stockholm-based film production company.

Anna Lenoir holds a Master's degree in Management of Cultural Organizations from the University of Paris Dauphine. She was assistant to the artistic directors of a major record company. She is now a freelance executive producer.

Guy Parmentier is Full Professor at Grenoble Alpes University. His research and teaching focus on creativity management and business model management in the digital age. At CERAG laboratory, he heads the ICO research team on Innovation and Organizational Complexity.

Juliette Passebois-Ducros is Professor at Bordeaux University. She has a PhD in marketing. She studies the value-creation process of museum visitor experiences and their long-term relationship development. She has published articles in French and international journals on museum visitors' immersive experiences, arts amateur communities, and cultural institutions' networking.

Estelle Pellegrin-Boucher is formerly a consultant at PwC Paris and currently an Associate Professor in Strategy and Management at the University of Montpellier.She is a member of the Montpellier Research in Management team (MRM). Her research centers on collective strategies, innovation management, and business model innovation within high-tech industries and the cultural and creative sectors, with a particular emphasis on the architecture and fashion industries.

Carole Poirel is Professor of Management Sciences at Aix-Marseille University. She teaches a socio-economic approach to the book trade and conducts research at Cret-log into distribution strategies in the cultural and creative industries.

Pierre Roy is Associate Professor in Strategy and Management at the University of Montpellier (Montpellier Management Institute) and lecturer at Sorbonne University, Paris. He is a member of the Montpellier Research in Management team (MRM). His research areas concern competitive strategies, disruption, and business model innovation in the cultural and creative industries (especially in the film, architecture, and fashion industries).

Émilie Ruiz is Associate Professor of innovation management at Savoie Mont Blanc University and a member of the Institute of Research in Management and Economics (IREGE). She is also an associate fellow at Strasbourg University (BETA). Her research, published in various journals, such as *R&D Management, Technovation,* and *European Management Journal,* focuses on open innovation, particularly with communities of innovation, organizational creativity, as well as cultural and creative industries.

Albéric Tellier is Full Professor at Paris-Dauphine University, PSL University. His field of research is the management of innovation. His works focus most notably on the configuration and workings of innovation networks, situations of technological competition, and collective strategies for innovation. He is currently working on the impact of dematerialization on the music industry and has already published articles on the adoption of open innovation practices and the formation of new business ecosystems in this industry.

1 Introduction and book overview

Estelle Pellegrin-Boucher and Pierre Roy

The cultural and creative industries (CCIs) play a central role in the functioning of modern economies, whether economically, socially, or politically. The CCI ecosystem accounted for approximately 3.95% of the value created in the European Union in 2021, employing 8 million people in 1.2 million companies that are at 99.9% small and medium-sized enterprises (source: European Commission). From a political point of view, and in a context of accelerating globalization, CCIs are an important source of soft power, helping to disseminate various cultural elements (references, values, worldviews, etc.) and showcase a nation's heritage and talents.

Beyond their economic, social, and political weight, activities linked to culture and creation are directly concerned by innovation issues. Indeed, CCIs have historically played a key role in innovation development, due to the very nature of their products/services, the creative profiles of their actors, or the technologies they use. In this way, CCIs provide a stimulating context for observing the emergence and development of different types of innovation, whether they concern the product/service, the production or distribution processes, the marketing side, the management, or the business model (BM) as a whole. We strongly believe that CCIs are a field of observation for various forms of innovation that can then spread to other industries in our contemporary economies.

In recent years, CCIs have been going through a difficult period with the 2020 pandemic. It is estimated that turnover in cultural and creative activities fell by 31% in Europe in 2020 (source: Ernst & Young). Since the end of the pandemic, cultural and creative businesses have been able to bounce back and take advantage of various types of innovation to accelerate ongoing transformations and return to their pre-pandemic performance levels. The pandemic also represented an opportunity to drive new practices linked, for example, to digitalization, the hybridization of certain offerings, and the consideration of social responsibility issues.

However, the academic world in management devotes relatively little attention to CCIs. Reasons for this certainly include the great heterogeneity of activities at the heart of CCIs, the difficulty of identifying the precise boundaries of this field, and the very high proportion of medium- and

DOI: 10.4324/9781032714462-1

small-sized companies. This relative lack of interest on the part of researchers is at the root of this collective book project, which aims to question them through the prism of business model innovations (BMIs).

Thus, this book proposes a comprehensive exploration of the main creative and cultural industries, examining them through the lens of new and innovative BMs. It encompasses the latest research in these fields and delves into the key evolutions of the environment that impact organizations' BMs, such as sustainability, new forms of competition, digitalization and data management, open innovation, and shifting social trends and lifestyles. The book not only analyses these influences but also highlights some best practices and key success factors based on compelling case studies.

Throughout the book, readers will gain a comprehensive understanding and practical guidance on the multifaceted realm of BMI. By exploring these topics and providing valuable insights, this book aims to equip readers with the necessary knowledge, tools, and inspiration to navigate the dynamic world of BMI and drive to sustainable growth within their own organizations in the specific field of CCIs. Before exploring the impact of BMI on CCIs, the following section proposes a short presentation of the main CCIs.

1 A presentation of cultural and creative industries

Different definitions of CCIs coexist in existing publications in economics, business, and social sciences in general. Several authors have tried to define the concept, the scope, and the characteristics of the CCIs. American economist Richard Caves is often referenced as the key author when it comes to define the concept of CCIs. According to this author, CCIs are industries "in which the product or service is the manifestation of the creativity or artistic abilities of an individual or a team" (Caves, 2000). Concerning the scope of the CCIs, it may vary from one source to the other, but authors and public institutions usually retain eight main CCIs (see Table 1.1).

In order to delimit the scope of CCIs, researchers working in this field have identified several characteristics common to these different industries. These include, of course, a creative or artistic dimension at the heart of the product or service design process (Caves, 2000). This creative dimension is sometimes a source of tension with the economic dimension specific to any industry. For example, CCI players are often called upon to manage the paradox between artistic intent and the economic profitability of their offering (De Bruin, 2007; Henry, 2007; Durand and Jourdan, 2012; Landoni et al., 2020). Such tensions are common in the fashion, visual arts, film, music, architecture, and publishing industries.

Secondly, some authors insist that consumers have a constant need for novelty in CCIs (Holbrock and Hirschman, 1982). We can easily illustrate this with the fashion, music, and television industries. Furthermore, CCIs are often concerned with highly unpredictable product/service demand and

Table 1.1 The main cultural and creative industries

CCIs	*Sectors and activities*	*Examples of organizations*
Architecture	Building design, interior design	Foster + Partners, Ateliers Jean Nouvel, Zaha Hadid Architects, Tadao Ando Architect & Associates
Fashion, luxury, beauty	Clothing, accessories, perfumes, cosmetics, wines	L'Oréal, Zara, Asos, Veja, Hennessy, Fenty Beauty
Heritage	Museums, monuments, galleries	Le Louvre, British Museum, Moma, Guggenheim
Advertising	Advertising and marketing companies	Publicis, WPP, JC Decaux, Omnicom group, Hakuhodo
Performing arts	Shows, theaters, concerts	Coachella, Live Nation, Cirque du Soleil, The Walt Disney Company, Royal Albert Concert Hall
Audio-visual media	Radio, TV, cinema, music, video games	Nintendo, King Digital Entertainment, Ubisoft, BBC, Warner, Netflix, Spotify, TF1, EMI
Visual arts	Plastic arts, design, photography	Christie's, Kartell, Alessi, The Conran Shop
Printed media	Press, books	Condé Nast, Penguin, Time, Hachette

performance. Films, books, and music albums are "prototypes" whose success is often unpredictable. Another source of tension within CCIs lies in the constraints on companies' access to resources. Indeed, the unpredictable performance and economic fragility of small structures often make access to resources and skills complicated (De Bruin, 2007; Rietveld, 2011).

Other characteristics shared by several CCIs include a value often revealed in experience, and the existence of institutions charged with assessing product/service quality (critics, journalists, academics delivering awards, etc.). Finally, many CCIs are concerned with a concentration of activities within geographical territories where resources and talents are plentiful (Caves, 2000; Vogel, 2011). Examples of such clusters include the concentration of film studios and activities in Hollywood, or the strong links between certain world capitals and fashion and luxury activities (Paris, Milan, New York City).

Similarities between the industries listed in Table 1.1 may sometimes be questionable but they share some patterns and characteristics, especially in terms of resources, talents, risks, and types of organizations. There are also some strong connections between many of them that reinforces their belonging to the common field of CCIs. For example, video games and cinema activities are connected through the visual effects technologies, record companies in the music industry have bonds with the performing arts sector, or visual arts and photography develop key resources that are used for the fashion and luxury businesses.

Over and above the common characteristics mentioned above, most CCIs are today facing new challenges that have their roots in technological, commercial, sociological or environmental change. Faced with these metamorphoses, a number of cultural and creative businesses have developed innovative BMs to redefine their activities and offerings and even sometimes the industry dynamics.

2 Business model innovation and CCIs

2.1 Definition of business model innovation

Various scholars have defined the BM as an architecture, statement, description, method, structural template, framework, representation, or conceptual tool (Zott et al., 2011). Generally, a BM describes how a firm generates, delivers, and captures value in its interactions within a network of stakeholders. However, various frameworks have been developed to conceptualize and organize the components of a BM. For example, Johnson et al. (2008) propose a BM that comprises a customer value proposition, a profit formula, key resources, and key processes. Chesbrough and Rosenbloom (2002) expand this view, suggesting that a BM encompasses a value proposition, market segment, value chain structure, cost structure, profit potential, position within the value network, and competitive strategy. Osterwalder and Pigneur (2010) introduce their BM Canvas framework, which identifies customer segments, customer relationships, channels, value propositions, revenue streams, key activities, key resources, key partners, and cost structure as essential elements of a BM.

Recent research shows that BMs are subject to innovation and change over time, with BMI often leading to superior value creation and the disruption of established market position (Magretta, 2002; Morris et al., 2005). Indeed, BMI refers to the process of enhancing advantage and creating value by making simultaneous changes both to an organization's value proposition and to its underlying operating model (Chesbrough, 2007). It encompasses the strategic reconfiguration of various elements, such as customer segments, value propositions, revenue models, distribution channels, and key partnerships (Demil and Lecocq, 2010). By innovating their BMs, organizations can gain a competitive edge, adapt to changing market dynamics, and seize new opportunities in an ever-evolving business environment. Innovative BMs allow companies to distinguish themselves from competitors with a new and distinctive value proposition in the market (Bucherer, Eisert, and Gassmann, 2012).

BMI can be viewed as a source of firm heterogeneity and competitive advantage, differing significantly from traditional firm-level product-market strategies (Markides and Charitou, 2004). Despite firms addressing similar customer needs and employing similar product-market strategies, they may utilize different BMs. Thus, BMI and product-market innovation complement each other rather than serving as substitutes (Zott and Amit, 2008). For example, some innovative BMs integrate processes and technologies that improve operational efficiency, resulting in reduced costs, better resource utilization, and overall optimization of operations (Teece, 2010). Finally, BMI can also benefit stakeholders, such as customers, suppliers, employees and provides a powerful means for companies to remain competitive, create value, and adapt to rapidly changing environments, ensuring long-term sustainability (Bucherer et al., 2012; Demil and Lecocq, 2010).

Concerning CCIs, some scholars argue that BMI clarifies the restructuring of the activity system which dictates how a cultural and creative firm (CCF) creates, delivers, and captures value, thus enabling the pursuit of entrepreneurial opportunities over time (Landoni et al., 2020). However, despite BMI's acknowledged importance for rapid growth and sustained competitive advantage, there is limited literature shedding light on its potential to assist CCFs in managing their distinctive structures and characteristics.

2.2 *Emerging trends within BMs and CCIs*

Innovative BMs within the CCIs have been reshaping traditional approaches to value creation, organizational architecture, and value capture. In these sectors, trends are constantly evolving, reflecting shifts in societal values, technological advancements, and changing consumer behaviors. Below are examples illustrating the intersection of various elements within these trends:

1. **Corporate Social Responsibility (CSR):** Companies within CCIs are increasingly prioritizing sustainability and ethical practices. For instance, architecture agencies like Foster + Partners created by Norman Foster are integrating sustainable design principles into their projects. In the fashion industry, outdoor apparel company Patagonia leads the charge in environmentally responsible manufacturing and activism. The company Veja is also a pioneer and a leader in the field of ecological sneakers.
2. **Diversity and Inclusion:** Organizations in the film sector, such as Disney and in the fashion and cosmetics industries like Fenty Beauty or Fenty Savage are championing diversity and inclusion in their marketing strategies. Disney's commitment to diverse storytelling and representation across its media platforms resonates with global audiences. Similarly, Fenty Beauty, founded by Rihanna, has revolutionized the beauty industry with its inclusive range of products catering to a diverse customer base.
3. **Marketing Innovations:** Brands like Louis Vuitton are leveraging artification, blurring the lines between fashion and art to create unique and immersive experiences for consumers. Additionally, emphasizing personalized experiences and celebrity endorsements in sectors like fashion and beauty has become increasingly prevalent. Brands collaborate with influencers and celebrities to amplify their reach and engagement with target audiences.

4 **Digital and Technological Integration:** In the film or publishing sectors, companies harness the power of big data to personalize content recommendations and enhance user experiences. Digital and technological integration also fosters freemium models, as seen in music streaming services and mobile video games, which offer basic services for free while charging for premium features. Peer-to-peer digital platforms like Vinted also enable users to buy and sell second-hand clothing, fostering at the same time a sense of community and sustainability.
5 **Managing Stakeholder Dynamics:** a large portion of film producers and video game editors embrace open innovation, collaborating with external partners to improve their products. Museums also collaborate to develop exhibitions and educational programs. Multi-sided BMs in video games also involve revenue streams from various sources, including game sales, downloadable content, and in-game purchases. Besides, coopetition, where competitors collaborate for mutual benefit, is evident in industries, such as architecture, television, and gaming.
6 **Cross-Industry Collaboration:** Companies are breaking boundaries by integrating elements from different industries. Netflix or Spotify, for example, combines elements of technology, music, cinema, and entertainment to deliver streaming content globally. Similarly, Cirque du Soleil merges art, acrobatics, and theater to create captivating live performances. Video games, with their interdisciplinary nature encompassing art, design, technology, and storytelling, exemplify the fusion of various industries.

Adapting to these trends is thus essential for organizations seeking to thrive in an ever-evolving landscape of creativity and culture. For example, freemium models and subscription-based platforms have become increasingly popular in CCIs and have transformed the way consumers access music and film content, with services like Spotify and Netflix offering a plethora of options for a recurring fee. This model is prevalent in software applications, design tools, and online gaming. Additionally, experiential entertainment, including virtual reality installations, offers consumers unique and memorable experiences they're eager to pay for. Moreover, collaborations between CCIs and brands have become increasingly symbiotic, blending creativity with commercial endeavors. Fashion brands often collaborate with artists to create limited-edition collections or host art-inspired events, merging the worlds of fashion and art to offer consumers unique and culturally enriched experiences. Similarly, influencers and celebrities are frequently enlisted by brands to endorse products or collaborate on exclusive releases, leveraging their social influence to enhance brand visibility and connect with target audiences authentically. In essence, these collaborations not only elevate brand presence but also enrich the consumer experience by infusing it with cultural significance and creativity. They represent a powerful strategy for brands to stand out in a saturated market and cultivate long-lasting relationships with their customers, all while monetizing data and communities, as seen in industries like fashion or publishing, exemplified by the "new romance" phenomenon.

The CCIs continue to evolve rapidly, driven by innovative BMs that capitalize on digital technologies, changing consumer behaviors, and shifting economic landscapes. Adapting to these trends will be crucial for businesses and entrepreneurs looking to thrive in these dynamic sectors since BMI within these industries poses several significant challenges. For example, organizations must remain vigilant in tracking emerging market trends to sustain competitiveness and it is imperative that they effectively manage organizational change for adapting to evolving business environments. Moreover, nurturing a culture of innovation within the company is essential for cultivating fresh ideas and approaches. Securing necessary resources, whether financial or human, will be critical for implementing innovative strategies since navigating intricate stakeholder dynamics, including relationships with artists, consumers, and partners, demands careful attention.

To effectively navigate these challenges and capitalize on the opportunities presented by BMI, organizations within CCIs must equip themselves with strategies and insights tailored to their specific contexts. It is the reason why this book intends to offer in-depth analysis and practical solutions to address some of these key challenges. In the chapters ahead, we will explore case studies and expert perspectives to illuminate the intricacies of BMI.

3 Overview of chapters' contents

The book comprises nine chapters based on case studies carried out in various CCIs. The authors of the chapters have been selected for their expertise in each of the industries concerned. We have deliberately chosen authors working in different CCIs in order to offer a wide range of innovative strategies at work in these industries. Together, these case studies enable us to analyze different forms of BMI, to decipher the reasons for their success and the best practices that can be transposed to other CCIs.

Chapter 2 explores the music industry through the theoretical lens of open BM. Albéric Tellier, Emilie Ruiz, and Anna Lenoir studied the evolution of record companies' BM following the major transformations that took place in the music industry and especially the rise of digital platforms. The authors demonstrate that record companies have changed their BM in order to shift their emphasis toward capitalizing on artists with proven potential, as opposed to exploration. The research unveils four essential artists selection criteria favored by record companies: community involvement, formulation of a robust marketing strategy, live performances, and the creation of an appealing artistic concept.

In **Chapter 3**, Gael Gueguen explores the board game industry's significant transformation driven by innovative publishers. As these companies push boundaries, understanding the ecosystem's dynamics becomes crucial, with French company Asmodee exemplifying rapid expansion and growth through a diversified BM. Embracing a classic dominator strategy, Asmodee strategically acquires companies at various levels, sparking a discussion on the correlation between such evolution and ecosystem expansion. Contrary to common belief, this approach not only challenges the negative perception but also contributes to the growth and structuring of the ecosystem.

In **Chapter 4**, Arthur Caré-Famchon and Pierre Roy discuss the increasing consideration of sustainable issues in the fashion industry. The authors analyze the construction and the development of the sustainable BM of the sneakers brand Veja. Data show that Veja has been able to explore uncaptured value in order to add social and environmental values aside from the economic value to its BM. The chapter discusses five main key success factors that can be tackled from the Veja case study: building a sustainable supply chain, limiting overconsumption by proposing timeless models, showing transparency about the BM, developing recycling activities, and updating the value chain in order to compensate with the additional costs due to sustainability.

In **Chapter 5**, Carole Poirel examines the resurgence of the romance sector, dubbed "new romance," which has revitalized the publishing industry with hits like *Fifty Shades of Grey* and *After*. Originating as fanfiction, these titles illustrate evolving author-reader dynamics. Beyond blockbusters, the market reflects the long-tail economy, encompassing niche products with lucrative combined sales. Traditional publishing adapts through hybridization, utilizing user-generated content for growth. Poirel analyzes Hlab/BMR, a French publisher in the romance sector, exploring necessary changes in traditional publishing's BM to address the market, particularly in romance. This study contributes to understanding BM hybridization and opportunities in cultural industries.

Chapter 6 is focused on the video games industry and the ecosystem of online games. Romain Gandia and Guy Parmentier study the openness of content with communities and the development of a creative ecosystem. Based on three innovative case studies (Ankama, Nadeo/Ubisoft, Vidcoin), research shows that organizations are adopting multi-sided BMs and that it helps managing the creative ecosystem by orchestrating creative resources and openness dynamics within dedicated spaces of exploration and exploitation. Data from the case studies also show the instrumental role of digital platforms in the structural interweaving of the creative ecosystem with the multi-sided BM.

In **Chapter 7**, Federica Antonaglia, Arnaud Fernandez, and Juliette Passebois-Ducros explore the luxury industry's resilience, highlighting how French luxury firms leverage the art world to enhance their creativity and market position. Through art patronage and collaborations, luxury brands transform into cultural symbols, strengthening their value proposition and market distinctiveness. The study focuses on artification strategies within luxury BMs, specifically in the wine and spirits sector, using Hennessy as a case study. By examining Hennessy's artification-driven BM innovation, the authors reveal how artistic connections reshape its value proposition and capture. This research underscores artification's significant role in driving BMI, especially within the LVMH conglomerate.

In **Chapter 8**, Paulina Knobloch discusses the issues of BMI in the film industry since the emergence of digital platforms. The research is based on a longitudinal study of two major film studios in Scandinavia: SF Studios and Nordisk Film. Data show that the studios opened up for online distribution channels, which generated a new source of revenue and new partnerships. The demand for content, especially high-quality content has been impacted and led the film studios to increase their own productions. This allowed them to better control the content and to become less dependent on other content suppliers while at the same time targeting the audience more directly.

Finally, **Chapter 9** delves into the concept of an open BM between competitors within the architecture sector. Estelle Pellegrin-Boucher et Pierre Roy examine the BM established among three competing architectural firms for the renovation of the Montparnasse Tower in Paris (Nouvelle AOM). Empirical findings reveal the construction process of the Nouvelle AOM BM and its operational methods. It elucidates how the competitors position the Nouvelle AOM offering in comparison to their individual agency offerings, the role of creating an autonomous legal entity, using dedicated and independent teams, formalizing governance rules, and implementing equitable profit distribution to mitigate tensions.

References

Bucherer, E., Eisert, U., and Gassmann, O. (2012). Towards systematic business model innovation: Lessons from product innovation management. *Creativity and Innovation Management*, 21(2), 183–198.

Caves, R. (2000). *Creative Industries: Contracts between Arts and Commerce*. Cambridge, MA: Harvard University Press.

Chesbrough, H.W. (2007). Business model innovation: It's not just about technology anymore. *Strategic Leadership*, 35(6), 12–17.

Chesbrough, H.W., and Rosenbloom, R.S. (2002). The role of business models in capturing value from innovation: Evidence from Xerox Corporation's technology spin-off companies. *Industrial Corporate Change*, 11(3), 529–555.

De Bruin, A. (2007). Building the film industry in New Zealand: An entrepreneurship continuum. In *Entrepreneurship in Creative Industries: An International Perspective* (pp. 87–103). Northampton, MA: Edward Elgar Publishing.

Demil, B., and Lecocq, X. (2010). Business model evolution: In search of dynamic consistency. *Long Range Planning*, 43(2–3), 227–246.

Durand, R., and Jourdan, J. (2012). Jules or Jim: Alternative conformity to minority logics. *Academy of Management Journal*, 55(6), 1295–1315.

Henry, C. (2007). *Entrepreneurship in the Creative Industries: An International Perspective*. Cheltenham: Edward Elgar Publishing.

Holbrook, M.B., and Hirschman, E.C. (1982). The experiential aspects of consumption - Consumer fantasies, feelings, and fun. *Journal of Consumer Research*, 9(2), 132–140.

Johnson, M., Christensen, C.M., and Kagermann, H. (2008). Reinventing your business model. *Harvard Business Review,* 86(12), 57–68.

Landoni, P., Dell'era, C., Frattini, F., Messeni Petruzzelli, A., Verganti, R., and Manelli, L. (2020). Business model innovation in cultural and creative industries: Insights from three leading mobile gaming firms. *Technovation*, 92, 45–77.

Osterwalder, A., and Pigneur, Y. (2010). *Business Model Generation: A Handbook for Visionaries, Game Changers, and Challengers.* New York, NY: John Wiley & Sons.

Magretta, J. (2002). Why business models matter. *Harvard Business Review*, 80(5), 86–92.

Markides, C., and Charitou, C.D. (2004). Competing with dual business models: A contingency approach. *Academy Management Executive,* 18(3), 22–36.

Morris, M., Schidehutte, M., and Allen, J. (2005). The entrepreneur's business model: Toward unified perspective. *Journal of Business Research*, 58(6), 726–735.

Rietveld, J. (2011). Profiting from digitally distributed cultural products: The case of content producers in the video games industry. In K.J. McCarthy, W.A. Dolfsma, and M. Fiolet (Eds.), *The Nature of the New Firm: Beyond the Boundaries of Organizations and Institutions* (pp. 100–120). Northamption, MA: Edward Elgar Publishing.

Vogel, H.L. (2011). *Entertainment Industry Economics*. Cambridge: Cambridge University Press.

Teece, D.J. (2010). Business models, business strategy and innovation. *Long Range Planning*, 43(2–3), 172–194.

Zott, C., and Amit, R. (2008). The fit between product market strategy and business model: Implications for firm performance. *Strategic Management Journal*, 29(1), 1–26.

Zott, C., Amit, R., and Massa, L.C. (2011). The business model: Recent developments and future research. *Journal of Management,* 37(4), 1019–1042.

2 Open business models in the music industry

Lessons from the transformation of record companies

Albéric Tellier, Émilie Ruiz and Anna Lenoir

1 Introduction

The music industry has undergone a profound transformation in recent years, driven by technological advancements, shifting consumer behaviors, and the rise of digital platforms. This chapter delves into the evolving landscape of the music industry, specifically exploring the paradigm shift toward open business models. Focusing on the lessons drawn from the transformation of record companies, one of the actors most affected by the transformations in the music industry, we aim to better understand the consequences of the open business model adopted by these companies.

Based on primary data (28 semi-structured interviews conducted between 2020 and 2023 with various music industry stakeholders), our chapter demonstrates that record companies have successfully navigated the transformations in their industry by embracing an open business model. This approach has allowed them to shift their emphasis toward capitalizing on artists with proven potential, as opposed to exploration. The characteristics of this business model are delineated, highlighting the essential activities that record companies have needed to cultivate and the ensuing implications for the artists themselves. Moreover, with a focus on the music industry, we aim to contribute to a better understanding of the circumstances under which creative industries (Caves, 2000) can adopt these open business models and the ramifications of such adoption.

The chapter is organized as follows. The first section describes the theoretical framework. We present the literature on open business models and position it within the context of the literature on open innovation. We conclude this first section by highlighting the relevance and gaps related to the study of the open business model in the music industry, particularly in the case of record companies. The second section presents the qualitative methods and the case study. Finally, we present our findings before we discuss it and conclude the chapter.

DOI: 10.4324/9781032714462-2

2 Open business model: theoretical background

2.1 *At the origins of the open business model: open innovation*

In past decades, the concept of open innovation has gained significant attention both in the academic and managerial realms. Open innovation is a paradigm introduced by Henry Chesbrough (2003). It is defined as "*the use of purposive inflows and outflows of knowledge to accelerate internal innovation (…).*" (Chesbrough, 2003: 1). In opposition to closed innovation, open innovation challenges traditional models by emphasizing the importance of leveraging external ideas and collaborations for the advancement of organizational goals. In other words, open innovation has been marked by a shift from closed, internally focused processes, to a more collaborative and externally inclusive approach.

Open innovation comprises inbound and outbound activities (Chesbrough, 2003, 2006). The inbound logic (also known as the outside-in approach), in which the company opens itself to external knowledge, is defined as "*a practice of leveraging the discoveries of others: companies do not need and should not rely exclusively on their own R&D*" (Chesbrough and Crowther, 2006: 229). In this case, the company acquires knowledge and ideas from stakeholders in both its internal and external environment with the aim of creating value. Dahlander and Gann (2010) indicate that companies must develop mechanisms for sourcing and acquiring external knowledge to enhance their internal growth. In this case, the company scans its environment with the idea of finding innovation opportunities with others. The advantage of engaging in an inbound innovation process lies in accessing a wide variety of resources for the company (Dahlander and Gann, 2010).

In the outbound logic (also known as the inside-out approach), the company seeks to leverage its intellectual property rights (such as licensing). Outbound open innovation "*suggests, rather than relying solely on internal paths, that companies can seek external organizations with more suitable business models to commercialize a given technology*" (Chesbrough and Crowther, 2006: 229). In this logic, the company licenses out ideas and technologies it has created to better exploit them, with the aim of capturing value. In this case, the company generates profits by granting property rights to others.

However, while open innovation offers numerous benefits, it also presents challenges. Literature first points out intellectual property concerns (e.g., Alexy et al., 2009) and organizational cultural shifts (e.g., Dabrowska and Savitskaya, 2014) as the main barriers to open innovation. In line with these challenges, Laursen and Salter (2006) have particularly explored solutions to these challenges, emphasizing the importance of establishing clear communication channels, trust, and appropriate incentive structures to overcome barriers. The literature also suggests that, in the case of inbound logic, when accessing various external resources, companies face several difficulties, including those related to relationships with external stakeholders or managing the "too" great diversity of resources it accesses (Sieg et al., 2010). Dahlander and Gann (2010) also highlight, in the outbound open innovation, challenges, including those related to managing licensing agreements or potential information leaks.

Indeed, open innovation calls for collaboration with (new) external partners beyond the organization. While Laursen and Salter (2006) initially identified suppliers, customers, competitors, research organizations, R&D private labs, and universities, the literature has since recognized additional actors and organizational forms, such as innovation communities (e.g., Berthinier-Poncet et al., 2023). These new partners also prompt organizations to evolve their activities (Chesbrough, 2003), leading them to open not only their innovation processes but also their business models (Chesbrough, 2006).

2.2 *From open innovation to open business models*

Chesbrough (2006) suggests that the successful implementation of open innovation requires the adoption of a new or, at the very least, updated business model, which is thus open. According to the author (2010: 354), "*while companies may have extensive investments and processes for exploring new ideas and technologies, they often have little if any ability to innovate the business models through which these inputs will pass.*" In other words, adopting open innovation leads companies to transform their organizational processes and adopt an open business model.

Although Chesbrough's seminal work had the merit of highlighting the concept of the open business model, it suffers from a clearer definition than the elements indicated. According to Weiblen (2014: 39),

> the term can be split into two components: an adjective – "open" – describing the noun "business model". (…) Open is generally seen as referring to a firm's boundaries and its collaboration with the outside world across these boundaries – be it with other firms, communities, or customers.

Open business models thus represent a strategic paradigm shift, transcending conventional approaches by not only embracing external collaboration but also exposing key elements of the business model to external stakeholders (Albats et al., 2023). This concept aligns seamlessly with the broader philosophy of open innovation, as both emphasize the essential role of external input in driving organizational success.

In our view, open business models are deliberately designed business models that incorporate elements of collaboration, sharing, and openness with external stakeholders. They revolve around (1) creating value through activities and resources that depend on collaboration with external partners and (2) offering value propositions through transparent interactions

Table 2.1 Four types of open business models

	Efficiency-centric open business model	*User-centric open business model*	*Collaborative open business model*	*Open platform business model*
Content	Efficiency-centered value proposition, enabled by reduction in transaction and coordination costs	User-centered value proposition, input from communities of users	Radical innovations and opening up of new target segment	Business model acts as open-innovation platform for multiple stakeholders
Structure	Redefinition of role of internal R&D system Efficiency-centered structure	Ideation phase of innovation process "outsourced" to the crowd	Users/suppliers customers/ competitors become key partner in innovation process	Re-organization of the production & distributional system Need for complementary internal network
Governance	Monetary remuneration for external knowledge provider Use of "integration experts" to absorb market-available knowledge	Monetary prizes or recognition for external knowledge providers Incentives to engage and manage communities of users for own employee	Contract based, sharing of rewards on organizational level with external knowledge provider Incentives for own employees to engage with lead users and alliance partners	Provide incentives for own employees to engage with multitude of knowledge partners (individuals, companies, communities) Re-distribution of risks & rewards

Source: Saebi and Foss (2015).

and dynamic relationships with the partners the company is open to. Concretely, Saebi and Foss (2015) identified four different types of open business models (see Table 2.1): (1) efficiency-centric open business model, adopting a market-based innovation strategy, (2) user-centric open business model, adopting a crowd-based innovation strategy, (3) collaborative open business model, adopting a collaborative innovation strategy, and (4) open platform business model, adopting a network-based innovation strategy.

2.3 *Characteristics of open business models*

Even if there may be different degrees of openness, the open business model has specific characteristics. While Table 2.2 provides a relatively more comprehensive overview of these characteristics and allows for comparison with the characteristics of the closed business model, four elements prove to be particularly important.

First, open business models are characterized by the sharing of resources, both tangible and intangible, with external partners. This sharing fosters collaborative innovation. The integration of shared resources encourages a more inclusive approach to problem-solving and product development. This collaborative approach embraces the principles of open innovation, where external ideas and contributions are actively sought to enrich the innovation process. Companies adopting an open business model are at the core of a network of relationships, leading them to rely on an ecosystem rather than simple partnerships (Weinblen, 2014).

Second, another distinctive feature of open business models is the use of open licensing strategies (Chesbrough, 2006). Companies may choose to share their intellectual property openly, allowing others to build upon or utilize it. This aligns with the outbound dimension of open innovation, where organizations actively seek avenues to monetize their internal innovations by licensing them to external entities. The interplay between open business models and open innovation becomes evident as organizations strategically leverage licensing and monetization to maximize the value derived from their intellectual assets (Saebi and Foss, 2015).

Third, open business models inherently promote agility and adaptability, traits essential for thriving in dynamic markets. By engaging external stakeholders, especially customers, in the co-creation process, organizations using open business models align with the customer-centric focus of open innovation (Kortmann and Piller, 2006). Customer feedback and collaboration become integral components, driving iterative improvements and ensuring that products and services resonate with market needs. This iterative feedback loop is a cornerstone of both open business models and open innovation practices (Ghezzi et al., 2022). In line with the customer-centric approach, the risk-sharing aspect of open business models, where multiple stakeholders contribute to and share in the success or failure of a venture, aligns with the collaborative ethos of open innovation (Purdy et al., 2012).

Table 2.2 Main characteristics of closed versus open business model

	Closed business model	*Open business model*
Innovation	Internally focused, relies on in-house R&D and expertise	Externally focused, actively seeks external collaborations and input
Knowledge sources	Limited to internal knowledge and resources	Draws on a diverse range of external sources, including customers, partners, and competitors
Collaboration	Limited collaboration, often within organizational boundaries	Emphasizes collaboration with external stakeholders, fostering a networked approach
Intellectual property (IP)	Guarded and protected, with a focus on proprietary IP	May involve open licensing, sharing IP, or collaborating on joint IP development
Flexibility and adaptability	Can be rigid and less adaptable to external changes	More flexible and adaptable, responsive to external market dynamics
Monetization strategies	Primarily focuses on traditional revenue streams	Explores diverse monetization strategies, including open licensing, freemium models, and data monetization
Customer involvement	Limited customer involvement beyond consumption	Actively engages customers in co-creation and feedback processes
Digital platforms	Limited use of external digital platforms for collaboration	Utilizes digital platforms to connect with a wider ecosystem of participants
Decision-making authority	Centralized decision-making within the organization	Decentralized decision-making, involving external stakeholders in strategic decisions

Sources: Chesbrough (2003, 2006), Teece (2010), Dasgupta (2023), Shahhoseini et al. (2023).

Finally, open business models often leverage digital platforms to connect diverse participants and facilitate collaborative endeavors (Romero et al., 2021). These platforms serve as catalysts for innovation by bringing together a wide range of stakeholders, including customers, suppliers, and even competitors. This collaborative network effect mirrors the open innovation landscape (e.g., Bogers et al., 2017), where platforms play a pivotal role in democratizing access to innovation and enabling organizations to tap into external expertise and ideas.

Recently, although open business models have start being addressed in the literature, work has been focusing on how large companies go from closed to open business models, especially when it deals with technological innovation from specific industries such as automotive or pharmaceutical (e.g., Lerro et al., 2022; Seiferlein and Kanbach, 2023). In contrast, limited studies have paid rigorous attention to cultural and creative industries (CCIs).

More broadly, the organizational aspects of artistic work have been understudied (Lindqvist, 2011). In other words, despite its relevance for studying such a topic, the CCIs, which have undergone several transformations, involving opening up the value chain to a range broad of actors, have been understudied in terms of (open) business models.

This is all the more unfortunate as the literature on open innovation itself suggests studying CCIs to better understand openness (e.g., Radomska et al., 2023). Confronting these questions within the music industry, and particularly with the case of record companies, which are among the actors most affected by the need to open up and transform, appears particularly relevant to explore knowledge about open business models.

3 Methods

Our research relies on a qualitative method, and more specifically on primary data (semi-structured interviews). The selection of our sample adhered to two key principles:

- The Principle of Key Positions: It was imperative for our research that each interviewee held a significant position within the music industry.
- The Principle of Maximum Variation: We aimed for interviewees to represent diverse roles within the music industry. This principle was also extended to the size of the companies where the interviewees worked, ensuring a varied perspective from professionals in major companies, streaming platforms, festivals, independent labels, and freelancers (artists and managers). This diverse approach allows us to capture insights from entities with varying influence and resources for artist development within the music industry.

We conducted 28 interviews between 2020 and 2023 with various stakeholders in the music industry, including one manager from an agency specializing in artist support; five artistic directors/managers from labels; seven artists in the development phase; three label managers responsible for detecting and recruiting new artists; three data analysts for labels and platforms; one talent scout for a label; two business developers for labels; one brand relations manager for a label; one director of digital strategy for a label; three project managers for labels; one concert scheduler. Representative quotes from these interviews are included for illustrative purposes later in this chapter.

To select the artists for the interviews, we employed the same definition of a "developing artist" as explained by those responsible for detection and recruitment in the labels. We thus define a developing artist as an individual under 30 who aspires to establish a career in music and has been actively working on their project for over a year. All seven artists interviewed met these criteria.

These interviews were semi-structured, intending to prompt interviewees to share their experiences and perspectives on the evolution of the industry, the business of record companies, and artist development. These interviews were complemented by diverse secondary data gathered from specialized press sources. Our objective was to cross-reference insights from these interviews with the perspectives of other professionals and authors in the field, enabling us to discern the main trends and common logics. To achieve this, we drew on several press and research articles related to the topic, in line with the 2021 Mama Festival, where lots of music industry professionals provided their insights on artist development in the digital age. The integration of these secondary data allowed us to compare the perspectives of professionals with those expressed by our interviewees.

To analyze the data, we conducted a multiple-round coding process. The objective was to extract key viewpoints and recurring themes that emerged across different interviews. To achieve this, we systematically coded the primary data, organizing it into distinct categories. This initial coding provided a visual representation of the main themes to be addressed and explored. Subsequently, after completing this first-level coding, we conducted a second-level coding exercise. This aimed to consolidate the various identified categories under broader and more inclusive headings, creating more generalized meta-categories. This step allows us to streamline the number of categories and generate an analysis focused solely on the most significant overarching themes.

Finally, one of the authors served as an artistic assistant in a record company while conducting this research. Consequently, she actively contributed to the development of artists and the management of their projects. These responsibilities not only enriched the collected data but also facilitated the real-time assessment of its robustness.

4 Case study presentation

The music industry originated in the late 19th century when it became feasible to record, reproduce, and distribute works on a large scale. From the early 1900s onward, recorded discs achieved commercial success. The music market experienced significant growth in the late 1940s with the introduction of 33 rpm and 45 rpm vinyl records, followed by the advent of the audio cassette in 1963.

When discussing this industry, several terms will be used, including major, record company, and label. Clarifications are necessary. A record company is responsible for creating, producing, and publishing phonographic works. It oversees the design, manufacture, distribution, promotion, and dissemination of these works. One of the subdivisions of the record company is the label, and there may be one or more labels per company. However, there are independent labels that operate autonomously, not affiliated with any record company. The label functions as a "brand" under which artists are signed, with each label having a distinct artistic direction. Its primary mission is to provide financial, promotional, and logistical support to artists with musical projects. This includes purchasing studio sessions, producing music videos, managing tours, manufacturing vinyl or CDs, and executing promotional campaigns. In exchange for these expenses, the label takes a share of the artist's income. Unlike a record company, a label does not handle tasks related to music publishing. However, despite the more limited scope of a label's responsibilities compared to a record company, the terms are sometimes interchangeably used for simplicity. Finally, majors refer to record companies that significantly dominate the market. Currently, the majors include Universal Music, Sony Music, and Warner Music.

Since the 1950s, the music industry has been predominantly controlled by record companies, overseeing the entire value chain from artist identification to the commercial exploitation of works, including the financing of recordings. During this period, record companies adhered to a closed business model. They aimed to identify new artists at an early stage in their careers (exploration) and then allocate the necessary resources to develop them commercially (exploitation). Given that artists lacked access to the resources required for music production, record companies were compelled to lead the search for new talent. From the 1960s to the early 2000s, major record companies such as Motown and EMI often organized in-house procedures for evaluating, selecting, and training artists.

To execute all these operations, they assembled extensive teams, including songwriters, composers, studio musicians, sound engineers, arrangers, artistic directors, talent scouts, label managers, press officers, salespeople, administrative staff, and more. Simultaneously, the largest among them acquired substantial material resources, such as equipment and recording studios, and leveraged their association with major industrial groups to access cutting-edge technologies. During its peak in the 1970s, EMI boasted several specialized labels, an R&D department, and the renowned Abbey Road studios in London, where top sound specialists collaborated. In the 1980s, Polygram capitalized on its affiliation with the Philips group to utilize state-of-the-art equipment for recording and mixing works, incorporating revolutionary digital technologies (Philips being the inventor of the CD).

Bringing exploration activities in-house involves significant financial risk. In an industry like music, predicting public tastes and the success of new artists has always been exceedingly challenging (e.g., the DECCA label turned down the Beatles). Simultaneously, the costs associated with developing a new artist are extremely high. For many years, major record companies deemed this risk "acceptable" as long as substantial successes could offset the costs of failures. In essence, it was believed that to enjoy the profits generated by the world's biggest stars, there was a "price to pay": that of numerous unsuccessful launches.

This closed business model brought immense prosperity to major record companies until the 1990s, marking the most lucrative period in the history of the music industry. The stakeholders successfully navigated the shift from analog to digital while maintaining their established business model. CDs continued to be sold like vinyl records. However, this golden era ended for three primary reasons.

First, music was among the first industries to feel the impact of the digital technology surge, which facilitated the emergence of new entities capable of providing innovative services and business models. Since the 1990s, record companies have grappled with challenges related to piracy, peer-to-peer networks, and dematerialization (Leyshon, 2014). The business model centered around selling tangible objects (records) through a network of physical shops is diminishing in preference for services that offer access to extensive catalogs of musical works.

Second, digital technologies and networking tools have empowered artists to undertake activities that were once exclusive to specialized entities, thanks to resources and skills now accessible to the artists themselves. The simplicity of networking has facilitated the rise of crowdfunding initiatives. New promotion and distribution models have surfaced, allowing artists to directly engage with their audiences (e.g., Bandcamp, SoundCloud, Jamendo). Simultaneously, advancements have enabled the creation of professional-quality musical works using a basic laptop equipped with specialized software.

Third, in the early 2010s, digital technologies facilitated the development of a legal online offering provided by music streaming platforms. In the history of the music industry, it has never been as convenient for listeners to access such an extensive collection of recorded works. A user would now require over 16 million years to listen to all the tracks available on streaming platforms. The ramifications of this abundance are manifold and paradoxical (Hracs, 2012). Despite expanding choices, digital technologies concentrate consumers' attention on the most popular hits and the largest platforms (Anderson et al., 2020). In 2017, in the United States, although 377 billion songs were "streamed," 99% of the listings were concentrated on just 10% of the tracks.

All the opportunities presented by digital technology have posed a challenge to the prevailing position of record companies, granting easier access to resources that were once exclusively under their control. The dematerialization of music and the widespread availability of production and distribution tools were initially viewed as an opportunity for artists to liberate themselves from record companies and establish direct connections with their audiences. Consequently, in the early 2000s, numerous experts were forecasting the eventual disappearance of these traditional players, to be supplanted by new entrants skilled in matchmaking and artists capable of independently managing their fan base.

However, record companies successfully repelled this threat and remained central players in the sector, undergoing a re-organization process initiated in the 2000s that prompted a transformation in their business model. Despite the decline of the CD, the three majors managed to retain their dominance, accounting for nearly 80% of the global recorded music market. This feat required a substantial transformation. Researchers have identified swift and substantial changes in the "ways of doing things" within record companies: new approaches to detecting and funding artists (Guesmi et al., 2016), innovative business models (Rogers, 2016), new composition practices (Léveillé Gauvin, 2018), and new project management approaches (Seabrook, 2015). All these works underscore the adoption of practices aimed at facilitating and leveraging connections within an openness-driven logic in the innovation process.

5 Findings

How have record companies adapted their business models to navigate the changes in their industries? What are the impacts of this openness on other stakeholders, especially emerging artists? Analyzing the qualitative data collected unveils several crucial components. Representative quotes from interviews are included for illustrative purposes.

5.1 The open business model of record companies: key characteristics

With the rise of the internet and social media, record companies find it significantly more accessible to engage various stakeholders to enhance the value of their products and services. Activities are now structured more as networks rather than linear sequences.

Our observations indicate that record companies have embraced an open business model by expanding their relationships with a diverse range of players to leverage synergy effects. Some of these actors assume responsibility for exploration activities (research and support for new artists), allowing record companies to concentrate on exploitation (commercial development). Innovation is thus the outcome of collaboration among multiple participants. To accomplish this strategic shift, record companies have reevaluated their decision-making processes to adapt to the often unpredictable trends in social networking and establish connections with their clientele. They have also renegotiated compensation models with streaming platforms and devised new contract types with artists, varying in binding nature depending on their potential and bargaining power. Table 2.3 outlines the key characteristics of the record companies' open business model, which can be viewed as a collaborative open business model (Saebi and Foss, 2015).

Three points are worth highlighting here. Firstly, the shift in focus for record companies toward adopting an open business model necessitates the development of new key activities (4.2). Secondly, as record companies refocus on exploitation, they have delegated some of the tasks previously conducted in-house to the artists themselves (4.3).

Table 2.3 Main characteristics of the open business model of record companies

	New procedures and practices
Innovation	More relationships with intermediaries specializing in finding and supporting new artists. Refocusing on commercial exploitation
Knowledge sources	Development of systems for monitoring and collecting data on consumer behavior on social networks and in fan communities
Collaboration	Collaboration with new actors in the music industry: intermediaries, data processing specialists, streaming platforms, etc.
Intellectual property (IP)	Development of new intellectual property management services. Creation of new types of contracts with artists
Flexibility and adaptability	Establishment of network monitoring procedures to detect and exploit fashionable trends at an early stage
Monetization strategies	New practices for monetizing works (freemium, subscriptions, etc.), and negotiations with streaming platforms to establish new rules for calculating remuneration
Customer involvement	Including customers in the process of assessing the potential of new artists (recommendations, feedback, etc.)
Digital platforms	Creation of platforms to connect with new artists and use of existing platforms (Tik Tok) to connect with target customers
Decision-making authority	Introduction of faster selection procedures for new artists, based on simple indicators and rules

5.2 *The need to develop new key activities*

The creation and commercialization of a new musical work involve exploration and exploitation activities (Figure 2.1). The former transforms more or less formalized artistic ambitions (incubation) into projects. The latter enables the commercial potential of the finally selected projects to be exploited. Traditionally, record companies managed this exploration-exploitation sequence by entering into contracts with artists identified during the incubation phase. Nowadays, they have shifted their focus to exploitation activities. In other words, record companies are becoming less like "talent scouts" and more like structures specializing in developing projects with potential. This choice significantly impacts the business model of record companies, requiring them to re-organize their detection and selection activities.

Firstly, if the exploration phase is outsourced, establishing mechanisms to identify artists who are on the brink of successful emergence from this initial development phase becomes crucial. Consequently, record companies now maintain close relationships with individuals orbiting around emerging artists. The withdrawal of labels from artist development coincides with the rise of numerous actors enabling artists to engage with professionals even before securing a label deal. In the music industry, there has been a surge in the

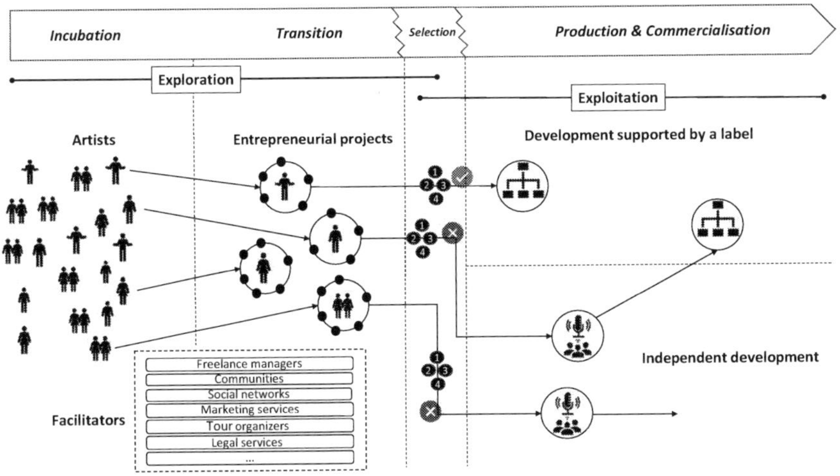

Figure 2.1 Artist development in an open business model context, a synthesis.

number and variety of companies dedicated to specific services: management, legal advice, artistic support, digital marketing, and more. These entities have taken over tasks that were traditionally handled by record companies. Many of our interviewees have highlighted the diversification and expansion of actors involved in artist development. Freelance managers, in particular, are re-emerging as key intermediaries catalyzing and facilitating new organizational forms and strategic partnerships among creative workers. The swift identification of artists is so crucial that some record companies are establishing their own initiatives, such as Universal Music and its SpinnUp platform, allowing artists to self-produce and gain visibility.

Secondly, with exploration activities delegated to external actors, record companies have had to devise new project detection and selection strategies. These activities come into play during the transition phase, where various criteria are employed to evaluate the suitability of signing a developing artist. Those selected gain access to dedicated career resources provided by the labels. Other artists, whether by choice or necessity (if not selected), may pursue independent development; some may even be identified and signed later. Figure 2.1 summarizes our findings.

5.3 *The impact of the open business model on new artists*

The expectations from professionals regarding what an artist must present to attract and convince them to develop their project have significantly intensified since the 2000s, primarily due to disintermediation leading to a larger pool of potential musicians and aspiring artists. Labels now require an initial product that is almost finalized and associated with a strong identity, essentially a "ready-to-use" artist. A case in point is a young electropop artist we interviewed, who seems to be a typical example. To secure a deal with Microqlima (a record label), he had to release an initial E.P. (consisting of five songs) and a track that garnered over a million streams on various platforms.

> The companies are more and more reassured by artists with already an environment. (…) An artist in the making is an artist who already exists, and there will be fewer and fewer newcomers who arrive with just a very good song or just a personality.
>
> (Artistic Director)

Our findings indicate that the record companies' shift toward exploitation has impacted artists' roles. Firstly, artists are now required to undertake entrepreneurial activities that were previously handled by the labels. To reach this, they can enlist various facilitators to assist in developing their projects and, consequently, attract the attention of record companies. Our interviews underscore the considerable challenge artists face in launching a career without the assistance of these partners. Having support remains a crucial step in the evolution of a musical project, even though labels no longer fulfill this role in the early stages of an artist's career. Secondly, it is imperative for artists to align with the evaluation and selection criteria of record companies if they aspire to secure a contract. Our data has allowed us to identify four key dimensions on which artists will be evaluated.

The creation of a community: The opportunities presented by digital technology have transformed the engagement with the audience into both an opportunity for emerging artists and a prerequisite for aiming to secure a contract with a label. Digital project managers, artistic directors of labels, and companies specializing in marketing support for artists have turned this connection into an indicator of an artist's potential and a selection criterion. Labels have initiated the development of tools to evaluate artists' potential, leveraging data from platforms and information gathered on social networks. Right from the initial phases of their project, artists must demonstrate that they have a modest yet devoted and consistent audience.

> Today, I get the impression that the strategy, especially on the part of the majors, is to sign projects that are already very well developed and not to take any risks with a project… Most of the artists who are signed are people who already exist, not necessarily through music, but who already have a community… It is one of the strategies to go after numbers. It is totally omnipresent.
>
> (Developing artist)

A coherent marketing strategy: Artist development is unattainable without a well-defined marketing strategy. Understanding one's audience, targeting it, cultivating it through social networks, and subsequently pursuing partnerships, innovative communication methods, or sales, along with creating visuals and images to generate discussions about one's music, all constitute stages of a marketing strategy that should be implemented right from the inception of the musical project. In formulating this marketing strategy, proficiency in digital and social networks has become indispensable.

> However, unfortunately yeah, you have to ask the artists to be digital experts.
>
> (Artistic director)

The emerging artist must stay informed about new communication methods, tools, and trends. TikTok serves as a prime illustration, reshaping the dynamics of the music industry in recent years. It currently stands as the social network that most effectively translates music presence on its platform into streams on other streaming platforms. Users discover a music snippet they like and promptly navigate to Spotify, Deezer, etc. Some artists leverage this to their advantage, using TikTok as a testing ground for their tracks. For instance, Sam Smith employed TikTok as a trial platform for his track "Unholy" by posting about 15 seconds online and gauging the audience's reaction before deciding on a full release. The track gained such popularity on TikTok that his label eventually released it.

Performing in public: Live music is central to the music industry's business model and is also crucial for artists' development. In the era of dematerialization, live concerts retain significant importance in the trajectory of an emerging artist. Firstly, numerous mechanisms for discovery, as well as platforms for launching artists, exist in the live environment.

> You see people like Christine and the Queens or Owlle, we programmed them, they were not signed yet, and you had all the producers and labels coming, so it is very interesting and important.
>
> (Festival programmer)

Formulating an attractive artistic concept: Like an entrepreneur tasked with "pitching" a project, an artist must adeptly convey its ambition in a compelling and attractive manner. These elements, instrumental in categorizing the artist, have gained immense significance in an era where web radios, streaming platforms, and, more broadly, commercial websites seek to leverage the connections between artists through recommendation systems to offer content tailored to listeners.

> Well, I think that in our label, what is most important for us when we sign, is that the artists already have quite precise and concrete ideas of what they want to do. That they already have a project in mind (...). For me, the number one rule, the very first thing, is to define an artistic

> project. You have to understand what you want to get out as an artist, know and have something to say, know why you want to address people and to whom too. Currently, making sound is so simple that we have moved on to the next stage, which is to have a project.
>
> (Assistant project manager in a label)

6 Contributions to business model innovation literature in CCIs

In the face of significant transformations associated with the rapid ascent of digital technology, record companies were compelled to undergo a metamorphosis or face extinction. It is widely acknowledged that well-established companies, particularly those dominating their sectors, encounter considerable challenges in maintaining their competitive positions amid technological disruptions (Chesbrough, 2003). Although dematerialization and the emergence of streaming services initially posed a direct threat, record companies managed to sustain their influential role in the music industry, making them an intriguing case for study at a time when numerous organizations in the creative industries grapple with challenges.

Our research demonstrates that record companies addressed the challenge of dematerialization by adopting an open business model. With the dematerialization of music, both the revenue model and the value proposition to listeners underwent a complete overhaul. Historically, record companies provided works recorded on various media to distribution networks (record stores, mass retailers, etc.) and broadcasters (radio, television, etc.), operating on a revenue model reliant on merchandise sales and royalty payments. Nowadays, record companies must negotiate with streaming platforms, receiving substantial remuneration based on the actual number of listens to their songs. Key actors like Apple, Spotify, and Deezer ensure listeners access a wide array of content, including new releases suggested via recommendation algorithms. Consequently, record companies are compelled to innovate to meet the streaming platforms' demand for novelty. Simultaneously, with digital technology, the proliferation of new releases contrasts with concentrated music consumption, prompting record companies to revamp their value-creation mechanisms. As our findings reveal, they shifted focus toward exploiting artists with demonstrated potential, sidelining exploration. This realignment necessitated the opening of their business model, leaving the exploration phase to artists themselves with the aid of facilitators. Record companies now depend on the resources and skills of external actors, instituting systems to connect with, evaluate, and select projects.

Our research also underscores that the adoption of an open business model by established actors, in this case, record companies, facilitates the transfer of specific resources and skills to upstream actors responsible for contributing to outside-in processes. It is now imperative for all new artists to undergo a phase of "self-development," taking charge of part of the development and production of their projects, irrespective of their main goal. This phase, even for those aspiring to sign with a label, requires self-production in terms of image, project, and audience development. This phase aids artists in getting noticed by music professionals and demands mastery of entrepreneurial skills traditionally held by labels. Our case study identifies four key skills that artists aspiring to collaborate with record labels must possess, contributing valuable insights, as existing research on open business models rarely delves into the key skills of external actors involved in outside-in processes. Our findings reveal that artists encounter challenges in implementing the new practices imposed by labels, with some artists highlighting difficulties in managing the economic aspects of their careers and navigating compromises between label demands and artistic ambitions.

Furthermore, we observe that artists' development necessitates collaboration with partners, with support remaining a crucial step even though labels no longer perform this function in the early stages of an artist's career. The advent of new actors in the industry stems from the need for new forms of artist support and the outsourcing of tasks previously handled by labels. Consequently, the introduction of an open business model in a creative industry leads to specialization and a distribution of tasks and roles among a greater number of actors. Notably, our results emphasize the significance of communities, identifying the ability to create and engage them as a key skill that artist-entrepreneurs must now master. This work underscores that one of the challenges of open innovation for a company is effectively engaging with diverse communities, either directly or through platform-type intermediation devices.

7 Conclusion

Our research indicates a notable shift in the focus of record companies toward the exploitation of artists whose potential is already demonstrated, moving away from the traditional emphasis on exploration. While these organizations historically took on the responsibility of early detection of new artists and swift allocation of resources to create their works, the current trend is to mitigate risks by concentrating on monitoring and evaluation activities that identify artists with proven potential. This transition signifies a gradual departure from a closed business model toward the adoption of an open one, transforming the recorded music sector into an arena where numerous actors actively participate in the innovation process, particularly in the launch of new artists.

In the contemporary music landscape, it has become indispensable for emerging artists to undergo a phase of "self-development" that facilitates recognition by music professionals. Our data analysis unveils four selection criteria favored by record companies: community involvement, formulation of a robust marketing strategy, live performances, and the creation of an appealing artistic concept. These criteria emerge as pivotal factors for the success of new artists in building their careers. While acknowledging the limitations of our chosen methodology, preventing broad generalizations, we believe this research holds significant managerial implications for both artists and professionals in the music industry.

For artists, our findings underscore the importance of cultivating and employing entrepreneurial skills throughout their projects. On the other hand, for record companies, the research highlights the essential conditions for the successful adoption of an open business model. Professionals across the industry can benefit from a deeper understanding of the evolving dynamics in the music sector, the diverse roles of actors involved, and the emergence of "artists-entrepreneurs." Those engaged in artist support structures may find valuable insights in our results to enhance their comprehension of the key success factors for emerging artists in the music industry.

While our study provides valuable insights, there is ample room for further research on these topics. The identified questions are pertinent and should be integrated into support programs for aspiring entrepreneurs in creative industries, ensuring a comprehensive and nuanced approach to navigating the evolving landscape of the music business.

References

Albats E, Podmetina D, Vanhaverbeke W. 2023. Open innovation in SMEs: A process view towards business model innovation. *Journal of Small Business Management*, *61*(6), 2519–2560.

Alexy O, Criscuolo P, Salter A. 2009. Does IP strategy have to cripple open innovation? *MIT Sloan Management Review*, *51*(1), 71.

Anderson A, Maystre L, Anderson I, Mehrotra R, Lalmas M. 2020. Algorithmic effects on the diversity of consumption on spotify. *Proceedings of the Web Conference*, April 20–24, Taipei, Taiwan.

Berthinier-Poncet A., Castro Gonçalves L., Dubouloz S., Ruiz E., Thévenard-Puthod. 2023. Understanding the role of innovation communities through a processual approach: The case of the outdoor sport industry. *European Management Journal*, *41*(4), 575–589.

Bogers M. et al. 2017. The open innovation research landscape: Established perspectives and emerging themes across different levels of analysis. *Industry and Innovation*, *24*(1), 8–40.

Chesbrough H. 2003, *Open Innovation – The New Imperative for Creating and Profiting from Technology*. Cambridge, MA: Harvard Business School Press.

Chesbrough H. 2006. *Open Business Models: How to Thrive in the New Innovation Landscape*. Boston: Harvard Business Press.

Chesbrough H, Crowther AK. 2006. Beyond high tech: Early adopters of open innovation in other industries. *R&D Management*, *36*(3), 229–236.

Dabrowska J, Savitskaya I. 2014. When culture matters: Exploring the open innovation paradigm. *International Journal of Business Innovation and Research*, *8*(1), 94–118.

Dahlander L, Gann DM. 2010. How open is innovation? *Research Policy*, *39*(6), 699–709.

Dasgupta, M. 2023. Open vs closed business model: Exploring its role in innovation in Indian small and medium enterprises (SMEs). *Journal of the Knowledge Economy*, *14*(4), 4973–5002.

Ghezzi A, Cavallo A, Sanasi S, Rangone A. 2022. Opening up to startup collaborations: Open business models and value co-creation in SMEs. *Competitiveness Review: An International Business Journal*, *32*(7), 40–61.

Guesmi S, Delfosse J, Lemoine L, Oliveri N. 2016. Crowdfunding et préservation du patrimoine culturel. *Revue française de gestion*, *42*(258), 89–103.

Hracs BJ. 2012. A creative industry in transition: The rise of digitally driven independent music production. *Growth and Change*, *43*(3), 442–461.

Kortmann S, Piller F. 2016. Open business models and closed-loop value chains: Redefining the firm-consumer relationship. *California Management Review*, *58*(3), 88–108.

Laursen K, Salter A. 2006. Open for innovation: The role of openness in explaining innovation performance among UK manufacturing firms. *Strategic Management Journal*, *27*(2), 131–150.

Lerro A, Schiuma G, Manfredi F. 2022. Entrepreneurial development and digital transformation in creative and cultural industries: Trends, opportunities and challenges. *International Journal of Entrepreneurial Behavior & Research*, *28*(8), 1929–1939.

Léveillé Gauvin H. 2018. Drawing listener attention in popular music: Testing five musical features arising from the theory of attention economy. *Musicae Scientiae*, *22*(3), 291–304.

Leyshon A. 2014. *Reformatted: Code, Networks, and the Transformation of the Music Industry*. Oxford: Oxford University Press.

Lindqvist K. 2011. Artist entrepreneurs. In Mikael Scherdin and Ivo Zander (Eds.), *Art Entrepreneurship*, pp. 10–22. Cheltenham: Edward Elgar.

Purdy M, Robinson MC, Wei K. 2012. Three new business models for "the open firm". *Strategy & Leadership*, *40*(6), 36–41.

Radomska J, Hajdas M, Wołczek P, Glinka B. 2023. Wide open? Creative industries and open strategizing challenges. *International Journal of Management and Economics*, *59*(2), 117–136.

Rogers J. 2016. Payer pour la musique à l'ère du tout-gratuit-pour-tous. In Philippe Le Guern (Dir.), *Où va la musique? Numérimorphose et nouvelles expériences d'écoute (pp. 109–125)*. Paris: Presses des Mines, Coll. Libres opinions.

Romero MC, Lara P, Villalobos J. 2021. Evolution of the business model: Arriving at open business model dynamics. *Journal of Open Innovation: Technology, Market, and Complexity*, *7*(1), 86.

Saebi T, Foss NJ. 2015. Business models for open innovation: Matching heterogeneous open innovation strategies with business model dimensions. *European Management Journal*, *33*(3), 201–213.

Seabrook J. 2015. *The Song Machine: Inside the Hit Factory*. WW Norton & Company.

Seiferlein B, Kanbach DK, Lehmann C. 2023. Internal antecedents for systematic business model innovation: Insights from the German automotive manufacturers. *International Journal of Entrepreneurship and Innovation Management*, *27*(1–2), 19–50.

Shahhoseini MA, Mollaahmadi F, Mokhtarzadeh N, Keymasi M. 2023. A systematic literature review of open business models. *Journal of Business Administration Researches*, *14*(30), 231–261.

Sieg JH, Wallin MW, Von Krogh G. 2010. Managerial challenges in open innovation: A study of innovation intermediation in the chemical industry. *R&D Management*, *40*(3), 281–291.

Teece DJ. 2010. Business models, business strategy and innovation. *Long Range Planning*, *43*(2–3), 172–194.

Weiblen T. 2014. The open business model: Understanding an emerging concept. *Journal of Multi Business Model Innovation and Technology*, *2*(1), 35–66.

3 Business model evolution and board game ecosystem expansion

The Asmodee case

Gaël Gueguen

Two major concepts related to strategic management emerged in the 1990s and have been theorized in subsequent years (Zott, Amit and Massa, 2011; Priem, Butler and Li, 2013). These are the business model (Chesbrough and Rosenbloom, 2002; Demil and Lecoq, 2010; Zott and Amit, 2010) and the business ecosystem (Moore, 1996; Iansiti and Levien, 2004; Teece, 2007; Jacobides, Cennamo and Gawer, 2018; Adner, 2021). In these concepts value creation is considered as being co-created by different actors. Business models and business ecosystems consider the firm in terms of its necessary external connections.

The use of the business model concept has become essential in management research and business practice (Adner, 2021; Zott, Amit and Massa, 2011). At the same time, several studies suggest that the notion of the ecosystem is equally essential (Adner, 2017; Teece, 2007; Jacobides, Cennamo and Gawer, 2018). Indeed, the sector level of analysis now seems insufficient to understand strategy (Moore, 1996) and business models (Jacobides, Cennamo and Gawer, 2018). The question then becomes one of understanding how value is created concerning the strategy of multiple actors and, thus, beyond a single firm or a few competitors (Adner and Kapoor, 2010).

Adner (2017) distinguishes between a business ecosystem, which is centered on a focal firm, and an ecosystem, which is centered on shared value creation. Firms may have different roles within an ecosystem and, therefore, need to adopt a business model that supports the development of their business. It is widely accepted that a strategy that facilitates keystone-type interactions is more profitable (Iansiti and Levien, 2004). A dominator-type strategy (Tellier, 2017, Yoon, Moon and Lee, 2022) is seen as limiting the development of the ecosystem. However, consideration of the ecosystem life cycle (Adner, 2021) leads to a more measured vision. The dominant design has not yet been established (Teece, 2010), and the dominant firm may have a business model that allows for the existence of numerous firms. These smaller firms will benefit from the dominator's efforts to expand the boundaries of the ecosystem.

Board games are part of a changing ecosystem. It is a cultural and creative ecosystem, with authors, publishers and specialized shops, where novelty has

DOI: 10.4324/9781032714462-3

become a permanent requirement. The French company Asmodee is a key player in this ecosystem. Asmodee stands out for its innovative approach to game development and distribution. Founded on a strategy of internal and external growth, the company has evolved significantly since its creation, making strategic acquisitions and diversifying its portfolio of games. By adopting a business model based on creativity and innovation, Asmodee has not only consolidated its position but also helped to transform the global board game ecosystem.

This chapter examines the relationship between business models and ecosystems from the perspective of leadership. After identifying the main contributions of the literature, we will present the modern board game ecosystem through its leader, Asmodee. Using a longitudinal case study, we will present the main movements. This will provide some answers to our research question, which is: How can a company exercising dominant-type leadership evolve its business model to maintain the growth and diversity of its ecosystem?

1 Theory

First, we will look at the conceptual relationships between ecosystems and business models. We will then consider the evolution of an ecosystem as a function of the evolution of the ecosystem leader's business model.

1.1 Ecosystem and business models

Business ecosystem analysis has emerged as a means of better understanding the complexity in which businesses evolve. This type of approach makes it possible to consider the business model more openly (Adner, 2017; Kohtamäki et al., 2019). Business model analysis is sometimes criticized for focusing too much on the strategy of the firm under study and less on the value proposition derived from the ensemble of different actors (Adner, 2017). For example, Chesbrough and Appleyard (2007) or Sjödin, Liljeborg and Mutter (2024) have stressed the importance of opening up the firm to its ecosystem. Thinking simultaneously in terms of ecosystems and business models allows us to take a broader view of this value proposition, which will be built on different resources (Demil and Lecocq, 2010).

This chapter aims to link ecosystems and business models. This relationship may be considered an important topic (Zott and Amit, 2013; Gomes et al., 2018; Helfat and Raubitschek, 2018; Teece, 2018; Kohtamäki et al., 2019). Indeed, Priem, Butler and Li (2013) believe that the joint integration of business models and business ecosystems opens up strategic thinking in research and practice; they speak of a holistic approach. The links between the two concepts are crucial for understanding business strategy (Madanaguli et al., 2024). As Garnsey, Lorenzoni and Ferriani (2008) point out: "A business model can be thought of as a design that specifies how a firm is connected to others in its ecosystem to create and capture value".

A business ecosystem has been defined as an economic environment in which disparate organizations and individuals interact with each other in many ways (Moore, 1996). For Iansiti and Levien (2004), it is formed by large networks of interconnected entities. A firm's success is linked to its ability to grow within a dynamic ecosystem of networks and relationships that combine competition and cooperation (Brandenburger and Nalebuff, 1996). For this reason, studying the business model in terms of the business ecosystem implies taking into account the openness of the firm to other, sometimes competing, actors.

The success of this concept has led to the global use of the term "ecosystem" (Adner 2017; Jacobides, Cennamo and Gawer, 2018), of which there are many: business ecosystems, innovation ecosystems, knowledge ecosystems, etc. According to Adner (2017), the use of ecosystem reflects the strong interdependence between organizations and their activities. Actors, activities, positioning within the ecosystem, and linkages are the enduring characteristics of ecosystems. Adner (2017) sees the ecosystem as a structured alignment of different partners that must interact to propose a value to be realized. Jacobides, Cennamo and Gawer (2018) consider that the most important characteristic of ecosystems is that they facilitate the coordination of independent organizations. The modularity of actors' contributions is crucial. In their view, an ecosystem is composed of a set of actors with variable multilateral and non-generic complementarities. These complementarities are not fully controlled hierarchically and affect both production and use (Jacobides, Cennamo and Gawer, 2018). From a business model perspective, the value architecture and the value proposition are affected.

However, Adner (2017) makes an important distinction between ecosystem as structure and ecosystem as affiliation. Ecosystem as structure are activity-centered, while ecosystem as affiliation are actor-centered. The "as affiliation" analysis is the most common and corresponds to the network within which a company will develop, especially in a platform logic. The "business ecosystem", which is centered on the focal firm, belongs to this category (Kohtamäki et al., 2019). The study of the central actor of the ecosystem is foremost. The ecosystem is that of this central actor. The "as structure" analysis goes beyond the framework of a single company, considering the configuration of different activities that make it possible to propose a value that is the central element. This value is shaped by the strategies of the different actors interacting with each other. Adner (2021) warns against an analysis that is too focused on a focal company, what he calls the "ego-system". The ecosystem approach must take into account the multiplicity of actors that will interact. This leads to it being less specific to a particular company. As a result, the company's business model must take into account the various external interactions.

In this sense, an ecosystem analysis is relevant to the study of business model evolution decisions. Zott and Amit (2010) see the business model as "a system of interdependent activities that transcends the focal firm and spans its boundaries". In other words, thinking in terms of the business model requires consideration of its openness to its ecosystem. A reading of business models in terms of value architecture, value proposition and economic profit equation (Moingeon and Lehmann-Ortega, 2010) can be achieved by integrating ecosystem characteristics.

1.2 *The leader's role in the business model and ecosystem evolution*

Chesbrough and Rosenbloom (2002) argue that one of the functions of the business model is to define the firm's position within a value network that includes suppliers, customers, complements, and competitors. Rather than seeing the firm as closed to its environment, it is possible to consider that for each of these dimensions, it will be in complex interrelationships with other actors. An analysis in terms of the business model runs the risk of assuming that one company must have all the resources, while several companies will contribute (Jacobides, Cennamo and Gawer, 2018). Thus, Adner (2017) speaks of ecosystem strategy, which is how a focal firm envisages the alignment of partners and secures its role in a competitive ecosystem.

Furthermore, while business models are often linked to issues of innovation (Chesbrough and Rosenbloom, 2002; Teece, 2010; Teece, 2018), they necessarily incorporate how the industry will evolve (Teece, 2010) and how dominant designs will exist within the ecosystem. In our view, thinking in terms of business models and ecosystems makes it possible to integrate consideration of the evolution of all the players involved in the value proposition (Madanaguli et al., 2024). A company's place in an ecosystem is crucial as it conditions its expansion. To build an ecosystem, a firm will first seek to establish a "minimum viable ecosystem". Then, it will try to move it forward, step by step, along a path that favors expansion. Finally, the firm will exploit any ecosystem gains (Adner, 2021).

An important issue in understanding value creation is the role of the leader of an ecosystem. Iansiti and Levien (2004) have considered the place of firms in business ecosystems. Their analysis focuses on the role of leaders. They identify several different behaviors, but two, in particular, seem important to us: keystones and dominators.

A keystone strategy aims to create value for the ecosystem and share it with other members. This strategy results in the creation of new resources and capabilities. Dominators, on the other hand, tend to reduce the diversity of the ecosystem and occupy a greater number of network nodes. The strategic orientation is to control and own all or part of the ecosystem. In terms of business models, the keystone strategy assumes a high degree of openness to the business ecosystem made up of independent players. The dominator strategy assumes openness to the ecosystem but with a desire to control external players. Both types of leadership are compatible with ecosystem development (Iansiti and Levien, 2004). There are "value dominators" and "classic dominators" who directly control the ecosystem. A classic dominator is characterized by being much larger than the other players and having a tendency to eliminate or absorb other companies (Yoon, Moon and Lee, 2022). Classic dominators follow a strategy of horizontal (competitors) and/or vertical (suppliers, distributors) integration. Nevertheless, the study of dominators in terms of understanding ecosystem evolution is less frequent than that of keystones (Kang and Downing, 2015; Cui et al., 2022), while their impact on the ecosystem is considered less positive (Fautrero and Gueguen, 2013; Tellier, 2017; Yoon, Moon and Lee, 2022).

To summarize the theoretical findings, we believe that the value of an activity is created by multiple actors (Jacobides, Cennamo and Gawer, 2018) and that strategic analysis must open the firm to its environment (Chesbrough and Appleyard, 2007; Teece, 2007; Adner, 2017; Sjödin, Liljeborg and Mutter, 2024). As a result, the business model is a means to explain this openness through its various constituent dimensions (Chesbrough and Rosenbloom, 2002; Zott and Amit, 2010; Helfat and Raubitschek, 2018; Madanaguli et al., 2024). Moreover, since the ecosystem must be considered at the level of an evolving set of activities (Adner, 2017, 2021), the role of the leader, and the configuration of its business model, appears crucial as it can share or capture value for its benefit (Iansiti and Levien, 2004).

In this way, we extend the question posed by Zott and Amit (2013), namely: How can firms adapt their business models to an evolving ecosystem? Therefore, we will analyze the role of a leader and the configuration of its ecosystem as it expands. The research question of particular interest to us is: How can a firm pursuing a classic dominator leadership strategy evolve its business model as its ecosystem expands?

2 Method

Our empirical research aims to study a firm that is attempting to develop its business ecosystem through a change in business model based on a new value proposition. While several cultural and creative ecosystems are suitable for our study, we have chosen to focus on so-called "modern" board games and to work on their leader, Asmodee, a company that is experiencing strong growth. Indeed, the company is working with other stakeholders to spread the practice of modern board games worldwide. Previously intended for children's use and infrequent purchases, board games have evolved significantly over the past 20 years and now extend beyond physical games to various cultural media and formats, demonstrating the ecosystem's expansion. The most important player is the French company Asmodee. Let us take a look at their strategic actions to understand their business model.

This chapter is based on a single case study (Yin, 1984). The author has been interested in the company and ecosystem concerned since 2017.

Based on an extensive review of secondary data (press articles, company websites, specialized websites, study reports, discussion forums, etc.), a chronological matrix was created to describe the company's actions and the ecosystem's movements. This first phase of collection allowed the production of a first case study for pedagogical purposes (Gueguen, 2018). This was written in different formats (from 5 to 20 pages) to meet different modes of administration (exam or work session). Regularly, for six years, this case was presented to graduate students two to three times a year. During this pedagogical exercise, the author interacted with his students, who were asked to analyze the company from a strategic perspective. The students were free to seek additional information. This resulted in a first set of field notes.

Over the past six years, the author has regularly modified the case and its interpretation in light of the work and discussions. He has continuously updated information about the company and its industry. He has interviewed experts in the field and people associated with the company under study. His knowledge of the issues involved facilitated interaction with these people. These discussions resulted in a series of field notes that were incorporated into the original chronological matrix and the interpretation of certain observed movements.

3 The Asmodee case

Asmodee is active in the board game industry. It has an estimated turnover of 1.1 billion euros. It employs 2,500 people and has a catalog of 400 games. The company started as a publisher and then became a distributor. It has evolved its business model to reach all parts of the board game ecosystem. Players, authors, publishers, distributors, specialty shops, toy libraries, festivals, and websites form a multifaceted ecosystem that is evolving and growing at over 10% annually worldwide. Asmodee's directors believe that their company must become a disruptive player in the world of entertainment. To achieve this, the company's ambition is to make its games available on all relevant media. A serious board game goes beyond the game itself. It represents a cultural universe that can be adapted to a variety of formats. Ownership of intellectual property is essential to take full advantage of new revenue streams.

With over 50 million boxes of games sold each year in some 50 countries, Asmodee is the second largest publisher (of games for the general public) and the number one distributor (of board games) in the world. Its goal is to become the world leader in this field by developing the various facets of board games. Many of its games are highly successful worldwide, and it has one of the most profitable catalogs in the sector (Ticket to Ride, Carcassonne, Unlock!, Splendor, Pandemic, A Game of Thrones, Jungle Speed, Catan, Spot it!, 7 Wonders, Time's up, Smallworld, The Werewolves of Miller's Hollow, Mysterium, Dixit, etc.). Creativity is at the heart of the company's business model for developing new games, but it has also acquired several companies, giving it a catalog of well-known games and a central position in the board game ecosystem.

3.1 *The board game ecosystem*

Asmodee operates in the modern board game ecosystem. In the 1990s, some small, local publishers, especially in Germany and France, contributed to the emergence of what we might call modern board games. In contrast to the classic games, mainly owned by Hasbro and Mattel, such as Monopoly, Clue, Scrabble, Trivial Pursuit, and Payday, these small publishers proposed games that limited the role of chance, allowed different types of victory, encouraged interaction, appealed to different age groups, and required a shorter playing time to complete. Today, these publishers are distributed through specialized boutiques and are constantly releasing new products. Unlike Hasbro or Mattel, they are rarely found in supermarkets. An estimated 3,500 new games are released worldwide each year. Some will become worldwide successes, while others will be forgotten. It is becoming increasingly important for these publishers to foster creativity and produce original games that are appreciated by critics and an ever-growing audience. Asmodee is the most successful company in the industry because it is perhaps one of the most creative.

Board games have been a fast-growing business in recent years. Worldwide, the industry is currently growing at a rate of 12%, with sales of $20 billion. The USA is the leading market, followed by France. France is experiencing growth of 15%, with 30 million game boxes sold each year. This corresponds to a turnover of 650 million euros. There are 150 publishers in France, many of them very small. Asmodee promotes the development of the sector by spreading the game culture and distributing a large number of them.

Games are not only for children but also for young adults. The trend is to develop this category of buyers. How can this craze be explained? Several factors can be taken into account. First of all, games are one of the cheapest leisure activities. For a few dozen dollars, it is possible to have several hours of fun. That is important in times of crisis. Gaming is also a shared activity and has benefited from the post-COVID period (+20% growth). This is true within families, where teenagers spend a lot of time in front of screens. It is also true among friends. Board games are a way to spend time together. In fact, when we say "board games" in English or "juegos de mesa" in Spanish, we are more likely to say "jeux de société" in French or "Gesellschaftsspiele" in German: these two languages emphasize the social dimension more than the physical one (the board).

The world's major publishers, such as Hasbro and Mattel, focus on a few historical blockbusters that are sold primarily through mass retail and television advertising. They keep some of the big games alive by trying to modernize them in small steps. Their goal is not to renew their portfolio of games but to continue to distribute them to an occasional audience. Conversely, some small publishers play the innovation card by releasing numerous new games each year. They do not advertise for lack of resources but target an audience of gamers who buy several games a year. The challenge is to maintain this creativity while managing to sustain their revenues. In other words, the challenge is to strike a balance between exploration and exploitation. Asmodee is a company that has been able to grow while maintaining a policy of constant creative innovation. In terms of size, it is well ahead of the smaller publishers and is aiming to take the place of Hasbro or Mattel while maintaining this aspect of exploration. However, it does not neglect exploitation. In 2023, for example, it grouped a dozen of its most popular games under a single label, "Unbox Now", to promote them with a consumer-oriented marketing campaign.

3.2 *The expansion and complexity of Asmodee's business model*

Asmodee was founded in 1987 to publish its own games. The company quickly realized that distribution in the industry was complicated. If the industry was to grow, distribution had to become easier. So, it became its own distributor. Then, it started to distribute the games of competing publishers, offering them a commercial and logistical package. Today, Asmodee presents itself as a creator, inventor, publisher and distributor of board games. These four elements are important for understanding its business model. Its goal is to "dust off the classic image of the gaming world". Ten years ago, Asmodee was releasing 20 new games a year; today it can release almost 300. On its corporate website, Asmodee presents itself as "We believe in the power of ideas, and encourage creativity and innovation. We believe that every idea can become a success story."

As far as the development of new games is concerned, Asmodee has developed an innovation and R&D model based on testing and learning, from publishing to distribution. A publisher selects games and then carries out a series of modifications: improving ergonomics and aesthetics, adapting rules, conducting numerous tests, and developing game strategies. The editing process takes between 6 and 24 months. The goal is to have a game whose rules fit on one page and can be played in half an hour. More emphasis is placed on the aesthetics of the game and the presentation of the authors. Today, publishers are actively looking for the best talent.

While innovating its games, the company has also expanded through numerous acquisitions of companies, both publishers (independent studios) and distributors (in different countries). It is estimated that 40% of Asmodee's growth is internal and 60% is external. To finance its development, it is owned by several investment funds. Asmodee is attractive to investors because, in addition to the development of its ecosystem, the company has a large catalog of well-known games, an ability to innovate, real marketing know-how, particularly in the development of games, and an extensive distribution network. The company has significant resources to expand internationally, which is rare in a sector that is beginning to consolidate. In 2022, the Swedish Embracer Group, which specializes in video games, acquired Asmodee for 2.75 billion euros.

Asmodee sees itself as a kind of "business angel" in the board game industry. The company will work on the publication, development, and distribution of high-potential games from various authors. In its role as publisher, it will review game concepts submitted by authors, select and perfect them, design the packaging, and promote them.

The company has developed its business model to reach the 15–30-year-old high-income segment by producing more dynamic board games. Asmodee has a panel of authors and it publishes their games. Game testing is critical to the success of the offering. Several months of it are necessary to simplify the rules and reduce the playing time. New products are first launched in specialized stores and are the subject of various events (e.g., tournaments). These stores are frequented by enthusiasts. It is in these stores, by interacting with the players, that Asmodee's teams find out if the new game will work or not. If the game is a success, it will be offered in specialized supermarkets and then, for a few, in general supermarkets.

Asmodee has 22 studios and as many distribution subsidiaries (in Europe, North and South America, China, Korea, and Australia). A studio is the unit that designs and develops the various games. The number of studios is linked to the preservation of a certain independence after the acquisition. Instead of integrating the acquired studios, Asmodee maintains its autonomy. It will also create new, equally autonomous studios. Among these different studios, three deserve special attention because they provide a better understanding of the expansion of the ecosystem.

- Twin Sails Interactive, formerly Asmodee Digital, is responsible for the digital porting of the games. Digital porting is an extension of the physical board game and helps drive sales. Players download a digital game application to their phone and then purchase the game in the store to play with friends. In some countries that do not have a board game culture, it is a way to reach customers, such as in China. In those that do, if gamers like a game, they will try to play it online thanks to its digital format.
- Asmodee Entertainment's mission is to exploit the intellectual property of its catalog to create films, TV series, comic books, and novels. In 2019, Asmodee created the subsidiary Aconyte, a publishing house that publishes novels based on the various Asmodee game universes. By 2022, more than 20 adaptations (books, TV series) inspired by Asmodee games were in development. The Werewolves of Miller's Hollow, for example, is to be made into a movie for Netflix. Conversely, Asmodee has been commissioned by Netflix to adapt The Queen's Gambit series phenomenon into a game.
- Access+ was created to develop or adapt games for people with cognitive disabilities. With the help of scientists, Asmodee's research department

proposes versions of its games that promote greater inclusion. It also supports research projects on the psychology of creativity.

Asmodee's development has been accompanied by numerous acquisitions. In the last ten years, it has acquired more than 40 companies. These include publishers (most recently Libellud (Mysterium, Dixit), Repos Production (Time's Up, 7 Wonders), Lui-Même (The Werewolves of Miller's Hollow), as well as regional distributors, such as Enigma Distribution, the leading distributor of board games in Northern Europe, and distributors in the USA, Germany, Brazil, Spain, Italy, Poland, and Canada. There is a strong link between publishing and distribution in Asmodee's acquisition policy. It will buy a foreign distributor that will distribute its games, or it will buy a studio whose games it will distribute.

As the chart below shows, its sales have grown significantly, by 27% per year in recent years (Figure 3.1).

Asmodee's development extends beyond publishing and distribution to the entire gaming ecosystem. For example, at the end of 2020, it acquired France's number one game e-commerce site (Philibert), as well as major board game information sites (e.g., Tric Trac). In 2021, it also acquired the startup Board Game Arena (five million largely international members) which offers digital versions of more than 250 games from all types of publishers.

Asmodee's choices are copied by other companies in the ecosystem. For example, the distributor Hachette Livre, in addition to its own studio (Studio H), has been buying up publishers (Gigamic, Blackrock Games, Le Scorpion Masqué) over the last two years and merging them into its Hachette Boardgames division. This allows it to copy Asmodee's business model.

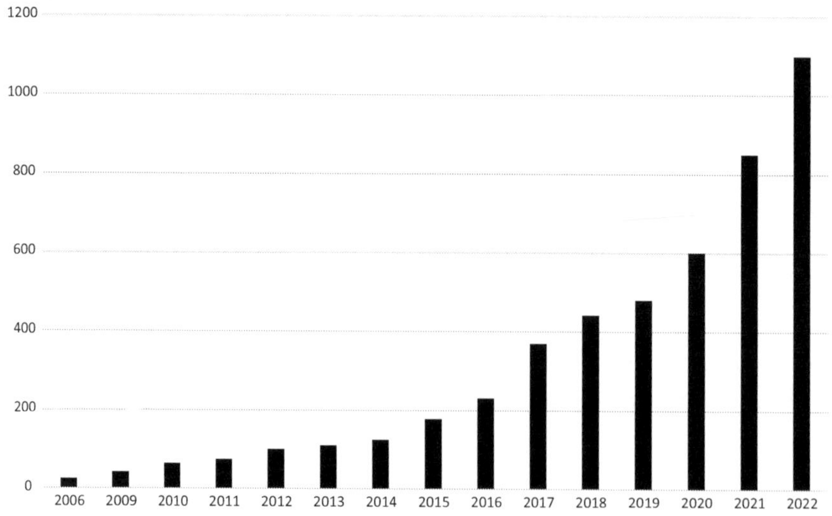

Figure 3.1 Evolution of Asmodee's sales

4 Key findings

The Asmodee case study provides insight into the development of a business model within the expanding board game ecosystem. Asmodee is part of this ecosystem and plays a leading role. Through its development initiatives (books, cinema, digital, new audiences, etc.), it contributes to expanding the boundaries of this ecosystem by spreading the board game culture. It is one of the key players in a value proposition focused on entertainment through board games. It has adopted a classic dominator strategy, with numerous acquisitions, both horizontal (other studios) and vertical (distributors, e-commerce).

4.1 An ecosystem and a business model driven by creativity

The board game ecosystem is made up of various heterogeneous players who contribute to the creation of greater value. In addition to game designers, publishers, graphic designers, distributors, various types of more or less specialized stores and buyers, other players influence the distribution of board games. Game libraries make it possible to borrow games for free. Game bars offer outdoor games. There are numerous game festivals and conventions around the world. E-commerce sites specializing in board games allow you to make specific purchases. Other websites and magazines provide information and recommendations about board games. There are dedicated YouTube channels. There is a large community of enthusiastic gamers, so we find companies, volunteers, enthusiasts, associations and independent creators who promote the development of board game culture.

This ecosystem is growing, as the figures in the case study show. This development is made possible by the spread of a gaming culture. In addition to the socio-economic dimensions (family structure, need to find oneself, value for money, etc.), the efforts of various publishers, including Asmodee, to launch new, innovative games are crucial. High-quality products contribute to the democratization and popularity of games. Beyond the quality aspect, the sheer number of games released each year means that only a small number will be profitable. A suitable business model is, therefore, needed to produce a large number of new games and remain profitable.

Asmodee has several processes in place to develop new products. It is clear that the best game idea alone does not guarantee commercial success. In the run-up to the market launch, thorough work is necessary to identify authors, edit, test, format, and clean up the rules. Downstream, distribution skills ensure a better presence in the various stores.

It acquires several independent publishers. The goal is to acquire well-known games and increase the value of the catalog in terms of intellectual property. However, this is not a one-time purchase of brands. Asmodee keeps its publishers as independent studios to preserve their creativity. In terms of cost rationalization, it would be more cost-effective to proceed with full integration within the parent company.

The case also highlights the importance of exploiting certain games. Asmodee can profit from the games that work best. For example, it selects its games for specialized and mass distribution. It is also able to develop mass marketing for a limited number of games.

4.2 *Business model expansion and ecosystem leadership*

Asmodee quickly realized that one of the keys to success was a business model that included distribution. The peculiarity of the industry is that games are mainly sold in small, specialized shops. The company needs to work with the various points of sale on the ground. Distribution is even more important when you consider the number of new games that are released each year. The sales staff in the stores are there to advise customers as the constant flow of new products creates uncertainty. Through its distribution activities, Asmodee is as close as possible to the sellers and, thus, to the buyers.

It is interesting to note the strong connection between publishing and distribution in Asmodee's acquisition decisions. The company will buy foreign distributors that it knows well because they distribute its games in those foreign countries. Conversely, it will buy publishers that it already distributes. This integration of publishing and distribution is a strength of its business model.

The case presents the evolution of Asmodee with certain players in the ecosystem. Asmodee is France's leading e-commerce site and the country's leading gaming information site. Its teams have a strong presence at festivals. It strategically considers all the players in the board game ecosystem and tries to reach out to them to ensure a strong presence. The innovation of its business model is particularly characterized by its focus on the ecosystem.

Asmodee's vision of the ecosystem extends beyond physical games. It is developing the value of its games by encouraging their transfer to cultural products (books, movies, etc.). This is a major area of development. One of its ambitions is to develop Walt Disney (entertainment) based on its games. Asmodee does not see digital games as a replacement but as a useful addition. Digital can be a gateway to physical games as well as a continuation of them.

By taking its ecosystem into account, Asmodee can develop its revenue sources and thus promote the expansion of board game culture worldwide. The choices it has made regarding its business model have allowed it to expand the impact of its activities by pushing back its natural boundaries. To understand Asmodee's business model, it may help to describe its evolution.

Regarding the value proposition:

Asmodee initially focused on providing entertainment through board games. Its evolution, linked to the expansion of its ecosystem, has led it to offer entertainment-related value within a multimedia universe linked to board games. The result is a much broader and potentially more profitable value proposition.

Regarding its value architecture:

> Asmodee started as a game publisher. To keep up with the expansion of its ecosystem, it evolved its architecture. It is still a publisher, but it consists of several studios. These studios retain their autonomy to foster creativity. It has added distribution activities that allow it to sell its games (as well as those of its competitors) worldwide. Asmodee's architecture allows it to acquire studios that own the rights to well-known games. In this way, it increases its intellectual property. It is also trying to spread the board game culture by expanding into digital, cinema, books, etc.

Regarding the economic profit equation:

> Asmodee's first revenues came from the sale of games. It continues to generate profits from sales, but also from distribution and e-commerce. In addition, new revenues are being generated, in particular by the digital business, which was planned as a supplement. Asmodee is also generating new profits from the exploitation of game licenses to which it holds the rights.

Our results show the growing complexity of Asmodee's business model. It actively participates in the development of its ecosystem by promoting the board game culture. This culture now extends beyond the physical games themselves, allowing numerous external players to develop within it. A virtuous circle is emerging between the business model and the ecosystem. The acquisition logic that drives Asmodee's strategy leads us to consider the company as a classic dominator. However, it manages to maintain a certain autonomy for its various studios. We can assume that it is the quest for creativity that guides this desire for autonomy.

5 How can we contribute to the understanding of business models?

The Asmodee case study is interesting for several reasons. The first is to observe the evolution of the business model of a player in a classic dominator role. This evolution of the business model is seen in the context of the expansion of the ecosystem. This leads us to observe a desire to integrate and control the ecosystem. Contrary to what the literature suggests, Asmodee's expansion strategy benefits the ecosystem as a whole.

The links between business models and ecosystems exist and seem necessary to understand the strategic evolution of firms (Chesbrough and Rosenbloom, 2002; Priem, Butler and Li, 2013). The openness of the business model or its interconnectedness with other actors is inevitable (Garnsey, Lorenzoni and Ferriani, 2008; Madanaguli et al., 2024). This may be obvious when a company follows a keystone strategy, but less so when it exercises classic dominator leadership (Iansiti and Levien, 2004). This openness exists on two levels. The firm has a business model that allows it to interact with multiple external actors (e.g., competitors' distribution), thus assuming a platform role. When the company integrates entities after acquisitions, it leaves a certain degree of openness because this encourages creativity. To integrate studios or distributors, the company must be in contact with them. This is a constant in Asmodee's development.

The business model is expanding, with a broader value proposition, a more complex value architecture, and multiple sources of profit (Demil and Lecocq, 2010; Moingeon and Lehmann-Ortega, 2010; Zott and Amit, 2010). This evolution of the business model exists because the ecosystem is also growing. A virtuous circle is created. The results suggest that Asmodee is establishing the dominant design within the ecosystem, a design that breaks with past practices (Hasbro or Mattel) (Teece, 2010). While Asmodee is not alone in promoting its business through modernization, it has succeeded in formalizing the approach and making itself more profitable. Its internationalization and ability to exploit a few high-profile games are a case in point. Spreading game culture (directly through game boxes or indirectly through digital or media channels) encourages the development of other players (authors-creators, independent publishers, specialized shops, etc.). This enables the success of a few who are then captured by the company. Broadening the ecosystem enables the success of companies that benefit from the democratization of the board game, a democratization that implies the search for new products and more frequent game purchases.

The strategic choices made by the company under study indicate a desire to control different dimensions of the ecosystem: publishing, distribution, online sales, information sites, use of licenses, etc. (Adner, 2021). The business model evolves to include new elements. However, internal and external growth coexist. The business model evolves in a hybrid way. Again, the desire to benefit from the creativity of the players seems to us to be a decisive factor in this evolution.

The results of the case study demonstrate the value of following a classic dominator strategy, not only for the benefit of the leading company but for the entire ecosystem (Iansiti and Levien, 2004). The figures show growth for the gaming ecosystem as a whole. This is interesting because the classic dominator is often viewed negatively (Iansiti and Levien, 2004; Fautrero and Gueguen, 2013; Tellier, 2017). We believe that the hybridity of its business model explains its positive impact on the ecosystem as a whole.

The temporal dimension, especially regarding the life cycle of the ecosystem, seems important to us (Moore, 1996; Adner, 2021). The modern board game ecosystem is a transformation of the classic board game sector: it consists of players with business models that are different from those of the companies in the sector. This ecosystem is young. It was created about 30 years ago and has been spreading globally for the past 15 years. This youthfulness may also explain the success of the business model of a company that adopts classic dominator leadership (Iansiti and Levien, 2004).

6 Conclusion

Asmodee stands out in the board game ecosystem not only as a leading publisher but also as a player actively redefining the modern board game landscape. By focusing on acquiring independent studios and preserving their creative autonomy, it aims not only to expand its game catalog but also to enrich the entire ecosystem with diversity and innovation. This strategy allows it to play a dominator role while fostering an environment where creativity and innovation are important. In this way, it not only contributes to the expansion of the board game ecosystem but also ensures that it remains dynamic, diverse, and constantly evolving.

This chapter aims to understand how a company can evolve its business model to contribute to the expansion of its ecosystem. The originality of the approach lies in the study of classic dominator leadership. By focusing on Asmodee's role within the board game ecosystem, our findings provide a more nuanced view of a classic dominator-type leadership, which is traditionally perceived as a constraint on the development of an ecosystem. Adopting Adner's (2017) vision of the ecosystem as a structure, and considering the issue of temporality (Adner, 2021), we find that the strategy employed helps to structure the ecosystem and promote its expansion. It seems to us that the youthful stage of the ecosystem helps to explain this positive impact. The evolution of the business model toward strong integration and diversification helps to support the development of the ecosystem.

In terms of limitations, the single case study reduces the external validity and the generalizability of our findings. We did not mobilize social network theory, which would have allowed us to model the different relationships between actors. The result is not an explanatory model that would allow us to isolate the variables at work in the relationship between the business model and the ecosystem. The quantification of impacts is also a shortcoming of this work. However, a more precise measurement of a reduced number of variables would have been detrimental to the overall understanding of the company and the ecosystem. In line with the case study proposed by Yin (1984), we thought it would be interesting to study the phenomenon of business model evolution in a more general context (ecosystem expansion), where the boundaries between phenomenon and context are blurred.

This research has many potential extensions related to the limitations mentioned above. An interesting avenue would be to consider the actors' representations concerning the ecosystem leader's strategy. Indeed, the ecosystem seems to be expanding and firms are taking advantage of this positive development. Nevertheless, the dominance exercised by the leader may lead to a perception of dependency and a limitation of available resources. This more negative vision can exist and lead to a sense of vulnerability. The degree of maturity of the ecosystem may be a variable that moderates this perception. It would also be interesting to look at our results linking the business model and the ecosystem in other creative industries, such as book publishing, music or film, to identify transferable practices and the specificities of each sector.

Bibliography

Adner R. 2017. Ecosystem as a structure. *Journal of Management* **43**(1): 39–58.

Adner R. 2021. *Winning the right game*. Cambridge: The MIT Press.

Adner R, Kapoor R. 2010. Value creation in innovation ecosystems: How the structure of technological interdependence affects firm performance in new technology generations. *Strategic Management Journal* **31**(3): 306–333.

Brandenburger A, Nalebuff B. 1996. *Co-opetition*. New York: Doubleday.

Chesbrough H W, Appleyard M M. 2007. Open innovation and strategy. *California Management Review* **50**(1): 57–76.

Chesbrough H W, Rosenbloom R S. 2002. The role of the business model in capturing value from innovation: Evidence from Xerox Corporation's technology spin-off companies. *Industrial and Corporate Change* **11**(3): 529–555.

Cui M, Li W, Cui L, Jia Y, Wu L. 2022. How do keystones govern their business ecosystems through resource orchestration? *Industrial Management & Data Systems* **122**(9) 1987–2011.

de Vasconcelos Gomes L A, Facin A L F, Salerno M S, Ikenami R K. 2018. Unpacking the innovation ecosystem construct: Evolution, gaps and trends. *Technological Forecasting and Social Change* **136**(C): 30–48.

Demil B, Lecocq X. 2010. Business model evolution: In search of dynamic consistency. *Long Range Planning* **43**(2–3): 227–246.

Fautrero F, Gueguen G. 2013. The dual dominance of the Android business ecosystem. In Ben Letaifa S, Gratacap A, Isckia T. (ed.), *Understanding Business Ecosystems*. Louvain: De Boeck: 211–230.

Garnsey E, Lorenzoni G, Ferriani S. 2008. Speciation through entrepreneurial spin-off: The Acorn-ARM story. *Research Policy* **37**(2): 210–224.

Gueguen G. 2018. *Asmodee, in search of leadership in board games*. CCMP G1950.

Helfat C, Raubitschek R S. 2018. Dynamic and integrative capabilities for profiting from innovation in digital platform-based ecosystems. *Research Policy* **47**(8): 1391–1399.

Iansiti M, Levien R. 2004. *The keystone advantage*. Brighton: Harvard Business School Press.

Jacobides M G, Cennamo C, Gawer A. 2018. Towards a theory of ecosystems. *Strategic Management Journal* **39**(8): 2255–2276.

Kang J-S, Downing S. 2015. Keystone effect on entry into two-sided markets: An analysis of the market entry of WiMAX. *Technological Forecasting and Social Change* **94**(C): 170–186.

Kohtamäki M, Parida V, Oghazi P, Gebauer H, Baines T. 2019. Digital servitization business models in ecosystems: A theory of the firm. *Journal of Business Research* **104**: 380–392.

Madanaguli A, Sjödin D, Parida V, Mikalef P. 2024. Artificial intelligence capabilities for circular business models: Research synthesis and future agenda. *Technological Forecasting and Social Change* **200**.

Moingeon B, Lehmann-Ortega L. 2010. Genesis and deployment of a new business model: A disarming case study. *M@n@gement* **13**: 266–297.

Moore J F. 1996. *The death of competition: Leadership and strategy in the age of business ecosystems*. New York: Wiley Harper Business.

Priem R L, Butler J E, Li S. 2013. Toward reimagining strategy research: Retrospection and prospection on the 2011 AMR decade award article. *Academy of Management Review* **38**(4): 471–489.

Sjödin D, Liljeborg A, Mutter S. 2024. Conceptualizing ecosystem management capabilities: Managing the ecosystem-organization interface. *Technological Forecasting and Social Change* **200**.

Teece D J. 2007. Explicating dynamic capabilities: The nature and microfoundations of (sustainable) enterprise performance. *Strategic Management Journal* **28**(13): 1319–1350.

Teece D J. 2010. Business models, business strategy and innovation. *Long Range Planning* **43**(2–3): 172–194.

Teece D J. 2018. Profiting from innovation in the digital economy: Enabling technologies, standards, and licensing models in the wireless world. *Research Policy* **47**(8): 1367–1387.

Tellier A. 2017. Whatever happened to the 'great escape'? Lessons from the rise and decline of the pinball ecosystem. *International Journal of Technology Management* **75**(1–4): 121–141.

Yin, R K. (1984). *Case study research, design and methods*. Newbury Park, CA: Sage.

Yoon C, Moon S, Lee H. 2022. Symbiotic relationships in business ecosystem: A systematic literature review. *Sustainability (Switzerland)* **14**(4): 2252.

Zott C, Amit R. 2010. Business model design: An activity system perspective. *Long Range Planning* **43**(2–3): 216–226.

Zott C, Amit R. 2013. The business model: A theoretically anchored robust construct for strategic analysis. *Strategic Organization* **11**(4): 403–411.

Zott C, Amit R, Massa L. 2011. The business model: Recent developments and future research. *Journal of Management* **37**(4): 1019–1042.

4 A sustainable business model in the fashion industry

Arthur Caré-Famchon and Pierre Roy

1 Introduction

Social and environmental concerns have been a key issue in modern society since the end of the 20th century. The maturity of Western markets is reflected in a broadening of the concept of value beyond economic and financial values. As a result, social and environmental values – the two pillars of sustainability – are increasingly present in customer expectations and in corporate strategies.

To explore these new opportunities, many companies have been trying to innovate by introducing a sustainable dimension to their business model (BM). Such companies include pioneers like The body shop in cosmetics, Patagonia in outdoor clothing and, more recently, Tesla in the automotive industry. The strategic management literature has attempted to conceptualise this development and question the issues involved. Over the last ten years or so, the concept of the sustainable business model (SBM) has emerged as perhaps the best description of how a company can place sustainability at the heart of its strategy. For the purposes of this chapter, we adopt the definition of an SBM as a BM that "incorporate[s] concepts, principles, or goals that aim at sustainability or integrate[s] sustainability into their value proposition, value creation and delivery activities, and/or value capture mechanisms" (Geissdoerfer et al., 2018, p. 403).

The research on SBMs mainly focuses on industries with a high environmental and social impact, such as transport, energy and food. Paradoxically, there has been little in-depth investigation of the sustainable strategies of the highly polluting fashion industry. In particular, there has been no research on how companies in the fashion industry can build SBMs by integrating sustainability into every component of their BMs.

This chapter aims to fill this gap. It first presents a summary of existing knowledge of the SBM concept and uncaptured value. It then empirically studies the fashion industry's Veja sneaker company to analyse the components of an SBM developed over the last 20 years. Finally, the results of the case study allow us to discuss the issues and challenges specific to BM innovation from a sustainability perspective within the cultural and creative industries (CCIs).

DOI: 10.4324/9781032714462-4

2 Theoretical background

2.1 The concept of the SBM

Since the end of the 20th century, the BM concept has attracted increasing attention from the media, researchers and professionals. Despite its novelty, there has been growing interest in this field of research from management science, particularly in the field of innovation, entrepreneurship, strategy and environmental sustainability (Massa et al., 2017). A BM is a mix of elements that describes how a company conducts its activities (Zott and Amit, 2010). Several formal conceptual representations of BMs have been proposed and are used by academics and professionals. The most famous of these are Richardson's (2005) triptych (value proposition; value creation and delivery; value capture) and the BM canvas by Osterwalder and Pigneur (2010).

Despite the environmental urgency and the pressure on organisations (from customers, politicians, media, etc.) to move towards sustainability, SBMs are rarely implemented and, of those that are, many fail in the market (Geissdoerfer et al., 2018). To date, researchers have mainly discussed SBMs and their specificities (Stubbs and Cocklin, 2008; Shakeel et al., 2020). These specificities have led researchers to link them to the existing literature on BM and BM innovation (Shakeel et al., 2020). Consequently, SBMs are defined in comparison to traditional BMs. For example, an SBM is a BM that "incorporate[s] concepts, principles, or goals that aim at sustainability or integrate[s] sustainability into their value proposition, value creation and delivery activities, and/or value capture mechanisms" (Geissdoerfer et al., 2018, p. 403).

With this in mind, Joyce and Paquin (2016) propose a revisited version of the famous BM canvas (Osterwalder and Pigneur, 2010) by adding two new layers (environmental and social layers) to the economic layer. The different dimensions of this triple layered BM canvas are summarised in Figure 4.1.

The first layer, (economic layer) incorporates the nine original dimensions of the BM canvas.

The second layer (environmental layer) is based on analysis of the life cycle and measurement of the environmental impact. The environmental impact is measured using evaluation methods of the goods and services produced by the company at all stages of their lives, that is, from the extraction of raw materials to elimination of the waste generated at the end (Cimprich et al., 2023). These analyses are based on various indicators, the best known and most widely used of which is "carbon dioxide emissions". The aim of this environmental layer is to put the environmental benefits generated by the company's activity into perspective against its impacts (Joyce and Paquin, 2016). Highlighting the most polluting activities can be a source for environmentally oriented innovations (Kuzma et al., 2020). This environmental layer comprises the following nine dimensions: functional value; supplies and outsourcing; materials; production; use phase; end-of-life; distribution; environmental impacts; and benefits.

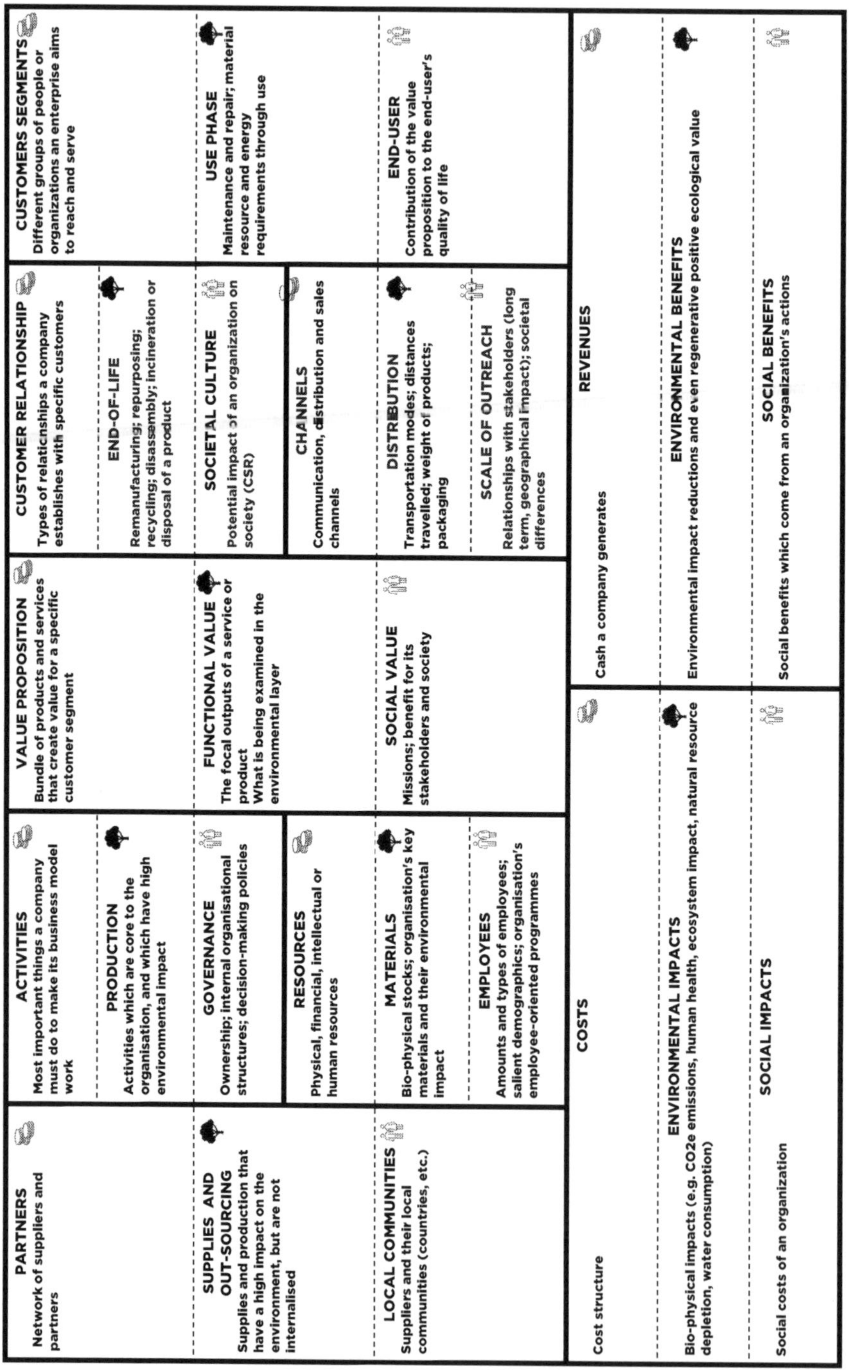

Figure 4.1 Triple layered BM canvas.

Source: Adapted from Joyce and Paquin (2016).

The third layer (social layer) focuses on the company's stakeholders in order to assess its social impact. Such stakeholders are all the individuals and groups of individuals who affect or are affected by that company. The most common stakeholders are shareholders, employees, competitors, customers, suppliers and the state. In the triple layered BM canvas (Joyce and Paquin, 2016), the notion of stakeholders is deliberately broad as stakeholders can differ widely from one company to another. The nine dimensions of this social layer are: social value; local communities; governance; employees; end-user; societal culture; scale of outreach; social benefits; and impact benefits.

The triple layered BM canvas focuses on the integration of sustainability into traditional BMs (Evans et al., 2017) and on innovation (Abdul-Rashid et al., 2017; Shakeel et al., 2020) in order to guarantee the economic sustainability of companies while they aim to develop sustainable alternatives. Thus, the most recent research uses the concept of SBM innovation as if the concepts of innovation and sustainability cannot be dissociated from one another (Joyce and Paquin, 2016; Geissdoerfer et al., 2018; Shakeel et al., 2020).

Shakeel and co-authors (2020, p. 8) define SBM innovation as follows:

> It deals with the modification of a business model to a more sustainable business model. This comprises either the creation of an exclusively new BM or changes the existing BM to innovatively address sustainability issues for its stakeholders for creating a long term sustainable competitive advantage. The change involves modification to its components.

In order to implement changes associated with sustainability, new tools and methods have also emerged for helping companies to innovate through their SBM (Evans et al., 2017; Yang et al., 2017; Geissdoerfer et al., 2018).

2.2 *Transforming uncaptured value into sustainable opportunities*

The notions of "sustainability" and "stakeholders" are at the heart of SBM issues. Whereas in traditional BMs value essentially refers to economic value, broader concerns are integrated into SBMs. SBM researchers are therefore invited to consider the notion of value in the context of sustainability (Yang et al., 2017). Value is no longer created solely for customers and shareholders, but for all stakeholders (Yang et al., 2014).

SBMs offer sustainable value but, in practice, value can be created and captured or destroyed (Bocken et al., 2015). Thus, to create social and/or environmental value through SBM innovation, authors suggest looking at "uncaptured value" (Yang et al., 2014, 2017). The sustainability of SBMs can be strengthened by taking account of "uncaptured value", which can be identified in four ways (value surplus; value absence; value destroyed; value missed – see Table 4.1).

Table 4.1 Characteristics of uncaptured value perspective

	Definition	*Sources*	*Illustrations in CCIs*
Value surplus	Value that exists but is not required	Waste (loss of heat, etc.); over-production; under-utilisation of resources; etc.	Lighting of shops at night (textiles); practice of piloning (destruction/ incineration of unsold goods; books); energy wastage (architecture); incentives for over-consumption, etc.
Value absence	Value that is required but does not exist	Unmet needs; lack of resources (labour, skills, technology, raw materials, etc.)	Sufficient supply of ecological raw materials (textiles, architecture); measurement of the environmental impact of dematerialised services, such as streaming (cinema, music, video games); ethical and ecological certification for most CCIs; etc.
Value destroyed	Value with negative consequences	Negative externalities (depletion of non-renewable energy sources, pollution, poor quality of products and services, poor working conditions, etc.)	Film sets; cultural homogenisation; intensive use of non-renewable materials; overuse of packaging (board games); etc.
Value missed	Value that exists and is required, but is not exploited	Under-exploitation of synergies between by-products, co-products, assets, resources, etc.; inefficient use (human resources, production capacity, etc.)	Poor management of unsold stock (books; textiles); vacant seats in cinemas and theatres; lack of coherence between the message conveyed by the creative medium and the creative process (film, books, board games on ecology), etc.

Source: Adapted from Yang et al. (2017).

Having identified the uncaptured value of a product, an existing BM or an industry, companies need to transform this uncaptured value into new opportunities. By seizing some of these opportunities, companies create or transform their existing BM into a more sustainable BM. In this chapter, we will apply this tool of uncaptured value to the fashion industry and illustrate the SBM concept through the case study of the Veja sneaker brand.

3 Research method

The SBM concept is a relatively recent research object in the field of strategic management. It stems from the intersection of research on BMs as a representation of corporate strategy on the one hand and work that explores sustainability issues on the other. As this is a rapidly developing area of research, the case study method seems appropriate (Eisenhardt, 1989; Yin, 1994) for defining its contours, understanding the issues and bringing out new theoretical elements.

Furthermore, the relative maturity of sustainable approaches in the fashion industry allows us to take a step back from the concept of the SBM. The existence of such BMs in the industry over the last two decades makes it possible to study their emergence and growth in a processual way. The fashion industry is directly affected by a number of issues that raise questions about sustainability. Such issues include over-consumption, over-production and waste treatment, the transport of goods and working conditions.

As the fashion industry is vast with numerous activities and sub-industries that specialise in terms of products and range, we chose to focus on a major industry: the sneaker industry. Within this highly competitive industry, several companies have opted to develop a sustainable approach. The French company Veja, founded in 2004, is a forerunner in this field and has established itself as a leading player in the sustainable sneaker segment.

Our research is based on a qualitative case study conducted between 2021 and 2023 with three objectives. The first objective was to understand how the sneaker industry works: its stakeholders, history, trends, key figures, key success factors, etc. The second was to understand the history of Veja: its creation, integration of sustainability into the various stages of its value chain, the company's growth, etc. The third objective was to understand the strategic challenges associated with an SBM in the fashion industry: competitors' reactions, impact on the industry, limits and obstacles to the large-scale spread of sustainable practices, etc.

The case study is based on the collection of primary and secondary data. The primary data was collected through 32 interviews with sustainability experts and fashion industry specialists in France. The secondary data was collected from pre-existing sources such as the website and social networks of Veja and those of its main competitors, press interviews with Veja's founders, websites that specialise in the fashion business, statistics, etc.

4 Case study presentation

4.1 Sneaker industry

4.1.1 A brief history of the industry

Since they first appeared in the footwear industry, sneakers have made steady progress both in terms of consumers' tastes and manufacturers' product ranges. The product emerged in the 19th century, when rubber was used as a key raw material in other industries, notably the automotive industry. In 1839, Charles Goodyear developed the process of vulcanising rubber to make it more flexible and resistant. Several decades later, this process was employed as an innovation for improving the quality of shoe soles and the material was used in the design of sports shoes, particularly tennis shoes.

The potential for the product to be used by the broader public started at the beginning of the 20th century. Forerunners included Keds (1916) and Converse (1917) in the USA and the Adidas brand developed by the two German brothers Rudolf and Adolf Dassler. The Adidas shoes quickly attracted the attention of the general public, particularly through high-profile sporting competitions. Subsequent differences of opinion between the two founding brothers led to the creation of two separate sneaker brands: Adidas and Puma.

From the 1950s onwards, the technical performance of the product and the fashionable nature of sneakers contributed to their democratisation. Sneakers became an essential part of the footwear market. They were also embraced by leading Hollywood celebrities, such as Marilyn Monroe and Marlon Brando. In the 1960s, a powerful new brand entered this booming market. Created by Phil Knight and Bill Bowerman, the American company Nike gradually established its global leadership. Sales grew rapidly and took off in the 1980s with the spread of hip-hop culture and sportswear. Another major competitor – the Anglo-American Reebok – appeared at the same time. Over the course of a century, sneakers had become a fashion staple and a mass market product.

4.1.2 *Market and competition*

The sneaker market has continued to grow. It is estimated that sneaker sales revenues will reach $90 billion in 2025, and in many developed countries sneaker sales account for more than 50% of the total footwear market. The sneaker market was internationalised very early on and is dominated by global players headquartered in the USA, Western Europe and Asia. Two market leaders stand out in terms of performance: the American company Nike (38.5% of the market in 2022) and the German group Adidas (18.4%).

In 2020, Nike's market capitalisation was worth $153 billion and that of its challenger Adidas was nearly $30 billion. There are several reasons for their hegemonic presence in the sneaker market. These include their historical presence in the market, the diversification of their products, the power of their brand and the existence of iconic products (bestsellers), such as the Adidas Stan Smith (1964) and the Nike Air Force One (1982).

Beyond these two leaders, the market remains competitive with many brands, some of which have been around for several decades and have a global presence: the American New Balance (1906), the German Puma (1948), the Japanese Asics (1949), the American Sketchers (1992) and the

American Vans (1966). Today, it is estimated that around one billion pairs of sneakers are sold each year worldwide.

4.1.3 *Sneaker industry value chain*

The sneaker industry has a relatively traditional value chain. In this highly globalised industry, the value chain is fragmented internationally. The high added-value activities (design, R&D, marketing) are mainly located in developed countries where the main competitors are headquartered, while production activities are mainly undertaken in developing countries.

The resources and skills required for the design and conception of sneakers are related to the creative activities in the fashion industry, such as identifying fashion trends in terms of product aesthetics. Sneakers also have a technical dimension, and are therefore subject to innovation in terms of resistance, weight, comfort, etc. Market leaders regularly introduce technical innovations, such as the "air" technology developed by Nike to better absorb shocks and improve customer comfort.

In terms of production, the dominant and historic key success factor has been the massive relocation of production to low-cost countries. Very early on, the industry envisaged the use of subcontractors in countries where an estimated 90% of production now takes place. The main production sites are in Asian countries, such as China, Vietnam, Indonesia and Cambodia. Local subcontractors enable brands to achieve economies of scale, reduce production costs and benefit from specialist skills in mass textile production. The fashion industry has seen a number of scandals over recent decades related to working conditions (employment of minors, intensive working hours, failure to comply with labour law), environmental impact (pollution of soil and rivers, greenhouse gas emissions, energy required for production, mass transport, etc.) and the raw materials used (plastics and materials derived from petrochemicals, animal leathers, non-natural dyes, etc.).

Marketing is one of the key activities in the industry's value chain. Market leaders invest much of their financial resources in brand image, sponsorship and communication campaigns. For example, Nike invests between 10% and 12% of its annual sales in marketing. Communication is intensive and uses a variety of media: TV commercials, billboards, press, product placement, social networks, etc. When it comes to sports-related business, marketing also involves sponsorship of individual sportsmen and sportswomen, sports teams and sporting events. Nike's total sponsorship expenditure is estimated to be around $1.3 billion a year. The slogans of the dominant brands in the industry include references to sporting performance and surpassing oneself: "Just do it" for Nike, "Impossible is nothing" for Adidas.

With regard to distribution, the leaders' sales strategies have changed to some extent over the last two decades, with increasing emphasis on directly operated shop networks alongside online sales. Direct sales now account for around a quarter of Nike's sales (1,000 outlets worldwide) and Adidas's sales (2,000 outlets). Online sales have also seen strong growth in recent years. This has considerably increased the margin (×7 according to some experts) compared with using specialist retailers. Sneakers are also better suited to online sales than other types of footwear as they are more flexible and comfortable, and they require less pre-purchase fitting than other types of footwear.

4.1.4 *Major market trends*

Over the last 20 years, the sneaker market has undergone transformations linked to various trends including the massive arrival of new competitors attracted by the volume of sales and the size of margins. These new entrants include luxury fashion brands, such as Chanel, Prada, Louis Vuitton, Dior and Balenciaga. The industry has also seen an increase in collaborations, for example, with sports stars and rappers.

Another key market trend is the diversification of product ranges and the increasing customisation of products. For example, the number of references offered by Nike has increased by 25% over the last two years and is said to have increased fifteen-fold compared with the range offered in the 1980s. This trend is facilitated by the rise of online sales and the development of flagships stores offering digital tools and customised services.

The sneaker industry has also incorporated profound changes associated with the rise of social media into its communication strategies. Targeting young customers in particular, sneaker brands have incorporated the rules of social networking into their communications and customer relation strategies. The power of market leaders can be analysed through the size of their follower communities. In 2023, Nike's Instagram account had more than 300 million followers worldwide.

The growing importance of corporate social responsibility (CSR) and ecological issues is reflected in another growing trend in the market. Like many other industries, the sneaker industry has witnessed an increase in the number of brands that adopt a responsible approach. This trend can be seen in the growth of the second-hand market through platforms such as Vinted. While there has been growing awareness among some long-established sneaker manufacturers (e.g. Adidas's search for less polluting materials), it seems that the CSR and ecological approach is really being adopted by new players who are making it part of their differentiation strategy. One of the new entrants that has chosen to position itself in this sustainable way is the French company Veja, which has established itself as one of the forerunners and, 20 years after its creation, has achieved undeniable success.

4.2 *The development of Veja*

4.2.1 *The brand's first steps (2003–2013)*

Two high school friends, François-Ghislain Morillion and Sébastien Kopp, launched their eco-friendly sneaker brand Veja in 2004 after their experience of working in and conducting an audit of the environmental practices of major French groups (Carrefour, Accor, etc.). They decided to create their own company in the sneaker sector of the textile industry. Their love of Brazil and the availability of the raw materials needed to make sneakers (organic cotton and wild rubber) led them to locate their production in the country.

After sourcing raw materials locally between 2003 and 2004 (meeting with producers and cooperatives), they made a commitment to producers and purchased three tons of cotton at twice the market price. In doing so, François-Ghislain and Sébastien applied the principles of fair trade, that is, advance financing of production and three-year contracts. They repeated the same process for rubber production and for the spinning, weaving and assembly stages. Veja was born in 2004. The brand's first pair of shoes (Veja Volley) was made from organic cotton with a sole incorporating 30% natural rubber.

The brand was launched in Paris in February 2005 and was soon followed by launches in the UK and Japan. Communication was based on participation in artistic events, trade fairs, blog and press articles extolling the virtues of the brand, and above all on word of mouth. Indeed, Veja cut back on advertising to offset its raw material costs. As a result, Veja sneakers are available at the same price as the competition, that is, around €100 a pair, and are sold in trendy and/or eco-friendly Parisian boutiques. Most of the sneakers are shipped from Brazil by sea, which consumes less energy than air freight. In France, the logistics are handled by a social reintegration association, "Atelier sans frontières".

From production of the sneakers in Brazil to delivery and points of sale, Veja is helping to build an ecological and ethical industry. With its advertising-free communication and referencing in hand-picked boutiques, Veja sold out the 5,000 pairs produced in just three months (2,000 pairs in the French market and 3,000 in the rest of the world). Buoyed by this success, in 2005 Veja extended its product range to younger children: "Veja Baby" and opened its website.

In 2009, Veja accelerated its development by multiplying its collections, collaborating with other brands and diversifying its offer. The founders launched "project number two", a line of Veja-branded leather goods, which, however, closed a few years after its launch. With six collections and a line of leather goods, the founders opened their first physical outlet in Paris in November 2010. In 2011, 120,000 pairs of sneakers were sold in more than 350 sales outlets in around 20 countries, and the cotton supply chain was now Fairtrade certified. The company's turnover exceeded €5 million.

4.2.2 *International growth (2014–2023)*

Following the closure of many independent shops, the founders chose to refocus their business and concentrate on internationalisation. They even gave up on Fairtrade certification because of the costs involved, which were so hard to obtain. As a result, 70% of the total €7.3 million in sales in 2015 came from sales abroad, mainly in Germany and Japan and more recently in the USA, where the brand had just set up shop. The following year, the US market became Veja's biggest market. Following in the footsteps of Marion Cotillard a few years earlier, it was Emma Watson's turn to share a photo with Veja on her feet.

From 2015 to 2017, sales and the number of employees almost doubled, from €7.3 million to over €18.6 million and from 18 to 35 respectively. This rapid increase in sales was not without consequences. It led to an increase in the volume of purchases, particularly of cotton and rubber, which at the time were suffering from drought and fire. Veja therefore decided to diversify its supply sources beyond southern Brazil. The company maintains an advantageous purchasing policy for producers in order to secure its supplies and combat the deforestation in Brazil. Rubber is purchased at twice the market price and 1.2 hectares of Amazonian forest are protected for each kilo of rubber purchased.

The brand's success continues. In 2018, the company opened its new website – veja-store.com – on which it is committed to transparency and goes so far as to provide access to contracts with suppliers and tracking of purchase volumes. It includes a page dedicated to the limits of its model, for example showing the results of its carbon footprint. In 2018, the company's turnover doubled again reaching €34 million with 1 million sneakers sold, half of which were in the USA. The company's marketing strategy and its decision not to advertise did not prevent it from being voted by Lyst as the most popular company on the Internet in 2018.

In 2019, sales rose to €65.6 million, boosted by the launch of six new collections, including a running shoe. From minimalist tennis shoes, the brand was moving into more technical footwear. Veja finished 2019 with the opening of its first shop. The following year, the company opened two new shops in New York and Bordeaux. The Bordeaux outlet aimed to take the brand's eco-responsible virtues a step further by taking charge of the end-of-life of its products through its shoe repair workshop and recycling. In 2021, the company extended its shoe repair service to the corner of a Parisian shop, then to its logistics warehouse and its new Berlin shop. Over two years, Veja repaired more than 13,000 pairs of sneakers.

By 2022, the company had sales of €160 million. The following year, it decided to produce 100,000 of the 3.5 million pairs it produced that year in Portugal. The V90 models produced exclusively in Portugal are reserved for European customers. Although marginal, this production could herald a change of BM for the company in the years to come.

5 Main results

5.1 Identifying sources of uncaptured value in the fashion industry

As explained in the theoretical section of this chapter, SBM authors stress the importance of companies identifying and exploring sources of uncaptured

Table 4.2 Uncaptured value perspective on fashion industry

	Sources	*Explanations*	*Opportunities to seize*
Value surplus	Over-production	Production of sneakers to meet customer needs Destruction of unsold products	Adapting production volumes to requirements Creating scarcity Encouraging customers not to over-consume
	Energy and logistics costs	Intensive and inefficient use of energy in the production process Higher cost of air transport than sea transport	Reducing the energy bill Reducing the transport bill
	Very high marketing expenditures	Marketing is a dominant key success factor in the industry	Reducing marketing costs Moving away from mass marketing (no advertising via traditional media)
Value absence	Insufficient volumes of responsible raw materials	Responsible sectors still at the development stage Responsible agricultural sectors more prone to natural hazards (drought, insect infestation)	Innovative components (e.g. vegan leather) and production processes (e.g. alternative glue) Creating responsible supply chains
	Difficulty in certifying raw materials	Certification not suitable for small-scale production Cost of certification too high	Breaking free from certification systems Creation of new labels
	Lack of recycling skills	Inability to recycle all or part of the product Recycling potential neglected	Reducing the raw material costs by recycling all or part of products Creation of new customer services (maintenance, repairs, etc.)
Value destroyed	Carbon footprint	CO_2 emissions	Innovating around components and production processes (e.g. natural dyes) Developing an image as a responsible company (like a food, cosmetics or car brand)

(*Continued*)

Table 4.2 (Continued)

	Sources	*Explanations*	*Opportunities to seize*
	Depletion of non-renewable resources	64% of the total mass of a pair of shoes comes from petrochemical materials	
	Soil pollution	Harmful components (e.g. carcinogens, etc.)	
	Poor working conditions	Production in developing countries (child labour, pay conditions, long working hours, etc.)	Improved brand image through better working conditions Play the local production card (e.g. Made in Europe)
Value missed	Customers' ecological values are underestimated	The sneaker industry is lagging behind the rise of ecological and social values	Developing more responsible offers
	Waste and scrap management	Non-recovery of scrap materials (e.g. pieces of fabric not used in the production process)	Developing an "upcycling" approach: using materials destined to be thrown away to reintroduce them into a new production process

Source: Adapted from Yang et al. (2017).

value. The literature distinguishes four types of uncaptured value that can be used to build an SBM. These are value surplus, value absence, value destroyed and value missed. By definition, the fashion industry is highly polluting and its dominant model is not based on sustainable elements. Therefore, to date, companies have not explored these forms of uncaptured value to any great extent. We attempt to illustrate the four forms of uncaptured value and the resulting opportunities for companies in the fashion industry by focusing our analysis on the sneaker product (see Table 4.2).

Strong competition within the fashion industry has led some companies, particularly new entrants, to explore these sources of uncaptured value in order to differentiate themselves through their SBM. The French sneaker brand Veja is a successful example of such a strategy.

5.2 *Veja's SBM*

Fashion industry practices are a source of both social and environmental damage. Highlighting these problems and raising consumer awareness can open up a wide range of commercial opportunities. From its introduction to

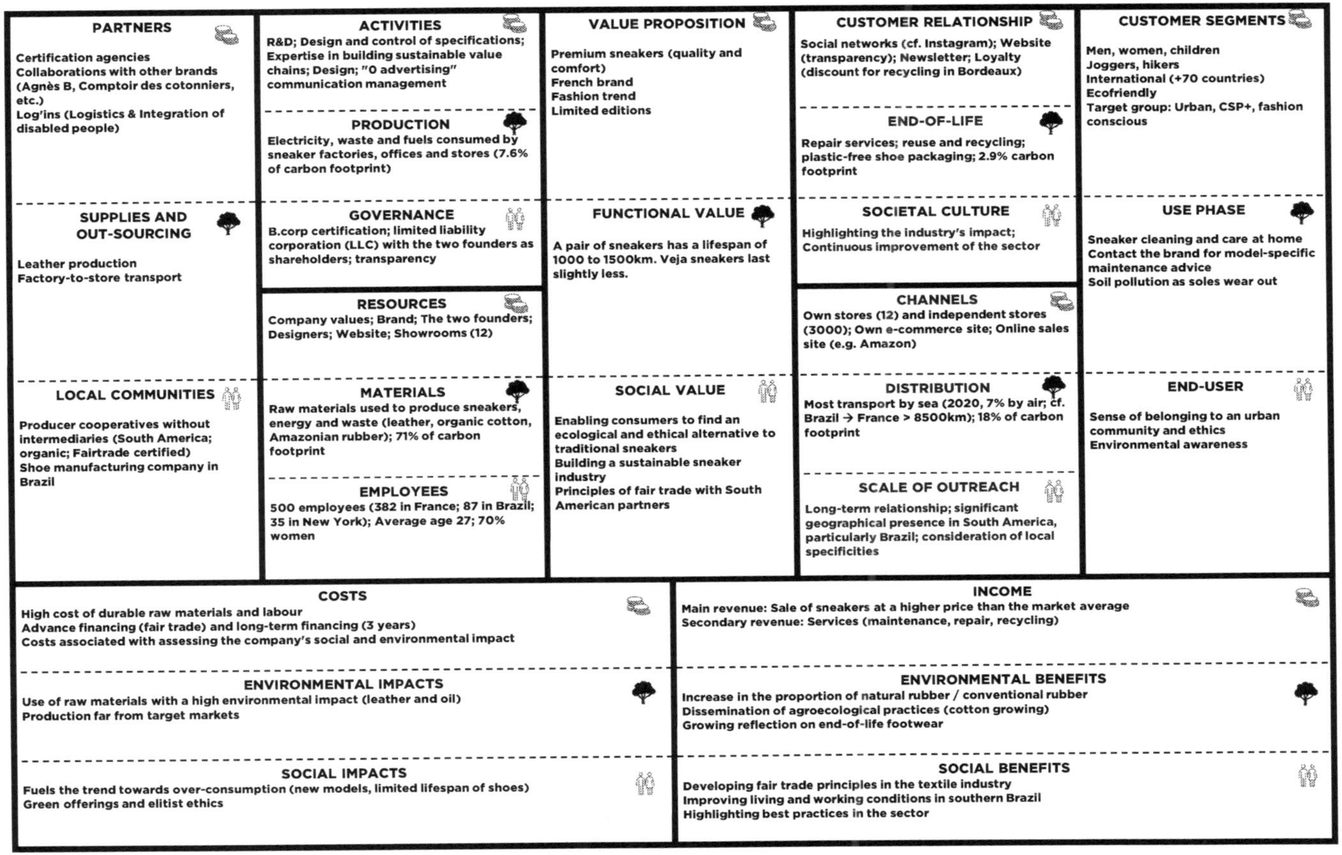

Figure 4.2 Triple layered BM canvas.

Source: Adapted from Joyce and Paquin (2016).

the sneaker industry in 2004 to the present day, Veja has developed its BM around the three dimensions of sustainability: economic, environmental and social dimensions (see Figure 4.2).

5.2.1 *Value proposition*

Veja's value proposition is similar to that of the industry leaders in that it has a range of premium sneakers with several collections and an increasing number of limited editions. However, the materials used to manufacture the sneakers are more ecological and ethical than the traditional ones. Although ecological, the use of new materials can have a negative impact on the functional value of the product. This limitation is highlighted on the company's website where it says: "*Working with natural materials can sometimes be a concession in terms of sustainability*". In other words, Veja shoes made from more environmentally friendly materials do not cover as many kilometres as a traditional pair of premium sneakers. Ultimately, technical innovations and the growing use of these materials should increase the functional value of eco-friendly sneakers.

The value proposition is differentiated in two ways. Firstly, Veja offers an eco-friendly and ethical alternative to fashion-conscious sneaker consumers. The company's strength lies in its promise to consumers to combine fashion and sustainability. Secondly, in order to fulfil the promise made to consumers, Veja has built up a sustainable sneaker production chain in South America. The principles of fair trade have been adapted to the specificities of the supply chain. As a result, the company reaches consumers who may or may not be sensitive to ethical and ecological issues through the design of their sneakers and/or through their social commitment. According to Sébastien Kopp (2017), "Initially, 5% bought out of conviction. Today, it's more like 15%. The others come primarily for the style, which remains the best Trojan horse".

5.2.2 *Value creation (partners; activities; resources)*

Building a sustainable supply chain is a key element of the company's value proposition. To achieve this objective, Veja needs to set up partnerships with producers of raw materials and with garment factories. The company has chosen to establish these partnerships in the south of Brazil and to extend them over time to other South American countries. The contracts respect the principles of fair trade, that is. advance financing of production and three-year contracts. Veja cuts out intermediaries and makes a commitment to communities. By 2022, 82 of the company's 500 employees were working in Brazil. The company adapts to the specific characteristics of local communities and offers fair pay.

From an environmental point of view, most CO_2 emissions are not emitted by Veja itself, but by its partners. In fact, analysis of the carbon footprint shows that Scope 1 represents only 0.003% of the total emissions of the company's activity.[1] The majority of CO_2 emissions are generated by the production of raw materials and therefore by the company's suppliers. This accounted for 71% of emissions in 2019, 97% of which came from leather production. The company is reducing the use of leather in the manufacture of its sneakers and is ensuring the traceability of its supplies (southern Brazil, which is not involved in the country's deforestation; skins from animals sold for their meat). The cotton used in the sneakers respects the principles of agroecology, which could eventually absorb some of the carbon emissions generated by the company. The energy used in sneaker production accounts for 7% of the total carbon footprint. Assessment of the company's main sources of CO_2 emissions highlights opportunities for its SBM to innovate with a view to reducing its environmental footprint.

The company is governed by the two founders, who are its sole shareholders 20 years after its creation. Decision-making is therefore centralised but, according to the founders, this enables them to protect their SBM from the excesses of capitalism. This form of governance is fairly common among companies with SBMs. The founder of the textile company Patagonia, known for its commitment to the environment, refused to go public. It is nevertheless possible to adopt other legal forms that would dilute power and ensure the development of the company's SBM after the founders have left.

5.2.3 Value delivery (customer relationship; channels; customer segments)

Veja is moving away from one of the common practices of companies in the sneaker industry: advertising. It has implemented what it describes as "zero advertising". This does not mean that the company spends no money on marketing; rather, it does not finance advertising campaigns or take on sponsorships. The company has built its reputation by capitalising on the confidential nature of the brand – a marketing approach that appeals to Veja's urban, eco-friendly customers. Today, Veja sells from its website, in independent boutiques and in 12 company-owned shops. These brand-owned boutiques are showcases and laboratories for experimentation. For example, the Veja X Darwin boutique (Bordeaux) was an opportunity for the company to test the introduction of new services, such as cleaning, repairing and recycling used sneakers.

A remaining problem is the fact that the sneakers must be transported from their place of production (South America) to the brand's customers (USA, Europe). The sneakers have to travel many kilometres before they reach the end customer. Transport is mainly by sea, but the company also uses air transport despite its well-known impact on the environment. Transport is the brand's second biggest CO_2 generator and accounts for 18% of the total footprint.

5.2.4 *Value capture (costs; revenues)*

The company's main source of revenue is the sale of its sneakers. The selling price of the shoes is close to that of the industry leaders, as Veja offsets higher raw material costs with lower marketing expenditure. The company also bears the costs associated with evaluating its practices, its environmental footprint and the entire supply chain. The recipe is working, and the sector leaders are not standing still in the face of this new market. The value opportunities (see Section 4.1.) exploited by Veja are now attracting industry leaders, such as Nike and Adidas. For example, Adidas aims to produce 90% of its products from environmentally friendly materials by 2025. Like Veja, the brand's website focuses on sustainability (measuring the environmental footprint, transparency, etc.). The challenge for Veja in the years ahead will be to defend or renew its competitive advantage in the face of growing competition from the market leaders.

6 Contribution to BM innovation and sustainability in CCIs

Analysis of Veja's success in the fashion industry sheds light on how a company creates value and develops its activities based on an SBM. In this respect, sustainability represents an opportunity to create an innovative BM. The analysis of the Veja case offers a number of lessons about the key success factors of such a strategy and the challenges encountered along the way, whether in the fashion industry or, more generally, in CCIs.

6.1 *Key success factors of SBMs in CCIs*

Exploration of Veja's case study enabled us to identify five key success factors for SBMs in the fashion sector and to draw parallels with practices observed in other CCIs.

The first key success factor revealed by Veja is the construction and management of a sustainable supply chain. Indeed, Veja's BM is based on thinking in terms of sustainability – environmental and social – throughout the supply chain, from suppliers through production and transport activities to distribution. In particular, securing supplies of sustainable raw materials is a key element of an SBM. This approach can be replicated by other players in the fashion industry, whether for sneakers or other products (clothing, accessories, leather goods, etc.). Companies in other CCIs can also draw inspiration from certain elements of Veja's SBM. One example is the architecture industry and the securing of supplies of materials used in the construction of eco-responsible buildings.

Secondly, Veja's SBM is also based on its decision to offer iconic and timeless sneaker models in order to reduce over-production and curb over-consumption linked to fashion trends. This key success factor seems to be closely linked to the sustainability levers available in the fashion industry, which is particularly concerned about the impact of over-consumption by customers dictated by fashion trends.

Thirdly, Veja has incorporated a degree of transparency into its sustainable approach. The company uses its website and social networks to develop an educational and transparent approach for customers. In this way, Veja explains its approach and highlights the limits of its model in terms of sustainability. This clear and nuanced approach certainly strengthens the company's credibility and limits accusations of green washing. Other CCI companies have developed similar approaches by displaying data relating to the environmental impact of their activity. This is particularly true of some music festivals which communicate this information before and during the festival (e.g. We Love Green, Terres du son, etc.).

The fourth key success factor in Veja's strategy relates to product end-of-life and recycling activities. The sneaker brand has developed a service activity which repairs products to give them a second life. This approach, which is fairly common in certain industries outside the scope of the CCIs, still appears to be underdeveloped within the CCIs themselves. Nevertheless, some, such as film and television production through the recycling of sets, may be interested in developing similar practices.

Finally, the Veja case illustrates how a company can review its value chain in order to reduce the cost of certain activities in order to offset the additional cost generated by the implementation of a sustainable approach. In the case of Veja, unlike the dominant players in the industry, it is the marketing activity that has been largely removed from the value chain in order to reduce the cost of the product. Similar approaches to reviewing the value chain can be found in the museum and major exhibition industry where the development of virtual tours makes it possible to reduce the budgets for welcoming the public on site, building sets and dealing with logistics and transport.

6.2 *Challenges of SBMs in CCIs*

As well as highlighting the key success factors identified, the Veja case study also reveals some of the challenges faced by companies that develop an SBM. One of the main difficulties that Veja has encountered is managing the tension between two paradoxical elements: its desire to implement a sustainable approach on the one hand and key elements of the fashion industry (roles played by the brand, design and fashion trends) on the other. Indeed, the frequency of new purchases by consumers to follow fashion trends is one of the historical pillars of the fashion industry's DNA. Sustainable strategies therefore come up against a fundamental principle of this industry and it seems that this will be a long-term obstacle to its development of SBMs. Several other CCIs also face obstacles to the development of SBMs because of how they operate: access to an unlimited supply of audio and visual content on streaming platforms (ecological impact of servers), the prototypical nature of cinema films each requiring specific sets, and shows and festivals involving the transport of equipment and spectators, etc.

Another challenge facing the fashion industry is that of scaling-up. While a variety of SBMs have emerged within the industry, they are often limited to niche markets. The fashion industry is currently undergoing great transformation, for example through the rise of mass consumption, which is generating major environmental problems. The many SBMs that have emerged include vegan textiles (Colorful Standard, nudie jeans, etc.); clothing made from recycled products (Patagonia, 1083, etc.); "made in" clothing (Peregrine, England, Le slip français, France; etc.); second-hand clothing (Flea markets, Vinted, etc.); made-to-order production (weargustin, Asphalte); and clothing rental (HURR, Le Closer, etc.). Even if some of the brands mentioned are now well known by the general public, the approach does not seem sufficient for scaling up a technology or a sustainable solution (product or service) beyond the company's SBM, given the pitfalls that an SBM encounters during its development. Indeed, SBM-initiated companies have to make certain trade-offs between the volume of their business and the sustainability of their SBM. Increased activity often compromises the sustainability of SBMs. As a result, companies often fall into the niche trap or expand their business rapidly, which has a negative impact on the environment.

The case of Veja shows that the process of scaling up is a long one involving trial and error (launch of a leather goods business, production in Europe, etc.). Companies can also choose to restrict their production. Like Veja, companies with ambitions to scale up their SBM can forge partnerships with incubators in the industry or related industries with a view to mobilising the key success factors mastered by these firms (collaboration with Agnès B for design skills, with Monoprix for the distribution network, etc.). In other CCIs, a number of sustainable initiatives are emerging, but they also seem to be facing the trap of being niche players (Bioviva in the board game industry, the "ecologically compatible editions" collective in the publishing industry, etc.). Not all industries are at the same stage of sustainability maturity. The food, cosmetics and fashion industries seem to be more mature than other industries. One explanation often put forward by experts in these industries is the relationship between the consumer object and the body. In the food industry goods are ingested, in the cosmetics industry goods are applied and in the textile industry goods are brought into contact with the body. The visibility of the negative environmental impact can also explain the different stages of maturity. Industries such as the automotive or energy sectors are being forced to move towards sustainability because of the visibility of the CO_2 emissions that are at their roots. Conversely, as the impact of digital technology is less perceptible to consumers, the sector's leaders are not being forced to update their BMs, even though its carbon footprint is significant.

7 Conclusion

In this chapter, we explored one of the avenues of BM innovation that has been frequently observed in the fashion industry over the last two decades: the construction of an SBM. The case of the French sneaker company Veja enabled us to show how a company can modify some of the industry's key success factors and identify sources of uncaptured value in order to develop an SBM. To better understand the innovative and sustainable dimension of this BM, we analysed the case using the triple layered BM canvas (Joyce and Paquin, 2016). Veja has designed a BM that incorporates environmental and social dimensions in addition to the traditional economic dimension. Based on this SBM, Veja has been able to transform sources of uncaptured value into opportunities for sustainability within a highly polluting industry.

Veja's success and growth over the last 20 years were the starting point for our research. Since then, a number of sneaker and clothing brands in the fashion industry have also developed SBMs. The relative maturity of these SBMs today raises new questions about their future development and the transformation of the fashion industry. Analysis of the Veja case revealed several major challenges that the company is now facing: the difficulty in reconciling sustainability with key success factors rooted in the industry (e.g. impulse buying, fashion trends, the role of design, over-consumption, etc.) and the simultaneous management of a scaling-up strategy while maintaining the principles of sustainability.

These new challenges call for future empirical investigation and analysis of other BMs that incorporate a sustainable dimension. In this respect, the Vinted app for selling second-hand clothes between individuals is another innovative BM in the fashion industry. It would be relevant to analyse its BM in detail and to understand how sustainability is present in its strategy as well as the limits of its model in relation to the abovementioned pitfalls, such as over-consumption or massification of an offer.

Note

1 VEJA CARBON FOOTPRINT 2019: Scope 1: The company's direct activities like driving the cars we own in Brazil; Scope 2: The energy consumption from the offices and shops ; Scope 3: All activities carried out by our suppliers and partners (from the fields to the factories and our offices).

References

Abdul-Rashid SH, Sakundarini N, Raja Ghazilla RA, Thurasamy R. 2017. The impact of sustainable manufacturing practices on sustainability performance: Empirical evidence from Malaysia. *International Journal of Operations & Production Management. Emerald Publishing Limited* 37(2): 182–204.

Bocken N, Rana P, Short S. 2015. Value mapping for sustainable business thinking. *Journal of Industrial and Production Engineering. Taylor & Francis* 32(1): 67–81.

Cimprich A, Sadayappan K, Young SB. 2023. Lightweighting electric vehicles: Scoping review of life cycle assessments. *Journal of Cleaner Production* 433: 139692.

Eisenhardt KM. 1989. Building theories from case study research. *Academy of Management Review* 14(4): 532–550.

Evans S, Vladimirova D, Holgado M, Fossen KV, Yang M, Silva EA, Barlow CY. 2017. Business model innovation for sustainability: Towards a unified perspective for creation of sustainable business models. *Business Strategy and the Environment* 26(5): 597–608.

Geissdoerfer M, Vladimirova D, Evans S. 2018. Sustainable business model innovation: A review. *Journal of Cleaner Production. Elsevier* 198: 401–416.

Joyce A, Paquin RL. 2016. The triple layered business model canvas: A tool to design more sustainable business models. *Journal of Cleaner Production* 135: 1474–1486.

Kuzma E, Padilha LS, Sehnem S, Julkovski DJ, Roman DJ. 2020. The relationship between innovation and sustainability: A meta-analytic study. *Journal of Cleaner Production* 259: 120745.

Massa L, Tucci CL, Afuah A. 2017. A critical assessment of business model research. *Academy of Management Annals. Academy of Management* 11(1): 73–104.

Osterwalder A, Pigneur Y. 2010. *Business model generation: A handbook for visionaries, game changers, and challengers*. New York, NY: Wiley.

Richardson JE. 2005. *The business model: An integrative framework for strategy execution*. Available at SSRN 932998.

Shakeel J, Mardani A, Chofreh AG, Goni FA, Klemeš JJ. 2020. Anatomy of sustainable business model innovation. *Journal of Cleaner Production* 261: 121201.

Stubbs W, Cocklin C. 2008. Conceptualizing a "sustainability business model". *Organization & Environment. SAGE Publications Inc* 21(2): 103–127.

Yang M, Evans T, Vladimirova D, Rana P. 2017. Value uncaptured perspective for sustainable business model innovation. *Journal of Cleaner Production* 140: 1794–1804.

Yang M, Vladimirova D, Rana P, Evans S. 2014. Sustainable value analysis tool for value creation. *Asian Journal of Management Science and Applications* 1(4): 312–332.

Yin RK. 1994. Discovering the future of the case study. Method in evaluation research. *Evaluation Practice* 15(3): 283–290.

Zott C and Amit R. 2010. Business model design: An activity system perspective. *Long Range Planning* 43(2–3): 216–226.

5 The long tail business model in publishing

The case of Hachette's romance division in France

Carole Poirel

1 Introduction

It Ends With Us, which has sold over 20 million copies worldwide since its release in 2016 in the United States! Author Colleen Hoover named one of the 100 most influential people of 2023 by *The Times*! The romance sector is the talk of the town. Its growth is pulling up a generally depressed publishing market. The sector has undergone such a revival since the 2010s that it is now referred to as new romance. This revival was marked by two titles published in 2012 that quickly became international bestsellers translated into several languages: *Fifty Shades of Grey* by E.L. James and *After* by Anna Todd. Both feature sex scenes and are not recommended for under-16s. The first is aimed at a discerning adult audience because of sadomasochistic scenes, and the second is aimed at a younger audience, teenagers and young adults. Initially, they were fanfictions, that is, stories that fans wrote to extend, amend or completely transform the story. They became sagas, with a trilogy for the first and five seasons for the second, plus spin-offs (*Before*, *Nothing More*) and then audio-visual adaptations (film, TV series and VOD). These two emblematic titles reveal the characteristics of the romance market: (i) authors who write and make a name for themselves on the Internet outside the traditional patterns of publishing; (ii) love stories that feature a woman who will make a dark man who couldn't get attached flinch; (iii) communities of readers, but above all of female readers who share their experiences on dedicated platforms and who are also authors, that is to say female authors.

The market is obviously not made up of bestsellers alone. It is made up of a very large number of titles, giving it the characteristics of the long-tail economy as described by Chris Anderson (2004, 2006): niche products that are sold in small quantities each, but whose combined sales make them profitable because of their low costs. The Internet and digital technologies have transformed the production, distribution and promotion of cultural goods. Amateurs create and exchange content online, without the need to go through a traditional publisher or print on paper. Books and texts circulate as digitised goods on platforms. However, traditional publishing is not being replaced by these new editorial forms initiated by user-generated content. It is

DOI: 10.4324/9781032714462-5

using them as new development opportunities to meet strong demand while keeping costs under control. As a result, its business model (BM) is being transformed, with a form of hybridisation that affects every stage of the value chain. What changes does traditional publishing need to make to its BM to adapt to the new long-tail market, and in particular the new romance market? How can it reduce the distribution costs of a large number of products while helping consumers to find what they are looking for in a plethora of offerings?

To answer these research questions, we chose a case from the French publishing industry, the Hlab/BMR publishing house. Hlab/BMR is managed by a small team and is part of the Hachette group, the number 1 French publisher with an international dimension. Created through organic growth in 2014, this publisher is not the leader in the romance market, but has been doing so for nearly ten years. The success of its bestselling author Sarah Rivens, discovered on Wattpad in 2022, has boosted its profile, particularly in dark romance, a controversial sector in the age of #MeToo.

In the chapter, we first present the theoretical background of the long-tail BM in book publishing, followed by the qualitative research method based on secondary sources. We then turn to the case study itself, that is, Hlab/BMR in itself and within the romance market in France. We analyse the main findings, using the Hlab/BMR BM diagram drawn up by Osterwalder and Pigneur (2010), and comment on the answers to the research questions. Finally, we propose a discussion on the contributions of the case study to the analysis of BMs in the cultural and creative industries (CCI), in particular by returning to the hybridisation of the BM and the way in which these industries can seize the opportunities offered by long-tail markets. The chapter ends with an overall conclusion.

2 Theoretical background: the long-tail BM

The long-tail concept was coined by Chris Anderson (2004, 2006) to describe a shift in the media business from selling a small number of "hit" items in large volumes towards selling a very large number of niche items each in relatively small quantities. It is represented by an asymptote as shown in Figure 5.1. The products are ordered on the x-axis by their rank in descending order of sales and the y-axis represents their sales. As a result, the head concentrate the few bestsellers since the long-tail gather countless niche contents. The long tail assumes that consumers prefer cultural diversity and that the internet makes it possible to present the full range of products available.

The long-tail hypothesis challenges Pareto's 80/20 law. Based on the cases of Rhapsody and Netflix, Anderson (2006) explains that 10% of products make 75% of sales and 66% of profits, while the remaining 90% generate 25% of sales and 34% of profits. But we have to keep in mind that the number of products is much higher online than in shop because the online retailers are not constrained by physical space. They have unlimited shelves

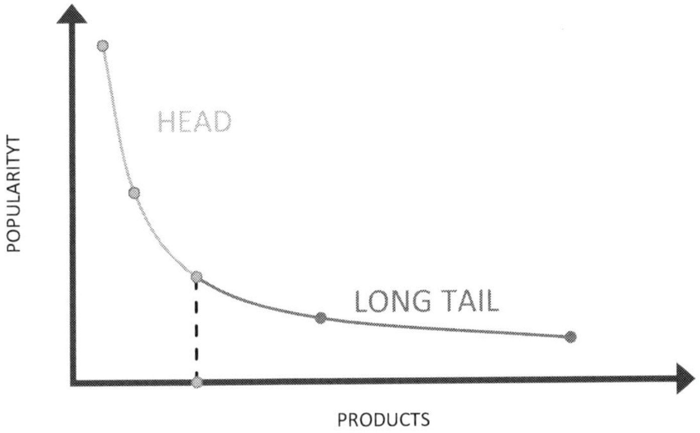

Figure 5.1 The long tail.

while the largest bookshops can offer just 50,000 different books out of the 350,000 available in France, that is, less than 15%. Above all, their storage and distribution costs are lower:

- (i) their warehouses are located in areas where the price per square metre is much lower than in the commercial locations of physical shops;
- (ii) they can sell without having first stocked the products by relaying the customer's order to the supplier on a just-in-time basis;
- (iii) and they have virtually zero costs for digital goods, such as e-books. A single server makes it possible to store millions of e-books, then distribute them by authorising a simple download. And the Internet serves as a transport channel.

By drastically reducing storage and distribution costs, a product that sells just a few units a month can become profitable for an online retailer.

Anderson (2006) deals with three main forces producing a marketplace of niche. The first is called the democratisation of the tools for production. He states the impact of this to be a population of content creation at a pace never seen before. As a matter of fact, anyone can publish a book by using self-publishing services as Amazon KDP or Lulu.com. Digital publishing breaks down the barriers to entry to the book publishing industry and allows amateur authors to do without a traditional publisher. The second force is a democratisation of distribution through internet, social media and mobile connections that allow everyone to distribute their contents. For instance, there are many literary applications, such as Wattpad that allow amateur and professional authors to have their work read and get feedback from readers. The third force is connecting supply and demand by lowering the search cost of finding the niche content. Consumers can easily find what they are looking for on the Internet thanks to powerful search and recommendation engines, user ratings and communities of interest. They are thus encouraged to go further into the niches to find what they want. Consumers are moving away from hit to niche that better match their preferences. The Internet and digital technologies are enabling amateur practices to develop in all areas of the CCI: to create and exchange content, with a certain porosity between creation and consumption, following the example of fan fiction in the romance sector (Jenkins, 1992).

The phenomenon of the long tail was the subject of a lot of studies after the publication of Anderson's book in the second half of the 2000s and up to the beginning of the 2010s. After that, research work became scarce. Economists have carried out research to quantify the long tail in various cultural industries (books, film, music) using a variety of measures and with contradictory results. We can cite the landmark work carried out by Brynjolfsson and his colleagues at MIT (2006, 2011), by Elberse (2008) at Harvard and in France by Benghozi and Benhamou (2008). Overall, the research shows that the long-tail phenomenon does not yet seem to be taking on the dimension that Anderson predicted. While the tail has been stretched, as more and more titles are available and consumed at least once, the conditions for a massive shift in demand towards products in the tail do not yet seem to have been met. This economic research studies sales statistics in shops and online in order to compare them.

We have another point of view based on business management since the long tail can support alternative strategies and BMs for publishers and retailers (Johnson et al., 2014). Two main research questions are raised to manage specific supply-side and demand-side challenges. First, how to mitigate the distribution costs of distributing a large number of products? Secondly, how can consumers be helped to find what they are looking for in a plethora of offerings? One of the characteristics of the CCI is the abundant and constantly renewed production according to the principles of supply-side economics (Caves, 2000). In France, the publishing industry produces an average of 38,000 new books each year, plus 15,000 self-published titles. Publishers face the challenge of capturing the attention of consumers for their own products. In a world of connected commerce, they need to develop all the relevant touchpoints with their consumers using multi-channel and omni-channel approaches (Palmatier et al., 2019).

We are using Anderson's long tail as an analytical and heuristic tool for discussing the changes taking place in the romance market because it details a fundamental comparison between traditional BMs and those of internet-based publishers. The BM reflects the company's profit-making strategy, that is, the choices made in terms of product-market combinations and positioning, as well as all the organisational means used to create value for customers, particularly in terms of the integration of activities and resources or the use of external partners. It is based on theoretical approaches to corporate strategy (Johnson et al., 2014). Osterwalder and Pigneur (2010)

Table 5.1 Comparison of two BM in Book Publishing Industry

	"Old model"	*"New model"*
	Traditional publishing	*Lulu.com*
Value proposition	Broad content (ideally "hit")	Self-publishing services Marketplace for each content
Customer segments	Broad audience	Niche authors Niche audiences
Customer relationship	–	Communities of interest Online profile
Channels	Retail Network	Lulu.com
Key activities	Content acquisitions Publishing Selling	Platform development Logistics
Key resource	Publishing knowledge Content	Platform Print-on-demand infrastructure
Key partners	–	–
Cost structure	Publishing Marketing	Platform management & development
Revenue streams	Wholesale revenues	Sales commissions (low) Publishing services fees

Source: Osterwalder and Pigneur (2010), pp. 70–71.

discuss transformations of the book publishing industry by comparing an *old model* bestseller-centric with a *new* self-publishing *model,* such as Lulu.com (see Table 5.1). The *old* model is built on the publisher selecting manuscript whereas the *new* one accepts all authors and provides them with services to publish and sell their books. The former gives rise to a publishing contract under which the publisher undertakes to produce and sell the author's books at its own expense and to pay the author a proportion of the royalties (around 5% plus the "à-valoir"). The latter is "à compte d'auteur" to the extent that the author is financially responsible. The cost structure and the revenues streams arising from these two value propositions are not at all the same, as shown in Table 5.1.

We want to highlight two major differences between these two BMs. On the one hand, Lulu.com is a multi-sided platform that serves and connects authors and readers with the long tail of user-generated niche content. The key activities and the key resources are focused on managing the platform. Traditional publishing uses bricks-and-mortar book distribution channels and online sales websites. In France, these channels all have roughly the same market share because of the law on the single price of books introduced in 1981 ("loi Lang") which forces retailers to apply a selling price set by the publisher. According to Ministry of Culture statistics for 2022, independent bookshops and Internet each have a market share of 23% and 22% respectively; 28% of sales are made by specialist superstores such as

Fnac, compared with 19% by general superstores; the remaining 8% come from traditional direct sales (excluding the Internet), book fairs, etc. Amazon accounts for over 80% of all Internet sales in France, along with Fnac.com.

On the other hand, another major difference between the two BMs lies in the production of paper books. This is limited to a few copies in the new model in response to demand because in a digital world the e-book is preferred. In the traditional model, the p-book is not an option as bestsellers are sold in hardcover book and then in softcover book. The cost structure is therefore very different. Traditional publishing is subject to high manufacturing, storage and distribution costs, whereas self-publishing is not. The failure of a particular title to sell is irrelevant to Lulu.com whereas in traditional publishing, it will have an impact.

3 Research method

The research method is qualitative, based on thematic content analysis of a corpus of secondary sources. The data collected concerns the romance market in France and its players, and more specifically Hlab/BMR, which is the subject of the case study. As shown in Table 5.2, the corpus includes press articles, publishing house websites and an internship report carried out by a second-year post-baccalaureate student in 2023 at Hlab/BMR.

Unlike the other sources, the internship report[1] enabled an introspective approach, from inside the structure, based on the criteria listed in Table 5.2. The quality of the work in this report in terms of data collection and analysis is guaranteed by the fact that its author has a university degree specialising in the book trade, and that she had the necessary knowledge to tackle the above-mentioned criteria in the best possible conditions. The 40-page written

Table 5.2 Nature of secondary sources

	Characteristics of the source	*Nature of data*
Press articles	Specialised press (*Livres-Hebdo*, *ActuaLitté*) Other press titles (*Le Monde*, *Le Figaro*, *Libération*, *Les Echos*)	Thirty-five articles including 25 articles of specialised press
Web sites	Hachette, Hlab, BMR, Hugo Publishing, HarperCollins, Editions Addictives	Consulted several times between September 2023 and February 2024 on: catalogue, new releases, authors, news, links to social networks.
Internship report	Internship report on Hlab/ BMR from 27 March to 20 May 2024 (40 pages)	Criteria for analysis: history of the company, construction of the catalogue, workings of the team, editorial process, market data and competitors

essay and the one-hour oral presentation were given high marks by a panel of professional and academic experts.

The thematic content analysis (Miles and Hiberman, 1994) was carried out manually in two stages: firstly, each source was analysed separately, followed by a comparative analysis. The themes were defined after the literature review using a hypothetico-deductive logic. They comprise the nine patterns of the BM designed by Osterwalder and Pigneur (2010), plus two additional categories relating to competition and the market to take account of an ecosystemic level of analysis.

4 Case study presentation: Hlab/BMR publishing

Hlab/BMR publishing are part of the Hachette group, an international publishing group, which in turn belongs to Lagardère Publishing, whose majority shareholder is the Vivendi group, officially since 2023 following approval by the European Commission. The Hlab/BMR story begins with Stéphanie Meyer's *Twilight* saga, the first volume of which, *Fascination*, was published in 2004 by Hachette Romans. A new collection called Black Moon was created to include the other volumes in the saga. In this collection dedicated to romance and fantasy, *Journal d'un vampire* by L.J. Smith and *Sublimes créatures* by Kami Garcia and Margaret Stohl were bestsellers. In 2014, with *Jamais sans toi* by Jessica Sorensen, the collection changed its name to Black Moon Romance and then BMR. BMR is breaking away from Hachette Romans and is being merged with Hlab, a new pure-play romance label due to be launched in 2019. Since then, Hlab/BMR has had its own editorial team within "Hachette illustré et collections" (which also includes children's collections, such as Gautier-Languereau/Deux coqs d'or and Hachette Jeunesse, manga with Pika, novels from the Bibliothèque Rose and Bibliothèque Verte, and the Disney licence). The team includes three publishers and a project manager, who is also in charge of communications and marketing, as well as two or three interns or apprentices, depending on the period.

It should be noted that not all romance titles published by the Hachette group carry the Hlab or BMR brands. Tillie Colle, a bestselling English author of romance and dark romance, is published in France by Hachette Romans (*Milles baisers pour un garçon*, 2016). The book that relaunched romance, *Fifty Shades of Grey* d'E.L. James was published in France in 2012 by Jean-Claude Lattès, part of the Hachette group. The Hachette group's famous paperback collection, Le Livre de Poche, includes bestsellers published primarily by Hachette, but also by other publishers such as Albin Michel, which has published bestsellers by French romance author Mélissa Da Costa. (*Tout le bleu du ciel*, 2020; *Je revenais des autres*, 2022; *Les douleurs fantômes*, 2023).

It was with Sarah Rivens that the brands gained visibility in romance, and more specifically in dark romance, with the publication of *Captives* in 2022. Dark romance is an eroticisation of the mistreatment of women by men. It combines sexuality, humiliation, control, rape, torture, abduction and toxic relationships. Dark romance is a niche revealed by Sarah Rivens' *Captives*. In the book, Ella falls in love with Asher Scott, a gang leader who has held her captive since she was a teenager, who abuses her and to whom she belongs. The publication of *Captives* is a good illustration of the romance publishing process. Registered under the pseudonym "Thebluerredgirl" Sarah Rivens published her first stories on Wattpad in 2018. Readers were thrilled! Fans created a hashtag #captivewattpad seen by millions of users. The content spreads on TikTok. It was a 2.0 success.

BMR describes itself on its website as "*an unashamed romance publisher*". BMR may stand for Black Moon Romance, but it could also stand for "*Beau Mec Rebelle*", which translates into English as "*handsome and rebellious guy*". Aimed at a discerning Young Adult audience, it publishes an average of 75 new titles each year. Whether BMR or Hlab, the contents are first released digitally and then, for many of them, in paper format within three to six months. Hlab is the digital label, but BMR also publishes digital books under its own imprint. The catalogue has a total of over 300 titles, 180 of which are in both e-book and p-book. Major titles are also available as audio books. Production is higher at BMR (around 240 titles) than at Hlab (around 60 titles).

In 2023, a paperback collection, Ito, will be launched, giving contents a new life after the digital edition, in addition to the hardcover book, and at a lower price: €6.90 or €7.90 or €8.90 in paperback, compared with a range of €17 to €20 in hardcover book. Digital books are generally priced at €5.99, €6.99 or €7.99 to the nearest cent. E-book and paperback prices are therefore close. The paperback makes it possible to reach a readership that is less keen on reading on screen. The company's sales have risen sharply in recent years. From 1 million euros in 2021, it has risen to 20 million in 2023.

We don't have the turnover of each main stakeholders of the romance market, but we do know their importance and reputation in the market (see Figure 5.2). Hlab/BMR's main rival is Hugo Publishing. It is the French publisher of bestselling American authors Anna Todd (*After*, 2015) and Colleen Hoover (*Jamais plus*, 2017) as well as French authors Morgane Moncomble, C.S. Quill and Laura S.Wild. The house regularly organises writing competitions on its own Fyctia platform to unearth new talent, and in 2016 created the *Festival de la New Romance*, which takes place every year. Founded in 2005 by Hughes Saint-Vincent and chaired by Arthur Saint-Vincent, Hugo Publishing generated sales of €80 million in 2023. It is the market leader in romance. Two other publishing houses with smaller sales than Hugo Publishing have been present on the market for ten years. On the one hand, Editions Addictives, founded in 2013, publishes bestselling authors, such as Emma Green, Erin Graham and Anita Rigins. With several subsidiaries abroad, it is easy to acquire rights for translation into several languages (English, Spanish, German, Italian) when a success appears in one of these subsidiaries. The American publisher HarperCollins, number 2 in the United

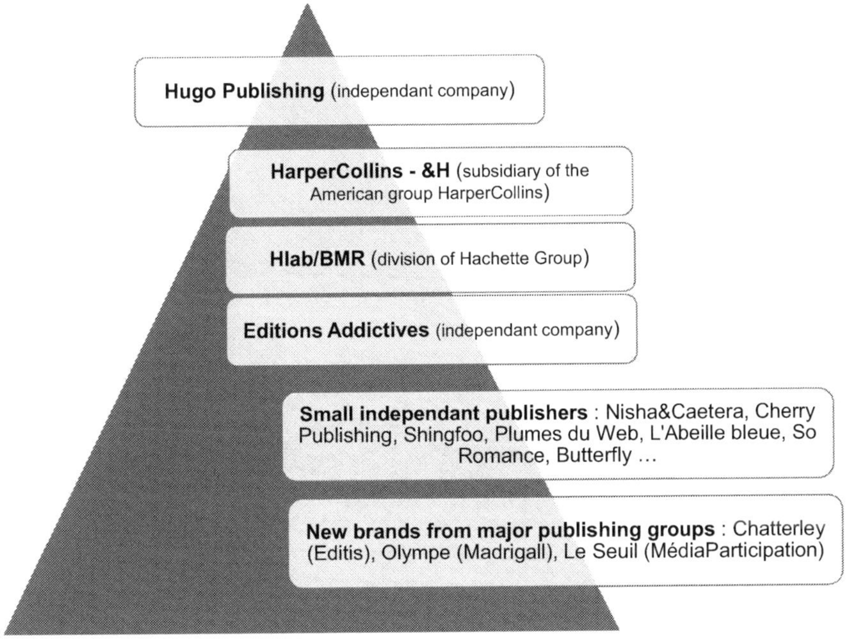

Figure 5.2 Main stakeholders of the romance Publishing in France.

States after Bertelsmann (Penguin Random House), has a French subsidiary which publishes romance under the Harlequin brand and the &H collection in particular. They have published L.J. Shen, Penelope Douglas and Emily Blain. Then there are a host of small publishers, such as Nisha&Caetera, Cherry Publishing, Shingfoo, Plumes du Web, L'Abeille bleue, So Romance and Butterfly, while publishing groups that initially shied away from this literature have begun to exploit the potential by creating new labels in 2023: Chatterley within Editis, Olympe within Madrigall, Verso within Le Seuil (MédiaParticipations group). The growth in sales has undoubtedly seduced the historic protagonists as well as new entrants.

As a matter of fact, sales of romance doubled in 2023 in France. With 6 million books sold, the niche now represents 7% of the book market, excluding e-books. One out of every nine novels sold is a romance. A best-seller in romance sells 10,000 copies, compared with hundreds of thousands for a novel. Their number has increased in 2023: 106 titles compared with 56 titles in 2022. According to the experts at GfK (2024), "*the dynamic of the market comes from demand, which can be seen in both long-standing titles and new releases*". In reference to Chris Anderson's asymptote, the head has thickened and the tail has lengthened. An external factor linked to France's cultural policy has played a part in this strong growth. This is the "Pass culture", introduced in 2019, which gives young people aged 15 to 18 a budget (€20 at 15, €30 at 16 and 17, €300 at 18) to buy books and other cultural products or services (concert tickets, cinema tickets, etc.). Books were the main beneficiaries, particularly manga and romance.

The profile of readers is well identified (in particular Nielsen, 2016 for the American public). The majority of readers are women (84% women, 16% men). They are young (6% are under 18, 25% between 18 and 30 and 28% between 30 and 45). They read fast and a lot of big books. Romance books are between 500 and 800 pages long and form multi-volume sagas. They are on the lookout for new releases as well as texts emerging on various platforms, such as Wattpad, Fyctia or We love word. They listen assiduously to their favourite female influencers on social networks (TikTok, Instagram, FaceBook, Youtub). While they read for free on the web, they also buy books: digital books, which they increasingly read on their smartphones, but also printed books when they go to the shops. "*Every day, students come here after class*", says a bookseller at a Parisian Fnac. "*They choose according to TikTok and only browse these shelves, smartphone in hand* (*Libération*, 13/6/2023)". So, the readership is young and female, and so are the authors. The readers feel close to their authors and develop a great admiration for them. They want to meet them, spend time with them and find out about their personal lives. Readers are passionate and the emotional dimension is very present.

According to the experts at Nielsen (2016), "*the relatively low cost and ease of access to e-books, combined with an increasingly younger fan base, suggest that romance readers are particularly open to trying out new titles and niches within the genre.*" In fact, the market is becoming increasingly segmented. The romance niche is giving rise to sub-niches or new niches: new romance (contemporary romance), dark romance (romance and sex), romance fantasy (romance and fantasy), romance with police plots, romance and the paranormal, etc. Boys also have their romance and dark romance. In France, they loved *Père riche, père pauvre* by Robert Kiyosaki, *Power* by the American Robert Green and *L'art de la séduction* by the same author. These three books are personal development manuals that date back more than ten years and have been rediscovered by BookTok. Romance is turning to social issues, such as bullying, eating disorders and mental health. The manager of a major bookshop in Bordeaux explains that "*the authors evoke family, illness and the trials of life. The characters are resilient. Their lives resemble the lives of readers. There's a strong sense of identification. It's like novelised personal development, novels that feel good in an age of anxiety* (*Le Figaro*, 19/1/2024)." These factors explain the success of the romance market and of Hlab/BMR in particular.

5 Results

Belong to Osterwalder and Pigneur (2010), "*the value proposition of a long tail BM is characterized by offering a wide scope of "non-hit" items that may co-exist with "hit" products*". At Hlab/BMR, this characteristic is satisfied.

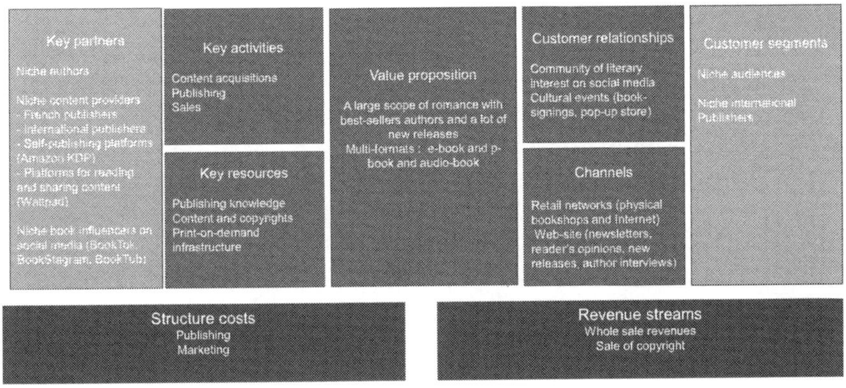

Figure 5.3 Hlab/BMR's business model.

But that's the case for publishing houses in general, who put a large number of books on the market each year without knowing how successful they will be, and who hope to find one or two bestsellers to balance the books. Thanks to Sarah Rivens, Hlab/BMR has become a top seller. Of the 300 titles in the catalogue, the *Captive* saga has sold 350,000 copies in print and over 50,000 in digital format. At the start of 2024, his new title, Lakestone, sold over 47,000 copies in its first week. Camille Creati has also had great success in 2023 with Hlab/BMR, selling 80,000 copies (paper) of *Fallen Angel*. These major successes coexist in the catalogue alongside the 98% of other titles in the house.

The results are summarised in the Hlab/BMR publishing BM shown in Figure 5.3. They are part of a traditional publishing model which they are transforming in order to remain successful on the romance market, without however moving into the self-publishing model seen above as a new BM. We observed three major transformations.

5.1 *First transformation: "Publisher looking for authors"*

The high demand for romance means that we have to produce a lot of titles quickly. Quantity and speed are the watchwords. The pace of publication is accelerated: tomes of the same saga have to be published one after the other; a new title is released on the market within four to eight months. Content research is therefore a key activity. But the process is reversed at Hlab/BMR compared with the traditional model: it is the publisher who seeks out the author, not the author who seeks out the publisher. This is the first transformation of the traditional publishing model that characterises Hlab/BMR's BM. There are many amateur romance authors on the Internet, either self-publishing their novels via Amazon KDP, for example, or writing texts that are popular with readers on platforms, such as Wattpad. These content providers are key partners for the publishing house, which faces stiff competition from other romance labels, such as Hugo&Cie and HarperCollins. On Wattpad, Hlab/BMR has unearthed Sarah Rivens and more recently Laura Swann for *Trouble Maker*. Hlab/BMR has developed a Young Adult partnership with Wattpad. It has been published in French by the American "Amazon" author Leia Stone in Urban Fantasy and Paranormal Romance. Generally speaking, Hlab/BMR scans these international platforms for promising content to pass on to the traditional publishing circuit. Romance is written on these platforms, sometimes with the help of a smartphone, chapter by chapter, according to readers' comments. In these romance fan communities, readers are also authors. Long-tail business may also facilitate and build on user-generated content. This is a far cry from the traditional writing model, where the author drafts his manuscript and then sends it to several publishers in the hope of being selected by a reading committee. The titles published via these platforms have not really been selected by the publisher as in the traditional model. They were first read and enjoyed by romance fans before going through the traditional publishing circuit.

To satisfy demand, the search for content also involves supply channels specific to the traditional model:

- in-house authors with whom publishing contracts have been signed and who can guarantee regular, lucrative production;
- an average of 500 unsolicited manuscripts sent to Hlab/BMR each year, of which only 1% are published after passing through a reading committee;
- the purchase of paperback rights (Ito collection) from French publishers, such as Shingfoo (for *Coloc malgré moi* by Virginie E.Gérard), Editions Plumes du web and Butterfly Editions;
- rights purchases from foreign publishers for French translations, such as the English successes *The Roomate* by Rosie Danan and *Ice Breaker* by Hannah Grace.

As far as copyrights are concerned, the company buys them but it can also sell them, which generates additional income over and above the sale of the books themselves. Successful titles can be sold at a high price to international publishers who will translate them into their own language. These publishers are both customers and suppliers (as key partners). Romance is an international market in which authors' rights are exchanged through traditional publishing channels (international fairs, literary agencies).

5.2 *A second transformation: e-books first, p-books perhaps!*

A second transformation of the traditional BM lies in the importance of digital books. When interviewed by the trade magazine *Livres-Hebdo* at the end of 2023, Marie Legrand, Director of Projects at Hlab/BMR, acknowledged that the paper collection alone was not enough after the wave of *Twilight* and *Fifty Shades of Grey* successes. "*We realised that* popular literature *was a digital phenomenon and that we couldn't afford to ignore it.*" The pure player label Hlab was created and BMR increased its number of first digital publications. As a result, an important key resource is publishing knowledge. In romance, the publication chronology starts with the digital book and not with the paper book, as in the traditional model (which, however, is increasingly releasing both formats simultaneously). Once a title has been released digitally by Hlab or BMR, it may go into production, depending on its sales score, in short runs of 100 to 1,000 copies at Hachette's in-house print-on-demand service (called Ritméo), or in conventional print for larger print runs.

The digital format responds well to market requirements (high production output) and at the same time makes it possible to limit production costs and editorial risks. This has a favourable impact on the cost structure, but less favourable on revenue streams insofar as digital books are sold at a lower price than paper books (between 20% and 25% cheaper than paperbacks, and at least 50% cheaper than paperbacks). Manufacturing and distribution are cheaper for digital books than for paper. And when there is print production (or paper books), quantities are adjusted to demand, with the possibility of reprinting at no prohibitive cost. Placing texts on platforms acts as a market test, thanks to the number of "likes" and views. Potential demand is thus assessed and risk-taking limited. It may also be thought that the creative costs themselves (or editorial costs) are reduced when the novels are written by their authors on collaborative platforms, such as Wattpad. After all, the content has been evaluated and validated by readers, and not by publishers (at least in the first instance) as in the traditional model.

The paper book is an option valued by Hlab/BMR readers, enabling the company to sell content at a higher price. It is an integral part of their value proposition. In April 2023, Hlab/BMR launched a paperback collection (named Ito), enabling it to catch up with its main competitors (Hugo&Cie and HarpersCollin in particular). In terms of publication chronology, paperbacks come after digital books and paperbacks. Romance customers like to have a physical object, even if they read in digital format, and often even for free in digital format. Books fulfil a social function that is easier to express through a collection of printed objects, especially when it comes to showing off one's library on social networks. But if customers want printed books, they tend to prefer the most affordable format, that is, paperback. Bonus editions and collector's editions allow the publisher to move upmarket in his value proposition and provide a differentiating service; for example, collector's editions of *Captives* or unpublished fan art in the novels (drawings of characters, scenes or the world of the novel). In recent months, the range has also been enhanced by audio books. This offers a new kind of immersive reading experience for major titles at prices over €20.

5.3 *Third transformation: "goodbye critics, hello influencers!"*

A third major transformation of the BM compared with the traditional publishing model concerns book promotion. Whereas in the traditional model, promotion is carried out by publishers for journalists and booksellers who act as relays with readers, in the romance sector it is handled by the Internet and social networks. These players are, on the one hand, influencers operating on YouTube, Instagram and TikTok and, on the other, romance readers who share their experiences on various platforms (Wattpad, Goodreads, Booknode, Gleeph, We love words, etc.). Influencers are key partners with whom the publishing house has agreements: press service mailings, quarterly information meetings on new releases, communication of exclusive information, invitations to launch parties, etc. Readers brought together in different communities of influencers are also key partners for the publishing house. Readers gathered in different communities of interest require customer relationship management. The publishers are developing community management around the brand, authors and titles. Hlab and BMR each have a FaceBook account (770 subscribers and 10,000 subscribers respectively) and BMR also has an Instagram account followed by 85,000 people. In these literary communities, publishers, authors, readers and influencers interact as equals. There is no longer any question of a book chain as in the traditional model, where some links occupy a hierarchical position over others.

Concerning channels, the approach remains traditional. Hlab/BMR each have a website that serves as a privileged touchpoint with customers. But neither of them sells direct. They use the usual distribution channels (bookshops, specialist superstores and online platforms). Their website provides information on the catalogue and new releases, offers newsletter subscriptions, relays readers' opinions and features the authors in short videos. The company regularly organises meetings between authors and readers in bookshops, in the traditional format of book signings. Readers are keen to attend events that allow them to get up close and personal with the authors, or to immerse themselves in the world of the fictional characters, like the pop-up store organised by Hlab/BMR in January 2024 in Paris to coincide with the release of *Lakestone*, the new saga by Sarah Rivens.

6 Case study's contribution to business model innovation in CCIs

The Hlab/BMR BM reveals the transformations of the traditional publishing model driven by the appeal of a growth sector. These transformations are taking place against a backdrop of dematerialisation of products and disintermediation of activities specific to the CCI. As mentioned above, they affect the entire value chain, from publishing (first transformation) to manufacturing (second transformation) and promotion (third transformation). Since books have been less severely affected by dematerialisation than music and film (Carrière and Eco, 2011), the BM has evolved by opening up to new editorial schemes driven by digital books and self-publishing, while retaining the old ones inherited from paper books (manuscript selection, rights management, distribution channels, etc.). In book publishing, the BM is thus undergoing a form of hybridisation. In other CCIs, long-tail BM have been more profoundly affected by dematerialisation to the extent that physical media, such as CDs and DVDs have disappeared. Hybridisation comes from the virtual sphere and concerns both upstream and downstream of the editorial process leading to the value proposition.

6.1 *Hybridisation and upstream of the editorial process*

Upstream, new supply chains are emerging with the digital platforms on which women authors write their fiction. When publishers succeed in capturing content - because competition with other publishers can be fierce - they find more than a text. They find a text that readers have already enjoyed. By signing a publishing contract with the author, they enter into a long-term relationship that enables them to secure their supply and respond to the market's demand for "lots and lots fast". In short, the virtual sphere provides the publisher with a title, a market and an author. It enables publishers to outsource a significant part of their editorial process. Creative costs are saved and editorial risks are minimised.

To access the most promising texts and turn them into copyrights, the means of proceeding differ from one publishing house to another. Hlab/BMR has built a partnership with Wattpad, while its main competitor, Hugo Publishing, has made a different strategic choice. By creating its own Fyctia platform, it has adopted an upstream integration strategy. This strategy is costlier but guarantees security of supply. It's a winning strategy. Four to five competitions are organised each year on Fyctia, each attracting between 350 and 850 manuscripts. At the end of the competition, the winning titles are published after being chosen by the readers themselves. The publisher offers the author €500 in advance and 15% of sales. The platform brings 60% of authors to the catalogue, and sales per title are generally higher for Fyctia authors. For example, *Adopted Love* by Gaïa Alexia sold 150,000 hard copies after being read by 1.8 million readers on Fyctia. Another example, halfway between the two, comes from Harper Collins' Harlequin, which launched a writing competition on the We Love Words platform and discovered Emily Blaine, one of the catalogue's leading authors.

6.2 *Hybridisation and downstream of the editorial process*

Downstream, an entire customer relationship management system needs to be created in traditional publishing. Table 5.1 of the BMs drawn up by Osterwalder and Pigneur (2010) shows that customer relationship management is not included in the old model. Traditional publishing uses distribution networks (to sell) and literary journalists (to promote) to reach readers without seeking to establish a more direct link with them. In the romance sector, it's a different story! Booksellers and literary journalists have been replaced in their prescriptive role by influencers and readers themselves, who comment on books. Hugo Publishing is once again breaking new ground when it comes to customer relations. It has been organising a festival dedicated to romance every year since 2016. In 2023, for the seventh edition, the event reached record attendance levels, according to the publisher: "*two hours after tickets went on sale, we had 5,000 registrations, i.e. more than 1,000 additional festival-goers, and 1,800 people were placed on the waiting list*" (*Livres-Hebdo*, 8/12/2023). If the readers were fans, the authors were acclaimed like pop stars, applauded to the rafters and protected by the staff from any outbursts. There were book signings, a dinner with karaoke and fellowship to Ellie Goulding's *Love Me Like You Do*, an awards ceremony and an escape-game with the authors. Over 45,000 books were sold during the evening, not including the impact in bookshops. For its part, Hlab/BMR is sticking to more traditional publishing practices, but it did try out an event popular with romance fans in January 2024: a pop-store to accompany the release of a book.

In the theoretical part of this chapter, we identified two major research questions from the literature review on long-tail BM. The elements that have just been developed to explain the hybridisation of the BM in the romance sector, based on the Hlab/BMR case, provide some answers.

- How to mitigate the distribution costs of distributing a large number of products?

  Concerning this first question, the digital sphere is capable of producing successful titles, some of which are virtually co-written with readers in the same way as fan fiction. Supply is perfectly matched to demand. Traditional publishing is building on the success of the web. For the other part of the catalogue, which is supplied by the more traditional channels, as shown in Figure 5.3 (seen the niche content providers as key partners), supply is less easily adjusted to demand. The house's authors are not always bestsellers, and foreign books are not automatic successes once translated into French. The demand for publications based on first novels submitted to the publisher is even more uncertain, in line with what makes the CCI prototype industries (Caves, 2000). Nevertheless, the digital format greatly limits storage and distribution costs, and when there is a printed version, print runs are adapted as closely as possible and reprints are possible without prohibitive cost. The catalogue as a whole can therefore react positively to the logic of equalisation formulated as early as the 18th century by Diderot: profitability is not achieved on a title-by-title basis but globally within the catalogue. This is also the principle of the product portfolio developed in corporate strategy (Johnson et al., 2014).

How can consumers be helped to find what they are looking for in a plethora of offerings?

> With regard to the second research question, the readership has unique characteristics in romance. They are loyal and eager to learn new things, and they know where the books are published, both virtually and in real life. Armed with a smartphone, they use all the technological resources available to them and are therefore hyper-informed. They are familiar with multi-channel and multi-format practices, moving from bookshops to online sales platforms and vice versa, alternating between reading on e-book and p-book, getting information from a bookseller or on TikTok. It is therefore up to publishers to act on the networks they use and to involve them actively, in a way that differs from traditional patterns, in the design of books and their promotion, as mentioned above and as omnichannel marketing theorists advocate.
> (Palmatier et al., 2019)

While we can answer these two research questions in qualitative terms in accordance with our methodological approach, it would have been interesting to supplement the answers with a quantitative approach. One of the major limitations of our work is that we were unable to obtain statistical data and economic data on the catalogue and publishing activity of the case studied. It is in fact difficult, if not impossible at present, to obtain an interview with the managers. In addition, among the secondary sources used, press articles focus on bestsellers and neglect lesser-known titles, which would have been of interest to us in dealing with the long-tail hypothesis, according to which the sum of sales of niche content is equal to or greater than that of bestsellers.

The long-tail BM does not just apply to books, music and films, but to any content industry in the broad sense, such as journalism (Cook and Sirkkunen, 2013). In a broader sense, any activity involving consumers in the BM is likely to create a long-tail effect in reference to the three trends mentioned by Anderson as giving rise to niche markets thanks to the Internet (democratisation of production tools, distribution and matching between supply and demand). Osterwalder and Pigneur (2010) take the example of eBay, FaceBook and Lego (with Lego factory and Lego users catalog). This approach places the consumer at the centre of the BM and value creation. Plé et al. (2010) have taken this approach a step further by redesigning the BM as a "customer-integrated BM". In the book, co-writing the text with readers in the manner of fan fiction breaks down the watertight boundary between supply and demand. Without going as far as co-writing, the fact that a book is written by the author with reference to the real or supposed expectations of readers raises questions about the notion of literature. Romance which is part of popular literature, is presented as commercial literature whose aim is to entertain the reader. Readers are offered a quick, easy read for a single purpose. Erudite literature, on the other hand, is legitimised by literary institutions and offers a slow, hard read that needs to be repeated.

Finally, the book industry has been more resistant to the introduction of digital than other CCIs. In France, where there is a dense network of independent bookshops (selling mainly paper books), digital books account for just 10% of publishers' sales (SNE, 2023). Digital books have not evolved in the same way in the CCIs. In music and film, the BM has been completely rethought because the value chain has disappeared under the effect of disintermediation but also of the devaluation of the offer. If romance lends itself well to hybridisation in the book sector, we might well ask whether it has already reached a limit, or whether hybridisation can go even further on the digital side, and in what way.

7 Conclusion

The romance market is a fast-growing long-tail market, where national and international bestsellers written by a few star authors coexist with many other titles that are less visible to the general public, but which fans discover on the networks and within their communities. This market operates in a way that is far removed from traditional publishing processes in terms of creation, production, distribution and promotion. The Hlab/BMR case study, a division of the Hachette group specialising in romance, highlighted three major transformations in the BM: (i) the Internet as a supplier of authors and texts, including and above all texts validated by readers; (ii) the primacy of the e-book over the p-book in terms of product technology; (iii) the inclusion of readers in the customer relationship, hitherto relegated to second place behind booksellers and other distribution channels. The BM is thus hybrid, with traditional processes being maintained alongside new processes derived from the principles of the long tail. Hybridisation occurs both upstream and downstream of value creation, resulting in a number of functions being outsourced to users and a stronger partnership with players operating on the Internet.

The long-tail BM raises an important question for CCIs: how do we move from produced diversity to distributed and consumed diversity? On the one hand, the Internet and digital technologies have created a porous link between creation and consumption, and on the other, they have strengthened the downstream dimension in these industries, which were previously managed on the basis of a supply-side economy. The use of the Internet as a distribution channel, the development of the e-book, and amateur practices made public on the networks, have increased the market and customer focus. The romance market is thus a testing ground for new practices, and its growth has served as a catalyst for transforming BMs. At the end of this chapter, we can wonder how these practices will develop once the romance market reaches maturity, and how the BMs of traditional publishers targeting this market will continue to change.

Note

1 Sztern, L. (2023) *Internship report Hlab/BMR at Aix Marseille University* [Confidential document]. This internship report is not a public document due to a confidentiality clause.

References

Anderson, C. 2004. "The long tail", *Wired Magazine*, Issue 12.10.

Anderson, C. 2006. *The Long Tail: Why the Future of Business Is Selling Less of More.* New York, NY: Hyperion.

Benghozi, P.-J. and F. Benhamou. 2008. « Longue traîne: levier numérique de la diversité culturelle? », *Culture prospective*, 2008-1, Ministère de la culture et de la communication, http://www.culture.gouv.fr/deps, consulted on 10 January 2024.

Brynjolfsson, E., Y. J. Hu and M. D. Smith. 2006. "From niches to riches: Anatomy of the long tail", *MIT Sloan Management*, Vol.47, n°4, pp.67–71.

Brynjolfsson, E., Y. Hu and D. Simester. 2011. "Goodbye pareto principle, hello long tail: The effect of search costs on the concentration of product sales", *Management Science*, Vol.57, n°8, pp.1373–1386.

Carrière, J.-C. and U. Eco. 2011. *This Is Not the End of the Book: A Conversation Curated by Jean-Philippe de Tonnac.* London: Harvill Secker [First edition: *N'espérez pas vous débarrasser des livres*, Paris, Grasset, 2009].

Caves, R. 2000. *Creative Industries: Contracts Between Art and Commerce.* Cambridge, MA: Harvard University Press.

Cook, C. and E. Sirkkunen. 2013. "What's in a niche? Exploring the BM of on line journalism", *Journal of Media Business Studies*, Vol.10, n°4, pp.63–82.

Diderot, D. 2023. *Historical and Political Letter on the Book Trade.* London: Newcomb Livraria Press [First edition in French: *Lettre sur le commerce de la librairie*, in Œuvres Complètes, Vol.18, Paris Garnier Frères 1876].

Elberse, A. 2008. "Should you invest in the long tail?" *Harvard Business Review*, HBS Centennial Issue, Vol.86, n°7/8, pp.88–96.GfK. 2024. "Plus de 350 millions d'exemplaires vendus en 2023 en France », https://www.gfk.com/fr/press/plus-de-351-millions-livres-achats-france-2023, consulted on 25 January 2024.

Jenkins, H. 1992. *Textual Poachers. Television Fans & Participatory Culture.* London: Routledge.

Johnson, G., R. Whittington, K. Scholes, P. Regnér and D. Angwin. 2014. *Fundamentals of Strategy.* London: Pearson Education Limited.

Le Figaro. 2024. "Plates-formes d'écriture en ligne: le nouvel eldorado des éditeurs », par Alice Devely, 19/1/2024.

Libération. 2023. « La dark romance sur BookTok comme un poison dans l'eau de rose », par Constance Vilanova, 13/6/2023.

Livres-Hebdo. 2023. "Une décennie de New Romance" par Olivier Dion, 8/12/2023.

Miles, M. B. and A. M. Huberman. 1994. *Qualitative Data Analysis, An Expanded Sourcebook*, Second edition. London: Sage Publications.

Nielsen. 2016. Romance readers by the number. https://www.nielsen.com/fr/insights/2016/romance-readers-by-the-numbers/, consulted on 10 December 2023

Ministère de la Culture. 2023. https://data.culture.gouv.fr/explore/dataset/chiffres-cles-pour-le-secteur-du-livre/information/ consulted on 17 January 2024

Osterwalder, A. and Y. Pigneur. 2010. *BM Generation: A Handbook for Visionaries, Game Changers, and Challengers*. New York, NY: Wiley.
Palmatier, R. W., E. Silvadas, L.W. Stern and A.I. El-Ansary. 2019. *Marketing Channel Strategy: An Omni-Channel Approach*. London: Routledge.Plé, L., X. Lecocq and J. Angot. 2010. "Customer-integrated BMs: A theoretical framework", *M@n@gement*, Vol.13, n°4, pp.226–265.
Syndicat National de l'Edition. 2023. *Les chiffres clés de l'édition 2021–2022 Synthèse du rapport statistique du SNE France et International*. https://www.sne.fr/economie/chiffres-cles/ consulted on 22 February 2024
Sztern, L. 2023. *Internship report Hlab/BMR at Aix Marseille University* [Confidential document].

6 The role of multi-sided business models in managing creative ecosystems

The case of the online video game industry

Romain Gandia and Guy Parmentier

1 Introduction: the economic and social explosion of online video games

The digital age and the explosion of mobile entertainment have made online gaming the most profitable segment of the video game industry. With more than 50% of worldwide sales, massively multiplayer online games and social games on mobiles have largely contributed to the popularization of video games as a modern form of entertainment, considerably increasing the number of gamers worldwide. Historically dominated by the console gaming model, the industry has been faced with a real paradigm shift, involving a complete restructuring of existing strategic and logistical models in favor of new, more open, community-based digital models. Digital technologies and mobile networks (4G, 5G) have largely contributed to the development of these new models, increasing the rapid accessibility of games to a growing population still seeking entertainment (permanent or occasional), connectivity, and social interaction. The digital era has thus fostered the cultural acceptance of video games, and is now stimulating the sector's economic growth. With sales expected to reach 282 billion dollars by the end of 2024,[1] the industry is growing by an average of 8%–10% a year, and now boasts over 3.2 billion players, over 60% of whom play online on their smartphones.[2]

In addition to these technological, cultural, and social factors, the incredible success of online games also lies in opening up artistic and narrative content to communities of players (Parmentier and Gandia, 2013). Relying on social digital spaces and toolkits for innovation, many online games (e.g., Minecraft, League of Legends, Fortnite, Pokémon GO, Trackmania, Dofus, FarmVille, etc.) have thus enjoyed global success thanks to the active contribution of millions of players worldwide. However, this sustainable strategic model relies on the development of a genuine creative ecosystem that engages players in a dynamic of innovation that benefits industry players. However, strategic management of this type of ecosystem is complex, not least because companies need to orchestrate different types of resources in different types of spaces with different types of players to create different types of value.

DOI: 10.4324/9781032714462-6

To meet this challenge, many organizations are adopting multi-sided business models (BMs), which have the advantage of decoupling value logics between different sides (different user groups) in order to multiply the sources of value creation and capture, via network effects (Gandia and Parmentier, 2017). Despite the significant development of research on this subject, **the question of the role of the multi-sided BM in the strategic management of creative ecosystem** is still poorly understood. The aim of this chapter is precisely to answer this question based on a three-stage plan.

As a first step, we articulate the literature on multi-sided BM with research dealing with ecosystems. Based on the limitations of literature, we suggest that multi-sided BMs can be adapted for managing the resource orchestration and the openness dynamics in a creative ecosystem. Secondly, we discuss the method used to study the online video game industry and the three companies Ankama, Nadeo/Ubisoft, and VidCoin. Finally, we present the main results of our research and the contributions they make to companies in the cultural and creative industries (ICCs).

2 Theory

As the economic success of many online video games depends on the ability of actors to strategically develop and manage a creative ecosystem, we begin this section with works on ecosystems. Understanding the challenges involved in managing a creative ecosystem then enables us to consider the link with the multi-sided BM.

2.1 *The creative ecosystem: the challenges of openness and resource orchestration*

The concept of ecosystem is linked to the work of Moore (1993), who defines it as a space and environment bringing together a diversity of players invested jointly in the production of a business logic. First popularized under the term business ecosystem, the concept was extended with the work of Koenig (2013) on community ecosystems, defined as common spaces in which communities interact around a common resource. One example is Open Source community ecosystems on the Internet, which show how different groups (developers, integrators, users, laboratories, etc.) can organize and exchange to develop, maintain, and evolve a common resource. Since the work of Koenig (2013), the community logic is seen as a constitutive dimension of a business logic. Other research has subsequently applied the ecosystem view to the logic of innovation and creativity, with both conceptions emphasizing the importance of coordination between actors. The innovation ecosystem is defined as a set of collaborative arrangements between different actors who seek to combine their individual offerings to stimulate innovation (e.g., Adner, 2006). The creative ecosystem describes the organization of the creative system (people, resources, and environment) that enables creative activity to take place (de Bernard et al., 2021). In order to create value (innovation or creativity), it is essential to coordinate the individual efforts and resources of the players toward a common goal (Adner, 2006).

This conception of the ecosystem as a mix of key ingredients (space, time, diversity of actors, resources, common purpose) raises two important challenges: openness and orchestration of resources. Openness refers to the ability of players to exchange ideas, knowledge, and resources with other players in order to create value (Chesbroug, 2006). Orchestration refers to the ability to select, assemble, deploy, and coordinate resources to meet a strategic objective (Sirmon et al., 2011). The functioning of an ecosystem requires these types of capabilities, as the actors involved must collaborate and perform value transactions to produce a common result. The ecosystem is thus based on a structure of exchange and open borders between partner actors (Malherbe and Tellier, 2022). While the selection of partners can play a role in ecosystem performance, research shows that it is the choice of resources and their orchestration that prove decisive (Linde et al., 2021). In the literature, these two challenges of openness and orchestration can be addressed using work on the structural approach and the interactionist approach to ecosystems (Hou and Shi, 2021).

The structural approach envisions the ecosystem as a structure of alignment between the needs and expectations of various partners, who must structure their exchanges to materialize a focal value proposition (Adner, 2017). The ecosystem is then characterized by four structural elements: (1) the activities required to realize a focal value proposition, (2) the actors managing these activities, (3) the position of actors in the flow of activities, and (4) the exchanges between actors. By analyzing these four elements, it is possible to reflect on the alignment structure between partners and thus reduce resource orchestration problems. The interactionist approach is based on a precise analysis of relationships between players and power relations, and seeks to qualify the organizational dynamics. So we see centralized ecosystems where relationships are orchestrated by a hub, while others opt for more community-based governance, in which decision-making power is distributed among the various players (Olk and West, 2023). The interactionist approach relies heavily on value transactions, while the structural approach emphasizes the alignment of partners toward a focal value proposition. Although these two approaches may seem very different, they nevertheless share common points and complement each other. Both pay close attention to the notion of value, and to the way in which players organize themselves and exchange in a balanced way (or not) to produce common value. This highlights the importance of managing openness and orchestrating resources, two challenges that are exacerbated in the case of creative and innovation ecosystems.

Creative and innovation ecosystems have the distinctive feature of focusing the efforts of players on a common objective of creating new value (new idea, concept, product, etc.). This newness implies more uncertainty and exploration than other types of ecosystem, which are more focused on exploiting a common resource (e.g., Open Source) or an existing business logic. However, the creative ecosystem is restricted to the production and dissemination of ideas, whereas the innovation ecosystem involves additional stages in the innovation process (design, prototyping, experimentation, etc.). This chapter focuses more specifically on creative ecosystems, for which specific elements need to be brought together to ensure the organization of creative activity: (1) the creative environment (space/place, creative climate, temporality), (2) individuals (personality, needs, expectations, etc.) and (3) technical resources (processes, tools, etc.) (Brem et al., 2016). Among these elements, openness and exchanges between individuals can prove complex, as the creative ecosystem brings together different types of individuals and collectives motivated by different and sometimes contradictory rationality (creative urge, artistic goals, recognition, politics, opportunism, economic needs, etc.) (Kirman, 2010). The resource orchestration can also be complex, as the creative ecosystem does not produce definitive results, but is used as a tool for developing and disseminating ideas in related spaces located at different levels within an industry or society. This is what Cohendet et al. (2009) call the "upperground" (firms, public organizations, universities, state, etc.), the "underground" (individuals, groups, communities), and the "middle-ground" (intermediate spaces where the two previous levels are mixed). The creative ecosystem thus develops within the middle-ground, through digital platforms, projects and events, and requires a difficult orchestration of resources from all levels to produce and disseminate ideas (Grandadam et al., 2013).

The literature tells us that the creative ecosystem must be based on an interactionist structure and must possess an environment conducive to framing creative activity, a set of complementary actors ready to open up to co-create value, and a set of adapted, well-orchestrated resources. Works on creative ecosystems are scarce and remain focused for the most part on physical spaces (e.g., Cohendet et al., 2009; Grandadam et al., 2013). A few rare studies mention the interesting potential of digital platforms to host such ecosystems (e.g., Novani et al., 2023), but the question of their strategic management remains under-studied.

2.2 *The multi-sided BM as a strategic tool for openness and resource orchestration*

Multi-sided BM is a particular BM architecture based on the delivery of several complementary and/or interdependent value propositions to several groups of customers who bring value to each other (Parmentier and Gandia, 2017). A face is thus characterized by a group of customers with similar behaviors, needs, and propensity to pay, which may represent all or part of a target market (Evans and Schmalensee, 2007). Developed in conjunction with multi-sided platforms, the multi-sided BM is fundamentally rooted in the digital age, since it relies on digital technologies to organize the creation, proposition, and capture of value with multiple user groups (Gawer, 2009). For this reason, multi-sided BMs are essentially based on a service business logic that implies the implementation of an open interactionist model (the connection between stakeholders to co-create value) rather than a closed industrial model of product distribution (Vargo & Lusch, 2016). An emblematic example is AirBnB, which markets tourism accommodation and experience service by connecting three user groups: hosts, travelers and experience makers. Using a multi-sided platform as a market space, the company has built a multi-sided BM that optimizes value creation and capture by relying on the contribution of users (Gandia and Parmentier, 2017). Multi-sided BMs thus require a more complex organization and management than a single-sided BM, because the dynamics of opening up and orchestrating resources with different actors is an essential condition for success.

To succeed, the multi-sided BM is originally based on a digital platform, which is itself considered a technological, economic, and strategic resource. The multi-sided platform acts as a socio-technical space of openness between users, who can interact thanks to the interfaces and functionalities available (Shuen, 2008). It is also a market space for transacting economic value (purchase, reservation, subscription, etc.), which will be self-sustaining as groups of customers become involved in the co-production of the service (e.g., Ebay) (Gawer, 2009). This economic approach enables a company to achieve economies of scale in both supply and demand by delivering a large-scale service directly to customers, while remaining connected to their needs and expectations (Gawer, 2014). Finally, the multi-sided platform is a strategic space for networking and orchestrating internal and external resources (contributed by groups of customers and partners), generating network effects (Hagiu and Wright, 2015).

In a multi-sided BM architecture, the value of the service delivered will depend on direct network effects (the value varies according to the behaviors and number of users of the service on the same side) and indirect network effects (the value varies according to the behaviors and number of users on another side) (Evans and Schmalensee, 2006). There are also cross-network effects (i.e., between faces) where the network effect is bidirectional, from one face to the other and vice versa (Hagiu and Wright, 2015). Network effects are therefore crucial to the economic performance of a multi-sided BM, and their production is intimately linked to the design and management of the dynamics of openness and orchestration of resources (Gandia and Parmentier, 2017). Within multi-sided BMs, openness is essential, as the aim is to involve groups of customers/partners in the co-creation of value. This is particularly the case in the video game industry, where communities of gamers are engaged in improving games and sometimes even creating narrative and artistic content. From a strategic design perspective, the multi-sided BM must therefore respect two imperatives (Parmentier and Gandia, 2017): (1) design a focused offer containing several complementary and/

or interdependent value propositions to engage mutually enriching customer groups and (2) provide the environment and resources needed for customer groups to engage in value-creating exchange behaviors. At this level, the platform is a true strategic asset, as it technologically, spatially, and temporally frames the opening of boundaries with user groups, and at the same time orchestrates the resources needed to create value (Gandia and Parmentier, 2020). These include toolkits for the creation of content, events, and projects, and processes structuring the organization of exchanges. Openness and resource orchestrations are therefore intimately linked, and their joint management relies on the technological potential of multi-sided platforms.

The challenges of openness and resource orchestration inherent in the management of creative ecosystems are addressed here by work on multi-sided BMs. Given the particularities of this type of BM, we suggest that the multi-sided architecture of a BM based on a digital platform can be a highly effective strategic tool for managing a creative ecosystem. This strategic and technological duality of the multi-sided BM provides key management principles:

- **The multi-sided BM can provide a stimulating framework for designing the value logic of a creative ecosystem:** that is, the way in which value creation, proposition, and capture are collectively envisioned within the ecosystem.
- **Multi-sided BM is based on a technological platform architecture that can help structure a creative ecosystem:** that is, how to define the creative ecosystem environment (the digital platform), how to define the types of actors to be involved (the definition of sides), and how to connect the actors to each other (the interfaces, functionalities, technological resources, and processes).
- **The multi-sided BM backed by a digital platform proposes mechanisms that can help manage the creative ecosystem in movement:** that is, how to manage the opening up and orchestration of resources between different types of players (the objective of producing network effects).

3 Method

This chapter focuses on the online video game industry. It is therefore particularly well suited to the issue of strategic management of creative ecosystems. With almost 2 billion online gamers worldwide (source: Digital Report, 2023), the industry possesses an unprecedented strategic and creative resource. Over the past 15 years, we have seen the gradual emergence of creative ecosystems (of varying sizes) associated with online games. Some games, such as Minecraft (over 300 million copies sold since 2009), have precisely built their gameplay on this creative principle, allowing players to concretely create the world in which they wish to evolve, thus contributing to the ongoing enrichment of the game environment.

Beyond these "extreme" cases of openness, other companies have sought to exploit the creative ecosystem in different ways. This is precisely the case with Ankama, Nadeo/Ubisoft, and Vidcoin, which we have studied in this chapter. We have adopted a qualitative approach to study in depth the role of the multi-sided BM in the strategic management of a creative ecosystem. This methodology is particularly well suited to emerging phenomena, for which it is important to understand in detail the mechanisms that govern their operation (Miles and Huberman, 2019). To this end, we have opted for a qualitative approach in order to gather the viewpoints of the players involved in the ecosystems under study.

Data collection was based on a series of interviews with each company (different profiles, such as the CEO, team leaders, and community managers) as well as with the various categories of partners involved in the ecosystem, including players. In all, more than 40 interviews were conducted over a period of around four years, in order to track the evolution of the BM and the creative ecosystem. The aim was to understand the company's history, the complete trajectory of the multi-sided BM, the link with the technology (the platform), and the management of the creative ecosystem (structuring, objectives, difficulties, mechanisms for managing openness, orchestration of resources, and results). These interviews were supplemented by an extensive set of secondary data, both internal to the companies (mainly project documentation and meeting minutes) and external (company websites, video game web pages, forums, press articles, press releases, video interviews). As online video games are a highly mediatized market, numerous documentary sources are available. The aim was to gain a better understanding of the creative ecosystems studied, and to corroborate the information obtained from the interviews.

The qualitative data were analyzed using standard lexical analysis and thematic coding techniques. The data were coded according to various codes and sub-codes from the literature, in the following structure: (1) the multi-sided BM, with codes relating to strategic decisions, value components (creation/proposition/capture), network effects, and temporal trajectory; (2) the digital platform, with codes relating to technical tools (toolkits), environment (digital spaces, interfaces, functionalities) and supporting processes; (3) the creative ecosystem, with codes relating to the focal value proposition, types of partners, activities, openness (interactions) and resource orchestration (resource provision, coordination, and results). Focusing on the strategic level of analysis (the BM), we cross-referenced coded data to identify causal relationships between the multi-sided BM, the digital platform, and the management of the creative ecosystem in each of the cases studied.

4 Case studies presentation

The three cases selected are examples of success in the online video game segment, and have exemplary a multi-sided BM based on digital platforms.

4.1 *Ankama case*

Ankama is an independent digital creation group specializing in entertainment (video games, animation, and publishing). Founded in 2001, the company is known for the international success of its first massively multiplayer online game: Dofus. Launched in 2004, the game now has over 85 million accounts (40 million in France). Building on this success, the company then developed a transmedia strategy to create a complete artistic and creative universe, exploited on three types of interconnected media: (1) video games (online/mobile), enabling players to interact and evolve within a heroic fantasy universe (Krosmoz) divided into various successful games (Dofus and Wakfu being the best known); (2) animation (TV/web), to tell certain stories from the universe and (3) editions (comics/manga), to tell the story of certain emblematic characters and thus helping to improve understanding of the animated series and video games. Today, this transmedia universe totals 15 video games, five animation series (broadcast on France TV, Netflix, etc.), and four manga and comic collections. The deployment of this transmedia strategy has prompted the company to gradually structure itself in the form of dedicated strategic units (Ankama Games, Animations, Editions, Products, Studio, and Convention) in order to control all the activities required to design, market, and distribute its artistic products. Distribution is international, mainly in Europe, South America and Asia. The Dofus and Wakfu transmedia games now have more than 7 million daily active users (more than half of whom are international). Ankama currently employs more than 500 people and generates average sales of over 40 million euros, of which over 70% come from video games.

Strategically, Ankama's transmedia offering is built around a multi-sided BM, with each side representing a media/customer category (see Table 6.1). The first category (side 1) is multiplayer online video games, which are at the heart of the transmedia offering, as they allow players to explore the Krosmoz universe in the present day. The second category (side 2) is TV animation, which tells viewers certain stories from the Krosmoz universe (e.g., Wakfu and Dofus) in advance of the video game. The third category (side 3) is editions, which allows readers to discover the historical past of the Krosmoz universe and its characters. The narrative and temporal connections between the media naturally create connections between the BM sides, which are thought of artistically and strategically as complementary. These connections produce positive network effects. Each side benefits from its own success, helping to attract more and more players, viewers, and readers (direct effects). Each side then contributes to the others thanks to narrative and temporal connections, which encourage players to become viewers and readers and vice versa, thus increasing the number of customers (indirect effects). Finally, the three sides are built around a collaborative digital platform that enables players, viewers, and readers to interact and enrich each other by creating value through discussion forums, content creation tools,

Table 6.1 Multi-sided BM of Ankama

Multi-sided BM	*Side 1 Video game*	*Side 2 Animated TV series*	*Side 3 Editions*
Value creation	*Players, viewers, and readers*: content creation and continuous improvement dynamic (on the platform), game dynamics, TV audience, readership		
	Ankama: creation and distribution of video games and contents	*Ankama*: creation of animated series	*Ankama*: creation and distribution of comics and mangas
Value proposition	*Players, viewers, and readers*: ideas and suggestions for improvement		
	Ankama: unique transmedia offering based on heroic fantasy universe		
Value capture	*Players*: recognition, virtual monetary *Ankama*: subscription revenues for full game access, iteming	*Viewers*: knowledge of the universe's future *Ankama*: revenues from exploitation rights	*Readers*: knowledge of the universe's past *Ankama*: revenues from sales of comics/manga
Network effects	Direct and indirect, as each side attracts new users not only to the same side but also to others. Crossed, because the players, viewers, and readers enrich each other through their interactions on the collaborative platform and their content creations.		

polls, and cross-effect competitions. In this way, the company benefits from the community's creative ideas to improve the elements of the transmedia offering. From an economic point of view, Ankama offers its video games online in freemium mode (free access to the game, followed by subscription and item pack purchases), while TV series are purchased by audiovisual distribution partners (France TV, Netflix) and mangas/comics are sold individually. A virtual money is also integrated into video games (the Kama), enabling valuable transactions (sale/purchase of objects, resources, items) to be carried out without any tax on Ankama's part.

4.2 *Nadeo/Ubisoft case*

Nadeo is an independent French video game studio founded in 2000, which made a name for itself with the international success of its massively multiplayer racing simulation game Trackmania. Launched in 2003, this game features simple graphics and an innovative gameplay concept, in stark contrast to the simulation games of the time. Trackamania is based on the principle of a community game that encourages creative player participation. Thanks to a circuit creation tool, players can design their own circuit before competing on it to appreciate its playability. Between 2003 and 2008, no fewer than seven extensions to the original game were developed and marketed (involving several million players), propelling Nadeo into the e-sport segment with Trackmania Nation (2006) and the creation of the Trackmania World Cup. This version is enhanced by a competition creation and management tool that uses the pool of tracks created to create original race sets on which players from all over the world can compete. On the strength of this success, the independent studio was acquired by Ubisoft in 2009, and continued to develop new versions and extensions (seven more, until 2017) for Nintendo DS, Nintendo Wii, PlayStation, and Xbox. A digital platform, Maniaplanet, is also launched to manage the online distribution of content and games developed by Nadeo. In 2017, the Trackmania Pro League was created, demonstrating the game's strong foothold in the growing eSports segment.

Strategically, Nadeo's Trackmania online video game is built around a multi-sided BM, with each side representing a different category of player (see Table 6.2). The first category (side 1) represents the creators, who play a strategic role in the diversity of content created within the game. They participate in the creation of tracks (hundreds of thousands to date), the creation of cars (via a customization tool), and the creation of race video replays (using a video editor). The second category (side 2) represents the managers, who also play a strategic role in the game, helping to create a multiplayer dynamic by organizing races and competitions. Each competition is organized in a unique

Table 6.2 Multi-sided BM of Nadeo/Ubisoft

Multi-sided BM	*Side 1 Creators*	*Side 2 Managers*	*Side 3 Competitors*
Value creation	Circuit creation, car customization, and replay *Nadeo*: toolkits for creation	Competitions and races management *Nadeo*: toolkits for competition creation and management	Participation in races, game dynamics *Nadeo*: race gameplay and ranking
Value proposition	Circuit sharing and content diversity *Nadeo*: community and creative game	Competitions and races schedule 7/7 *Nadeo*: community and creative game	Presence and ideas for improvement *Nadeo*: online multiplayer game
Value capture	Social recognition (by Nadeo and players), virtual monetary reward, free game versions *Nadeo*: economies of scale (profiting from user creativity) and revenues from game sales		Cash prize (economic) and reputation (medals) *Nadeo*: revenues from game sales
Network effects	Direct and indirect, as each side attracts new users not only to the same side but also to others. Crossed, because the three types of players enrich each other through their creative behavior and participation.		

way, as the managers themselves choose the circuits on which to compete, promote their competition to attract players, organize the media coverage of the races themselves using the video tool, and report the results on the leaderboard. The third category (side 3) represents the competitors, who are regular or occasional players competing on the circuits created by the creators and taking part in the competitions proposed by the managers. These three categories of players are interdependent because they bring value to each other. Creators bring diversity to the game, which benefits managers and competitors alike. Managers provide an international and permanent (7/7) multiplayer game dynamic that values the work of creators and attracts competitors. Competitors bring the competitions to life with their presence, and add value to the work of creators and managers. This interdependence benefits the company, which derives positive network effects. The company is remunerated by the sale of the game, but also by a virtual money, the Copper, which organizes value transactions between players (purchase of blocks for circuits, sale of circuits and cars, cash prizes for competitions, etc.). Players can obtain this money by earning medals (race podiums), winning competitions, or selling content (circuit, car). Nadeo receives a commission for each transaction carried out.

4.3 Vidcoin case

Vidcoin is a company specializing in integrated video advertising for the online and mobile social gaming segment. Founded in 2013 and benefiting from a €1 million fundraising round in 2014, Vidcoin has rapidly established itself as a key intermediary in the advertising business. This service, backed by online and mobile social gaming platforms, offers to broadcast sponsored video ads within the games themselves. The special feature of this service is that the ads are non-binding. Players themselves choose to watch certain ads (according to their preferences and interests) in order to earn virtual money. This highly incentivizing principle enables Vidcoin to generate a voluntary audience, motivated by the remuneration of in-game items. This principle is far more lucrative than traditional banner advertising (€20 per 1,000 views for video versus €1 per 1,000 views for banners), and has the advantage of not disrupting the player's experience. As soon as three ads have been viewed (short format under 45s), the player can purchase an item within the game of their choice. The more videos the player watches, the greater his or her power to purchase items within the games. This system makes it possible to monetize an audience that doesn't have access to payment methods, or that doesn't want to pay, even if it has the means to do so. While the online and mobile social gaming segment is structured around a free-to-play model and culture, Vidcoin has succeeded in developing a remunerative system for players, game publishers, and advertisers alike.

Strategically, the Vidcoin online service is built around a multi-sided BM, with each side representing a category of players/customers (see Table 6.3).

Table 6.3 Multi-sided BM of Vidcoin

Multi-sided BM	*Side 1 Publishers*	*Side 2 Advertisers*	*Side 3 Players*
Value creation	Integrate Vidcoin's advertising service on the gaming platform	Create advertising campaigns and pay for audiences	Create audience and gaming dynamics
	Vidcoin: create and manage the advertising system and data analysis		
Value proposition	Provide a qualified player database (panel)	Provide short ads (under 45s)	Give up your time to watch ads
	Vidcoin: provides a targeted and non-intrusive advertising service for social gaming platforms		
Value capture	Advertising revenue *Vidcoin*: cost savings (share installation costs)	Audience (number of views and clicks) *Vidcoin*: commission on advertiser billing (30%)	Virtual money *Vidcoin*: ideas and suggestions for improving the audience targeting
Network effects	Direct and indirect, as each side attracts new actors not only to the same side but also to others. Crossed, because the three types of players enrich each other through resources they bring (player panel, money, and time)		

The first category (side 1) represents game publishers who adopt Vidcoin technology and deploy the advertising system on their online and mobile game platforms in exchange for remuneration based on the number of exposures to sponsored videos. The second category (side 2) represents advertising agencies and advertisers who integrate the Vidcoin video format into their large-scale digital advertising campaign and pay in exchange for a qualified audience voluntarily engaged in viewing the videos. The third category (side 3) represents players who voluntarily select advertising videos to watch in exchange for payment (virtual money). Multi-sided BM is based on the principle of volume. The aim is to aggregate as many gaming platforms as possible, in order to engage as many players as possible in video viewing, and thus convince as many advertisers as possible to pay for advertising campaigns. Vidcoin is remunerated by a 30% commission on each campaign, with advertisers invoiced according to the number of video views. This multi-sided BM generates positive network effects. Firstly, directly on each side, since service performance increases the customer base. The more publishers, advertisers and gamers use the service, the newer publishers, advertisers, and gamers are won over. Secondly, the three categories of player are interdependent. If one of them disappears, the model no longer works. For example, the more publishers install the Vidcoin service on their online gaming platforms, the larger the community of gamers becomes and the more videos they view, resulting in a greater number of advertising campaigns broadcast by advertisers. By 2015, this model had enabled Vidcoin to integrate its advertising network service into more than 300 applications, while simultaneously launching more than 2,500 advertising campaigns in over 25 countries (reaching nearly 100 million players).

5 Main results

The data analysis shows the existence of an interlocking structural relationship between the multi-sided BM and the creative ecosystem of each case studied. This relationship is essential, as it enables the creative ecosystem to be nested within the value logic of the multi-sided BM. Secondly, the comparative analysis of the cases reveals the common elements that explain the role of the multi-sided BM in the strategic management of the creative ecosystem, in particular the management of openness and the orchestration of resources.

5.1 The interlocking structural relationship between the multi-sided BM and the creative ecosystem

The originality of cases lies in their differences, describing several structures of creative ecosystem: distributed (Ankama), integrated (Nadeo), and centralized (Vidcoin).

Ankama has structured its creative ecosystem in a distributed way, using several interconnected multi-sided platforms that multiply the gateways into the artistic universe of Krosmoz. At the center are the two main platforms on Dofus and Wakfu, which articulate the core of the transmedia offering, around which gravitate other platforms exploiting other products in the offering. The artistic theme of the platforms allows Ankama to bring together of its customers in the same place, in order to stimulate exchanges and value creation. Each platform therefore hosts forum-style interaction areas and tools enabling users to create content, particularly in the Dofus Lab and Wakfu Lab. These areas are mainly dedicated to improving video games, and provide a forum for players' opinions and ideas, which benefits Ankama. For example, on the Wakfu multi-sided platform, users can exchange information, organize new teams of players, suggest solutions to improve combat management or encourage Ankama to develop new areas seen in the series but not yet present in the game. This structural organization allows creativity to be distributed across several areas, and enables Ankama to link user needs with the operation of its multi-sided BM (see Figure 6.1).

Nadeo has structured its creative ecosystem in a way that is fully integrated with its Trackmania game and the player community. To achieve this, the company has organized different digital spaces inside and outside the game, and provided a set of technical resources adapted to the three categories of players. Within the game, the interface provides access to separate areas based on the toolkits available: (1) the "creation" area

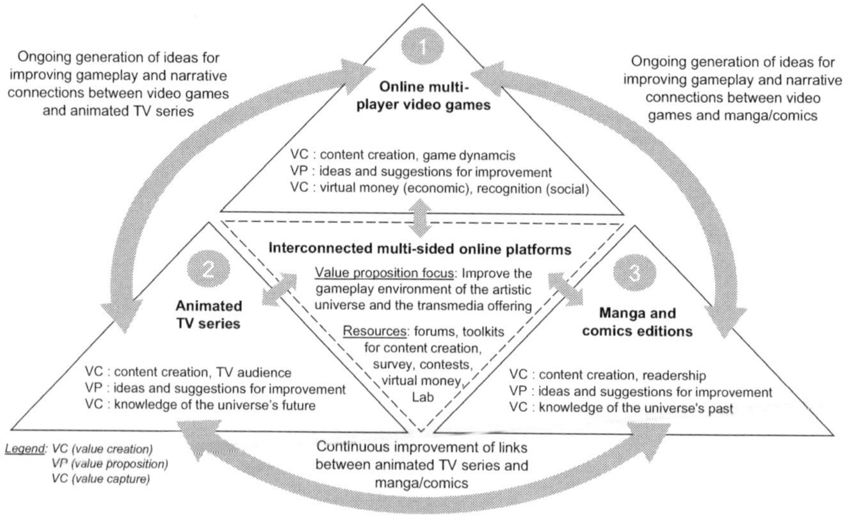

Figure 6.1 The structural interweaving of Ankama's multi-sided BM and the creative ecosystem.

for creators, with the track editor, garage, replay editor, and access to other players' creations; (2) the "events" area for managers, with the competition organization tool; and (3) the "game" area for competitors, with access to solo and multiplayer races. Outside the game, these areas are structured around official forums for exchanging information, ideas, and suggestions for improvement, as well as for promoting races and competitions. In return, Nadeo promotes the most deserving players, giving them official and public recognition for their talent. Players also promote each other's creations. Obtaining virtual money and regional rankings are also part of this process. Some of the most deserving players have even been hired by the company to animate and energize the game and the community on a full-time basis. Thanks to this creative ecosystem integrated into a multi-sided online gaming platform, Nadeo is able to capitalize on the creativity of its community of players and take advantage of their ideas to continuously improve the game, thereby enhancing the performance of its multi-sided BM (see Figure 6.2).

Vidcoin has structured its creative ecosystem in a centralized way, by aggregating a maximum number of online social gaming platforms owned by publishers. This structuring is strategic, as the advertising service needs to centralize access to player panels (made available by publishers) in order to then effectively exploit targeting and remuneration technology. To achieve this, the company has opened offices in the major video game production hubs (the American West Coast, from San Diego to Vancouver) as well as in New York and San Diego, to get closer to the major American advertising agencies and advertisers. The aim is to be close to the players

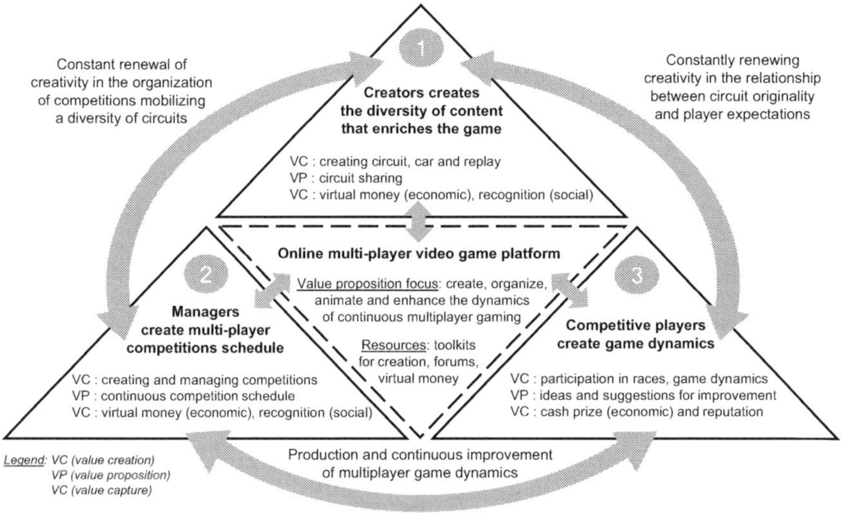

Figure 6.2 The structural interweaving of Nadeo's multi-sided BM and the creative ecosystem.

in order to continually improve the service and the targeting and remuneration technology. After all, the more efficient the advertising service, the higher its returns. For publishers, the aim is to improve the gaming experience, while offering non-intrusive, organic exposure to video advertising. On the advertisers' side, the aim is to work on improving the quality and reliability of targeting, in order to offer videos that are most likely to be watched by players. On the players' side, the aim is to work on qualifying players' preferences and interests for video ad viewing. Through voting systems, forums and polls, players can express their preferences and thus improve the quality of targeting, while also proposing ideas for improving the gaming experience. All these players and their interactions contribute to constantly improving the performance of the advertising service, and thus the multi-sided BM (see Figure 6.3).

5.2 *The role of the multi-sided BM in the strategic management of the creative ecosystem*

A comparative analysis of the Ankama, Nadeo/Ubisoft, and Vidcoin cases shows that the strategic management of creative ecosystems depends on the presence of four common strategic elements linked to the multi-sided BM (see Table 6.4). (1) First, the presence of a focal value proposition that commits all ecosystem players to a common endeavor: creativity and improving the service/offer delivered. (2) A diversified set of actors/users who provide the resources and transactions needed to realize the focal value proposition. (3) The use of a multi-sided platform as an environment conducive to

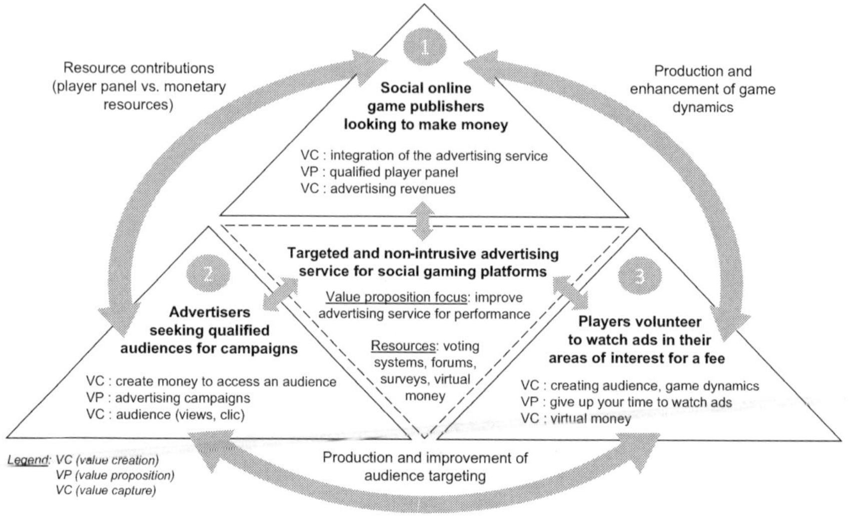

Figure 6.3 The structural interweaving of Vidcoin's multi-sided BM and the creative ecosystem.

Table 6.4 Strategic requirement for managing a creative ecosystem

Strategic requirements	*Ankama creative ecosystem*	*Nadeo creative ecosystem*	*Vidcoin creative ecosystem*
Focal value proposition	Improve the gameplay environment of the artistic universe and the global transmedia offering	Create, organize, animate, and enhance the dynamics of continuous multiplayer gaming	Improve advertising service (targeting technology and remuneration) for the benefit of all
Types of actors	Players, viewers, readers	Creators, managers, competitors	Publishers, advertisers, players
Creative environment	Interconnected, multi-faceted platforms with spaces for exchange and value creation (forums, labs)	Multi-sided game platforms with areas for creativity both inside and outside the game (forums)	Multi-sided platform with spaces (forums) for exchange about the improvement of the ads system
Technical resources	Toolkits for content creation (ideas, suggestions), creative contests, surveys, virtual money	Toolkits for creativity (circuit, car, video) and competitions, discussion tools, virtual money	Toolkits for feedback and content creation (ideas, suggestions), voting system, surveys, virtual money

opening up and orchestrating the resources needed for actors/users to interact. (4) The provision of toolkits for creativity and collaboration (openness), enabling ecosystem actors/users to engage in value-creating behaviors.

These strategic requirements are naturally integrated into the design of the multi-sided BM, which thus enables us to consider the creative ecosystem as a strategic resource useful to the functioning of the value logic and the components of value creation, proposition, and capture. In fact, the multi-sided BM of the cases studied relies on one or more multi-sided platforms, using digital technologies to frame openness (in dedicated spaces, such as video games, forums, etc.) and orchestrate resources between groups of actors, with a view to creativity. Orchestration is achieved by selecting and making available open tools (toolkits for creation) but also closed tools (surveys, voting systems, contests) to guide player behavior. This approach limits excesses, as creativity can only be expressed within the technological limits of the tools made available. These tools also enable actors to share in the value they create and capture a return on their investment (social recognition, virtual money, etc.). Multi-sided architecture is a real support for organizing openness and orchestrating resources, as the division into complementary and/or interdependent sides helps to structure the creative ecosystem and network effects.

Finally, the multi-sided BM of the cases studied enables effective management of a creative ecosystem because the BM's value components (creation, proposition, and capture) are designed to sustainably exploit the results of creative activity. Value creation is open and collaborative thanks to the support of the creative ecosystem, which optimizes alignment with customer needs and expectations. The value proposition is enriched by the contributions of the actors in the creative ecosystem, and is renewed daily, thus improving the sustainability of the BM. Value capture is multiple (for the company and the actors in the ecosystem), both economic and social, and self-sustaining through a set of positive network effects that also maintain the commitment of all actors in the co-production of value logic.

6 Case study's contribution to BM innovation in CCIs

Multi-sided BMs based on digital platforms are becoming widespread in CCIs as well as in other industries strongly impacted by digital transformation (e.g., tourism & hospitality, banking & insurance, real estate, or education). The platform era implies more collaborative economies, repositioning the customer and value logic at the center of strategy (rather than economic profit alone) (Gawer, 2014). This new approach to strategy implies an overhaul of historically closed BMs in favor of more open and innovative ones, involving more stakeholders. Therefore, the multi-sided architecture technologically framed by digital platforms is a lever for BM innovation, as it paves the way for more systemic BMs that optimize long-term value creation and capture (Gandia and Parmentier, 2017).

Our results show that the multi-sided BM is fundamentally linked to the notion of resource orchestration (Sirmon et al., 2011) and refers well to the conception of the BM as a system of interdependent activities (Zott and Amit, 2010). But designing a multi-sided BM is rather to designing a collaborative system of interdependent activities, involving a set of stakeholders who will co-produce a value logic. It is therefore not a purely utilitarian approach (as a network can be), but rather an ecosystemic approach that assumes the sustainable commitment of stakeholders within a common value objective (Adner, 2017). This ecosystemic vision is very important, as it enables managers to understand all the complexity involved in designing and implementing a multi-sided BM (Zhao et al., 2020), and all the importance of alignment between stakeholders (Malherbe and Tellier, 2022). In the cases studied, the interweaving of the BM's multi-sided architecture with the structure of the creative ecosystem demonstrates this complexity. To achieve this, companies need multi-sided platforms, which provide the socio-technical space required for networking and orchestrating internal and external resources (Hagiu and Wright, 2015). By relying on this type of platform, the multi-sided BM orchestrates resources within dedicated exploration and exploitation spaces. This ambidexterity is made possible by the strategic management of the creative ecosystem, which provides an ideal place for exploration (Novani et al., 2023). The transition to exploitation is then instrumentalized by the multi-sided platform, which organizes the mechanisms for creating, delivering, and capturing value for different user groups (Gawer, 2009).

Our results also show that multi-sided BM is fundamentally linked to the notion of openness (Chesbrough, 2006), as it organizes exchanges and value transactions between groups of customers/users in order to produce network effects (Parmentier and Gandia, 2017). Here too, the platform plays an important instrumental role, as it provides the spaces and functionalities needed to organize the dynamic of openness between users (Shuen, 2008). This openness is fundamental in the creative ecosystem, as creativity is not solely individual but results from exchanges between creative people (Brem et al., 2016). To ensure the production of value, the openness dynamic must also rely on toolkits, which provide the technology needed to collectively create, share, evaluate, and validate creations (Parmentier and Gandia, 2013). This technological framework is advantageous for companies, as it enables them to more easily manage the opening of their borders with a user community or stakeholder ecosystem (Gandia and Parmentier, 2020). However, it is important to choose the right mode of governance (centralized or decentralized) in order to avoid conflicts or the disengagement of players within the creative ecosystem (Olk and West, 2023). At the same time, social recognition and reward mechanisms (tokens, virtual currencies, symbolic rewards, etc.) need to be implemented to maintain the dynamic of openness and motivation to create (Jeppesen and Frederiksen, 2006).

Our results contribute to enriching work on multi-sided BMs and creative ecosystems in connection with CCIs, but also more generally in connection with the digital era.

7 Conclusion

This chapter focuses on the role of the multi-sided BM in the strategic management of a creative ecosystem in the online video game industry. It makes three important contributions. Firstly, it reveals that the multi-sided architecture of the BM must be interwoven with the structure of the creative ecosystem in order to ensure sustainable exploitation of the results of creative activity. Next, he explains that strategic management of the creative ecosystem depends on two key parameters within the multi-sided BM: (1) the orchestration of resources within dedicated spaces of exploration and exploitation (the faces of the BM) and (2) the organization of the dynamic of openness between stakeholders that produces network effects. Finally, it shows the fundamental instrumental role of the digital platform, which technologically articulates the various strategic, organizational, and operational levels relating to the management of creative activity and the BM. This chapter thus demonstrates the success of an unprecedented strategic recipe for sustainably exploiting the fruits of a creative ecosystem.

Notes

1 Source: Statista, 2024. https://www.statista.com/outlook/dmo/digital-media/video-games/worldwide
2 Source: Digital Report, 2023. https://wearesocial.com/fr/blog/2023/01/digital-2023/

References

Adner, R. 2006. "Match your innovation strategy to your innovation ecosystem," *Harvard Business Review*, Vol. 84, no 4, p. 98.

Adner, R. 2017. "Ecosystem as structure: An actionable construct for strategy," *Journal of Management*, Vol. 43, no 1, pp. 39–58.

Brem, A., R. Puente-Diaz and M. Agogué. 2016. "Creativity and innovation: State of the art and future perspectives for research," *International Journal of Innovation Management*, Vol. 20, no 4, pp. 1–19.

Chesbrough, H. 2006. *Open business models: How to thrive in the new innovation landscape*. Boston, MA: Harvard Business Press.

Cohendet, P., D. Grandadam and L. Simon. 2009. "Economics and the ecology of creativity: Evidence from the popular music industry," *International Review of Applied Economics*, Vol. 23, no 6, pp. 709–722.

de Bernard, M., R. Comunian and J. Gross. 2022. "Cultural and creative ecosystems: A review of theories and methods, towards a new research agenda," *Cultural Trends*, Vol. 31, no 4, pp. 332–353.

Evans, D.S. and R. Schmalensee. 2007. "The industrial organization of markets with two-sided platforms," *Competition Policy International*, Vol. 3, pp. 151–179.

Gandia, R. and G. Parmentier. 2017. "Optimizing value creation and value capture with a digital multi-sided business model," *Strategic Change*, Vol. 26, no 4, pp. 323–331.

Gandia, R. and G. Parmentier. 2020. "Managing open innovation through digital boundary control: The case of multi-sided platforms in the collaborative economy," *Journal of Innovation Economics & Management*, Vol. 32, no 2, pp. 159–180.

Gawer, A. 2009. *Platforms, Markets and Innovation*. Edward Elgar.

Gawer, A. 2014. "Bridging differing perspectives on technological platforms: Toward an integrative framework," *Research Policy*, Vol. 43, no 7, pp. 1239–1249.

Grandadam, D., P. Cohendet and L. Simon. 2013. "Places, spaces and the dynamics of creativity: The video game industry in Montreal," *Regional studies*, Vol. 17, no 10, pp. 1701–1714.

Hagiu, A. and J. Wright. 2015. "Multi-sided platforms," *International Journal of Industrial Organization*, Vol. 43, pp. 162–174.

Hou, H. and Y. Shi. 2021. "Ecosystem-as-structure and ecosystem-as-coevolution: A constructive examination," *Technovation*, Vol. 100, pp. 102–126.

Jeppesen, L.B. and L. Frederiksen. 2006. "Why do users contribute to firm-hosted user communities? The case of computer-controlled music instruments," *Organization Science*, Vol. 17, pp. 45–63.

Kirman, A. 2010. *Complex Economics: Individual and Collective Rationality*. Routledge: London.

Koenig, G. 2013. "Business ecosystem revisited," In Ben Letaifa, S., A. Gratacap and T. Isckia (eds.), *Understanding Business Ecosystem*. Louvain-la-neuve: de Boeck.

Linde, L., D. Sjödin, V. Parida and J. Wincent. 2021. "Dynamic capabilities for ecosystem orchestration A capability-based framework for smart city innovation initiatives," *Technological Forecasting and Social Change*, Vol. 166, pp. 1–12.

Malherbe, M. and A. Tellier. 2022. "Explaining the nonalignment of ecosystem partners: A structuralist approach," *Strategic Organization*, pp. 1–30.

Miles, M.B. and A.M. Huberman. 2019. *Qualitative Data Analysis: A Methods Sourcebook*. 4th ed., Sage Publications.

Moore, J.F. 1993. "Predators and prey: A new ecology of competition," *Harvard Business Review*, Vol. 71, no 3, pp. 75–86.

Novani, S., C. Cyntiawati, K. Kijima, V. Hasyimi, A.S. Trianto, L. Mayangsari, D.T. Alamanda and G. Anggadwita. 2023. "Empowering digital creative ecosystem using problem structuring method and a service science perspective: A case study in Cimahi and Bandung, Indonesia," *Asia Pacific Management Review*, Vol. 28, no 2, pp. 215–228.

Olk, P. and J. West. 2023. "Distributed governance of a complex ecosystem: How R&D Consortia orchestrate the Alzheimer's knowledge ecosystem," *California Management Review*, Vol. 65, no 2, pp. 93–128.

Parmentier, G. and R. Gandia. 2013. "Managing sustainable innovation with a user community toolkit: The case of the video game trackmania," *Creativity and Innovation Management*, Vol. 22, no 2, pp. 195–208.

Parmentier, G. and R. Gandia. 2017. "Redesigning the business model: From one-sided to multi-sided," *Journal of Business Strategy*, Vol. 38, no 2, pp. 52–61.

Shuen, A. 2008. *Web 2.0: A Strategy Guide*. Sebastopol, CA: O'Reilly Media Inc.

Sirmon, D.G., M.A. Hitt, R.D. Ireland and B.A. Gilbert. 2011. "Resource orchestration to create competitive advantage: Breadth, depth and life cycle effects," *Journal of Management*, Vol. 37, no 5, pp. 1390–1412.
Vargo, S.L. and R.F. Lusch. 2016. "Institutions and axioms: An extension and update of service-dominant logic," *Journal of the Academy of Marketing Science*, Vol. 44, pp. 5–23.
Zhao, Y., S. von Delft, A. Morgan-Thomas and T. Buck. 2020. "The evolution of platform business models: Exploring competitive battles in the world of platforms," *Long Range Planning*, Vol. 53, no 4, pp. 101–123.
Zott, C. and R. Amit. 2010. "Business model design: An activity system perspective," *Long Range Planning*, Vol. 43, no 2–3, pp. 216–226.

7 Luxury business model innovation

The case of Hennessy

Federica Antonaglia, Arnaud Fernandez and Juliette Passebois-Ducros

1 Introduction

Globalization, corporate social responsibility imperatives, digital shifts, and broader access to luxury, particularly from China and India, invite luxury companies to adapt. Despite crises, their resilience and agility have driven success, with the luxury market growing 6.5%[1] in 2023 and projected to be near €400 billion by 2025.[2] French luxury firms lead globally, with eight major French groups securing over a third of the top 100 luxury group revenues (Deloitte, 2023). LVMH exemplifies this success with €79.2 billion in 2022 revenue and a 23% growth rate from 2021 to 2022, highlighting the resilience of French luxury firms.

This chapter presents how historic French luxury houses create innovative business models (BMs). We add to the luxury BM literature by analyzing how artification strategies add to BM innovation. We suggest that the success of French luxury houses is influenced by their creativity, enriched through deep ties with the art world. The most successful brands share a commonality: their engagement with art, which is evident in patronage, artistic collaborations, exhibition centers, and the role of charismatic artistic directors.

This intersection between art and luxury has gained scholarly interest over the past decade (Styhre & Eriksson, 2008). As discussed by Massi and Turrini (2020), the concept of ratification involves transforming non-art into art, impacting people, objects, and actions. This sociological principle has been adopted in strategic management, particularly within the luxury sector, to combat commoditization and reposition products as art pieces.

In our article, we attempt to answer the question, "How and to what extent does an artification strategy contribute to innovating the BM of a luxury brand?" In an original way, we focus on the wine and spirits sector, which is under-investigated compared to other luxury segments, particularly under the artification lens (Passebois-Ducros, Trinquecoste, & Pichon, 2015).

Through a fresh case study, we explore how associations with the arts modify the value proposition, transform the value architecture, and affect the value capture of luxury brands. We assume that artified BM have the power to spin innovation and foster creativity in luxury brands.

DOI: 10.4324/9781032714462-7

We investigate the unique case of the world leader of Cognac, Hennessy, and the iconic wine and spirits group division brand of LVMH (the "H" of the LVMH name), leader of the Cognac segment (83M bottles sold, 50% of global sales). In the Cognac market, which has been globally challenged by a decline in consumption, Hennessy is particularly resilient and, thus, is an intrinsic case study (Stake, 1994). The brand has nurtured close relationships with the art world since the 1980s and continues to work with artists (e.g., recent collaborations are those with brand ambassadors, such as Jackson Wang and Alicia Keys). Furthermore, the extensive and deep use of artification pushes employees to collaborate within the boundaries of the LVMH conglomerate, thus designing an open innovation process.

2 Theoretical background

2.1 *Exploring BMs within the luxury sector*

2.1.1 *Toward a delimitation of the luxury sector*

Two perspectives exist in describing luxury products. The narrow perspective focuses on shared physical characteristics, viewing luxury products as possessing inherent qualities, such as material quality, technical craftsmanship, and creative talent. These qualities are supported by the transmission of intangible values like tradition, craftsmanship, and the pursuit of perfection (Chevalier & Mazzalovo, 2021). In contrast, the broader perspective sees luxury as encompassing individual and collective symbols contingent upon social context and time. Luxury integrates excellence in craftsmanship, unforgettable experiences, and resonance with the consumer's ideal self, emphasizing experiential value (Berthon, Pitt, Parent, & Berthon, 2009). Thus, luxury businesses offer exclusive and expensive products that provide material, individual, and social benefits through strategic actions. Research acknowledges luxury in each of these spheres, considering the superior value of luxury brands in their functional, experiential, and symbolic dimensions.

2.1.2 *Luxury BM principles*

A BM describes how an organization creates, delivers, and captures value (Osterwalder & Pigneur, 2010). Framing the "logic of the firm" at a given moment (Casadesus-Masanell & Ricart, 2010), it is composed of three areas: value proposition, i.e., the specific value developed for the targeted clients by a company (Chesbrough, 2010), value architecture, which refers to the firm's internal organization as "organizational structure, governance mechanisms, corporate culture and values, and the organization of work, activities, and resources (Johnson, Christensen, & Kagermann, 2008; Osterwalder & Pigneur, 2010; To, Chau, & Kan, 2020)" (Roy & Pellegrin-Boucher, 2024, p. 44); and value capture, which describes how a company handles finances, such as revenue streams and cost structure (Chesbrough & Rosenbloom, 2002; Demil & Lecocq, 2010; Osterwalder & Pigneur, 2010; Teece, 2010).

The BM of luxury brands has been poorly investigated; additional inquiry is thus relevant (Poisson-de Haro, Espejo, & Martí, 2022; Roy & Pellegrin-Boucher, 2024). Yet, considering the context of changing consumers' behaviors, with a shift from conspicuous to inconspicuous consumption (Eckhardt, Belk, & Wilson, 2015) as well as from conspicuous consumption to conspicuous conservation (Cervellon, 2013; Griskevicius, Tybur, & Van den Bergh, 2010), it appears crucial for luxury firms to build a BM that is able to

> leverage resources able to satisfy new customer expectations (Klaus & Manthiou, 2020; Ritala et al., 2018) by identifying new sources of value creation (Presenza & Messeni Petruzzelli, 2019) that trigger customers' willingness to pay (Bowman & Ambrosini, 2000; Teece, 2018).
> (Franco, Presenza, Messeni Petruzzelli, & Peruffo, 2022, p. 487)

2.1.3 *A traditional luxury BM*

By considering the specificities of luxury firms and relating them to BM components, an archetypal luxury BM can be drawn.

Tradition: Luxury businesses rely heavily on tradition, which yields potential advantages in both value creation and authenticity sought by customers (Franco et al., 2022). This tradition often stems from family origins, facilitating knowledge transmission despite acquisitions by conglomerates.

Quest for excellence: The quest for excellence is another common BM element for luxury and creative activities (Poisson-de Haro et al., 2022). In the luxury field, the quest for excellence is exploited for superior financial performance (value capture).

Communication codes: Luxury communication involves discreet strategies, including exclusive messaging and celebrity endorsements, shaping the value proposition (Patrin-Leclère, Marti de Montety, & Berthelot-Guiet, 2014).

Industrial production and handcrafts: Luxury balances industrial production with handcrafted pieces like haute couture, impacting both value architecture and capture by balancing the high-cost structure to produce the highest luxury portion with the margins allowed by the volumes reached through affordable luxury sales.

Distribution and global popularity: Global distribution enhances value capture, while international popularity strengthens the value proposition. However, maintaining selective coverage impacts cost structures (value capture).

Luxury faces challenges amid socioeconomic changes and acquisitions by conglomerates. Wine and spirits brands, for instance, balance luxury with widespread availability (Chevalier & Mazzalovo, 2021). Artisanal production no longer solely defines luxury, prompting brands to engage in artistic collaborations for legitimacy and differentiation (Kapferer, 2014). Through partnerships with artists, artistic directors, and museum exhibitions, luxury brands maintain their exceptional aura in an artification process.

2.2 *When art enhances the luxury BM*

2.2.1 *Artification as a strategy for luxury firms*

Artification originating from sociology is defined by Shapiro and Heinich (2012) as transforming the non-art into art, thereby altering the perception and status of objects, people, and actions to be recognized as "art." The concept has gained traction among luxury scholars and practitioners. It is seen as a strategy for battling commoditization by presenting products as "artworks" to overcome the challenge of creating artificial rarity, making items uniquely valuable (Baumgarth, 2018; Jelinek, 2018).

Massi and Turrini (2020) delineate three processes of artification in luxury: synergy, contamination, and hybridization. Each entails different degrees of collaboration with artists. Synergy is the initial stage; brands engage with the art world through collaborations or patronage without fundamentally altering their status. An example is the Louis Roederer Foundation, which supports art, artists, and museums. Contamination marks a deeper integration, where brands (e.g., Louis Vuitton or Cartier) open museums and set up exhibitions, influencing the artistic landscape and enhancing their image through associations with art attributes of rarity and prestige. Finally, within hybridization, brands themselves become works of art, intertwining art and luxury to create unique, collectible products under the direction of artistic directors, akin to Duchamp's transformation of a urinal into art through signature (Heinich & Shapiro, 2012).

2.2.2 *Artification as the generator of symbolic and intangible organizational value*

Whatever the degree of artification, it creates intangible organizational value at two levels (Carlucci & Schiuma, 2018):

First, art is a resource for organizations to elevate customer and employee engagement by creating aesthetic experiences. This involves sensory experiences in ordinary consumption or encounters with artworks, objects, or artistic events (Venkatesh & Meamber, 2008). Associating artwork with luxury goods adds symbolic and intangible values for customers and contributes to memorable brand experiences (Baumgarth, 2018; Kapferer, 2014). Meanwhile, aesthetic work environments stimulate sensorial expression among employees, enhancing well-being and creativity (Smiraglia, 2014). Recognizing the importance of human capital, businesses prioritize employee well-being as a value driver (Carlucci & Schiuma, 2018). Therefore, artification supports businesses in delivering high-value propositions to both external stakeholders and internal employees.

Second, art serves as a dynamic "learning platform" for organizations, facilitating value creation (Carlucci & Schiuma, 2018). Engaging with artists and artistic products inspires new business and organizational models that emphasize aesthetic, emotional, and energetic dimensions. Artistic processes encourage innovative thinking, enhancing creative cognition through analogical models (Schiuma, 2011). They inspire the blending of rationality and technical aspects with intuition and emotions, empowering transformative effects on human and organizational capital (Carlucci & Schiuma, 2018).

Finally, artistic associations foster connections among employees and stakeholders, regardless of age, gender, or ethnicity, and they promote cohesion, teamwork, and intergroup cooperation. Artification thus acts as a mechanism for creating aesthetic experiences that add value to organizational components and products for consumers (Carlucci & Schiuma, 2018). To conclude, artification transforms BMs internally by enhancing workspaces and externally by creating unique experiences, thereby improving stakeholder engagement and brand reputation.

3 Method section

Our research aims to shed light on the transformative power of artification strategies on luxury BMs.

As research lacks exploration of such a subject, we decided to conduct a qualitative analysis, which appears appropriate. Our aim is to reach a deeper understanding of an overlooked topic (Eisenhardt, 1989; Yin, 1984).

Access to the world-leading company in the Cognac industry, Hennessy, which belongs to the biggest luxury conglomerate, LVMH, legitimizes our choice of a unique case study.

We collected primary data in early 2024 through qualitative, semi-structured interviews with two employees in the creative sector. Interviewee 1, who belongs to the group and holds a relevant position in the marketing department, gave us a one-hour interview. Interviewee 2, who also belongs to the creative team in the marketing department, shared two meetings with us, lasting one hour each. These interviews were preceded and followed by written exchanges. The Interviewee allowed us to plunge into the creative team, which, as part of the marketing department, oversees all artistic and creative collaborations of the brand worldwide.

Second, data collected since 2023 completed our field search, triangulating the data analysis. These included interviews given by the Chief Executive Laurent Boillot, previously CEO[3] and president of Guerlain, and by Khoa Dodinh, the current artistic director of Hennessy. We also collected internal data, such as recent financial reports of the group (LVMH[4]), and external secondary data, such as press articles (national[5] and local press[6]) and economic reports (Xerfi analysis of the luxury sector, 2022, and the wine and spirits sector, 2022). We also analyzed the Hennessy website, spotlighting past artistic collaborations and featuring interviews with artists.

The geographical scope is global. Hennessy is a world leader in the Cognac industry, selling its products worldwide and applying artification everywhere as an adaptative winning strategy. The level of analysis is at the company level and has consequences for the entire luxury sector, as it is currently largely driving artification strategies.

4 Case presentation: Hennessy

Cognac is a grape-based eau-de-vie produced exclusively in the French region of Charente. Cognac benefits from a protected appellation (AOP: Appellation d'origine protegée). Maison Hennessy is a pivotal player in the Cognac market.

4.1 The global Cognac market

Cognac boasts a robust local economy, supporting over 17,000 direct jobs, including 4,400 winegrowers, and involving 265 trading houses with approximately 85,000 hectares of vineyards dedicated to production. Beyond direct employment, over 60,000 individuals benefit indirectly from the Cognac industry, encompassing barrel manufacturers, cooperatives, and distillers. Despite numerous family-owned houses, the market is dominated by four major players: Hennessy (LVMH), Rémy Martin (Rémy Cointreau), Martell (Pernod Ricard), and Courvoisier (Fortune Brands), accounting for 80% of sales. This global market sees Cognac exported to over 150 countries, with 97.2% of consumption occurring abroad. In France, Cognac is perceived as a business or digestive drink with a lower domestic consumption. Conversely, in the US, it is popular in bars and nightclubs, and it is considered a high-end beverage in China.

The Cognac market is valued at nearly $4 billion, with approximately 165 million bottles sold annually. Hennessy leads the market, exporting around 83 million bottles and accounting for almost half of global sales. Its main markets are the US and China, followed by Europe and South Africa. Despite global declines in alcohol consumption, the Cognac market has consistently grown in both volume and value over the past two decades. This resilience can be attributed to Cognac's status as a premium drink, often consumed sparingly, aligning with the trend of preferring quality over quantity.

The year 2023 was tough for Cognac, with a decline in demand and adverse economic policies (e.g., potential taxation threats in China). Shipments worldwide plummeted by 22.2% to 165.3 million bottles, notably with a severe 45.4%[7] downturn in North America. Hennessy also experienced a global volume drop of 11.8%,[8] particularly in the US. Strict containment measures in China further impacted sales, while mixed signals in Europe contributed to a 5.6% decrease in sales. However, these negative trends were partially offset. In 2020, despite the COVID-19 pandemic, the global market showed extraordinary growth, with increased demand in countries like South Africa, Nigeria, and Vietnam. Moreover, prices surged, with a value increase of 8.4% to €3.9 billion, making it one of the best years for Cognac. Logistic issues related to COVID-19 led to overstocking and a significant rise in distributor prices, prompting Cognac houses to adjust their prices to cope with inflation. This changed consumption patterns, particularly for popular qualities like VS and VSOP, which constitute 90% of global Cognac sales.[9]

4.2 *Hennessy presentation*

4.3.1 *Pioneering the Cognac market*

Hennessy was founded by Richard Hennessy, an Irish officer in the service of Louis XV, in 1765. Leveraging Cognac's strategic location and the Charente River for trade, he supplied his fine nectar to Europe's royal courts, prospering his business. After accidentally discovering that aging eau-de-vie in oak barrels during transport enhanced its color and taste with amber and vanilla notes, the Hennessy family began aging part of their production in oak, creating the distinct Hennessy Cognac flavor.

Under James Hennessy, the company expanded globally, exporting to the US, India, and Asia, and focused on standardizing the aging process to maintain quality worldwide. In 1803, the partnership with the Filloux family, master blenders tasked with ensuring consistent quality, was key to answering the question, "How can we guarantee Hennessy Cognac's exceptional taste globally?" This collaboration, still enduring with the Filloux heirs, has been vital to preserving Hennessy's heritage and excellence.

One of Hennessy's major achievements was the invention of its own classification of Cognacs based on years of aging in oak barrels. Taken up later by other Cognac companies, multiple stars represent the number of years of maturation, and common denominations would gradually appear after that:

- Very Special—VS (minimum two years of aging)
- Very Superior Old Pale—VSOP (minimum four years)
- Extra Old—XO (minimum ten years).

It is worth noting that the US primarily imports VS, while Asia has a higher consumption of VSOP and XO.

4.3.2 *Adapting to modern challenges*

Throughout the modern and contemporary era, the company successfully faced times threatening its activities (e.g., prohibition in the US, great wars, and crises of the 20th century). First, Hennessy successfully scaled up by merging with other major players in the wine and spirits sector: Moët in 1986 and Louis Vuitton a year later, creating LVMH, the world's largest luxury group. Since then, LVMH has become the leader in the luxury industry with a turnover of €79 milliards in 2022, holding 78 brands in six main activities: wine and spirits (Moët, Don Perignon, Yquem, Ruinart, etc.), fashion and leather (Dior, Chanel, Berlutti, Celine, Louis Vuitton, etc.), selective retail (Sephora, Le Bon Marché, etc.), make-up and perfumes (Guerlain, For Ever, etc.), watches and jewelry (Chaumet, Bulgari, Tiffany, etc.), and other activities (media, hotels, etc.).[10]

Second, Hennessy has taken advantage of the change and growth in global demand for Cognac. At the end of the 1990s, demand increased, as Cognac became very popular with the US Hip-Hop movement and Black community.[11] Cognac, especially Hennessy, became one of the most tendential drinks during parties. The Hennessy bottle of "Very Special-VS" became a social marker of wealth and success. The art of cocktail mixology became a new reason to put Cognac on the lips of consumers and enter a new market segment worldwide. Today, 80% of Cognac consumption is in cocktails. This new drinking trend also benefits the brands Courvoisier, Martell, Rémy Martin, and Camus.

As demand increases, Hennessy proposes new ways to support their high-quality standards. In addition to the three segments, Hennessy creates Cognac *Rare Editions* or *Re-Editions,* which are hyper-customized single offerings. In 2021, Hennessy sold its most exclusive Cognacs to date, exemplified by the sale of two unique Dames Jeanne formats, each containing 10 liters and fetching a staggering price of €600,000 each.[12]

Third, Hennessy wants to reinforce its presence in the minds of consumers through a strategy of getting inside their heads and hearts through key markets. Since the 1990s, Hennessy has implemented a global distribution strategy (off-trade liquor stores, supermarkets, bars, restaurants, hotels) through a joint venture with Diageo, the world leader in wine and spirits distribution. The "Hennessy experience," aligned with different sales channels, is thus as important as the product's physical characteristics. Their retail network offers a considerable competitive advantage for Hennessy. A new challenge is to preserve the Hennessy DNA while continuing to develop the brand universe.

5 Case study analysis: main results

The data analysis reveals the evolution of the artification process within the company and how artification leads to BM innovation regarding value proposition, architecture, and capture.

5.1 Hennessy and the arts: evolving through the artification process

Art manifests at Hennessy in three ways. The first is through collaborations with artists, a tradition dating back many years. In particular, the brand has a long-standing relationship with the Hip-Hop community, which revitalized its popularity in the 2000s. Recognizing the synergy with its consumers, Hennessy initiated collaborations with Hip-Hop artists, such as Nas, a prominent American rapper. In 2023, Nas created a commemorative bottle to mark 50 years of Hip-Hop, showcasing the potential of cultural and artistic brand marketing. Building on this success, Hennessy expanded its co-creative partnerships with renowned artists worldwide, recognizing their role in revitalizing brand equity.

As Khoa Dodinh (Hennessy AD) says, "It's not about a job for the sake of a job, but about enriching the brand and its history. Each of these individuals, with their own language and universe, comes to meet ours, where creation is central."[13] They selected partnerships and gave artists the creative freedom to interpret the brand equity and the brand history. Khoa Dodinh explains, "To give artists the opportunity to express their own perception of the historical know-how, the philosophy, and the style of the Maison Hennessy."[14] This logic has given rise to emblematic collaborations with iconic personalities like Frank Gehry, Kim Jones, Lorenz Bämer, Jackson Wang, and Alicia Keys, which marked a real artistic turning point for the brand and its marketing between 2015 and 2024.

The interviewees revealed that two types of limited editions are co-created with artists. The first is commissioning artists to create unique, limited-edition bottles and/or packaging. A recent example is Julien Colombier, an urban artist who redesigned the bottle of VS in a singular way. Another example is the collaboration with the Chinese artist Zhen Enli. The artist created unique carafes that serve as precious jewel cases for the Paradis cuvée. These decanters are hand-decorated and inspired by the work of the artist.[15]

The second form of collaboration with artists is the masterpieces (e.g., XO by Frank Gehry or Kim Jones). These are limited and numbered creations, directly crafted by the artists and sold as artworks. Rare editions were reinforced by artistic masterpieces. Painters, architects, singers, and designers develop special brand programs during key moments of the year. Chinese New Year is one of the most famous of them. Each year, Hennessy creates a special edition and collaborates with Chinese artists. To celebrate the Year of the Dragon (2023), the artist Yang Yongliang created an art piece in a bottle.

Third, sponsorship plays a significant role. Hennessy acts as a patron for the arts, supporting artistic creation by commissioning artworks. For instance, Chinese artist Zhen Enli created a painting inspired by the essence of the House and its Cognacs, which now belong to Hennessy's collections. These artworks are then showcased across various communication channels to reach a wider audience. Additionally, Hennessy sponsors museums and exhibitions, contributing to initiatives like the restoration of the Jardin des Tuileries at the Louvre, Notre Dame Church, and local heritage sites, such as Bassac Abbey.

Finally, the brand itself is communicated as an artwork and progressively becomes part of French cultural heritage. To keep the brand's memory and legacy alive, its history is scenarized. First, the brand leverages its website, with an entire section dedicated to showcasing artistic collaborations. The brand also offers exclusive tours to "discover the history of Maison Hennessy, a saga forged by the constant quest for excellence." To this end, the brand proposes "multi-sensory experiences designed to suit every taste and are available in a variety of languages. All our visits include guided tastings."

Regarding Massi and Turrini's (2020) work, we deduce that Hennessy is an example of brand artification. While collaborations with artists first enabled the brand to benefit from synergies with the art world, the brand quickly embarked on a more advanced artification process, akin to contamination, composed of genuine collaborations with artists who co-create works with and for Hennessy. While this is part of the brand's heritage and history, it also enriches and affects the art world.

5.2 *How art changes the value proposition for consumers*

The competitive Cognac market faces challenges from various alcoholic and non-alcoholic beverages. Hennessy distinguishes itself by offering Cognacs renowned for aging and unique aromatic profiles, enhancing desirability through rare editions co-created with renowned artists, infusing the product with a distinctive narrative and aesthetic appeal, elevating its perceived value among consumers. Hennessy's strategic selection of artists who deeply resonate with the values and preferences of their communities enables the brand to craft packaging that transcends mere aesthetics. Through thoughtful collaborations, Hennessy effectively imbues its products with functional, symbolic, and social significance, fostering a profound connection with consumers and reinforcing its position as a cultural icon.

Furthermore, the strength of Hennessy's artistic collaborations relies on the personalization of the value proposition in various markets. Indeed, the challenge for the brand is to sell a wide range of products of different quality levels all around the world but with a unique promise of excellence. As Interviewee 2 explains:

> We cover a very wide range. It goes from entry-level VS that costs €30, but we can go up to more than €2,000. And all our qualities are for the whole world, and the particularity of Hennessy is to be sold in almost all continents and countries.

Hennessy and artists co-create new and exclusive products to serve different markets. Interviewee 1 elaborated, saying:

> For Chinese markets, it's going to be Chinese artists. It can also be Chinese artists if we want to target the Asian community in the US. We did a special limited edition for the 300th anniversary of Richard

> Hennessy, who was Irish. So, we worked with Irish artists. These elements are part of the brief for selecting the artists we work with.

Interviewee 2 said:

> In terms of consumption, the product and the experience will not be the same in each country. In the US, for example, the focus is very much on pop culture, Hip-Hop, and sports. We look for artists in this universe. In China, on another hand, we're aiming for something more intimate. There is an idea of intellectualization, of selling premium products like VSOP or XO. In these markets, consumers go for the taste, to get to the bottom of the product. So we'll choose artists who have a high level of recognition and a certain reputation.

This enables the brand to enter at the foundation of cultural communities. Artistic collaborations for a sole edition of Cognac are just the starting point for a series of activities that enable the brand to meet consumers and create experiences:

> We worked with the designer Stephane Asphool to promote VS in France. The artist wanted a bottle that had his own style, a little offbeat, with bold colors, and the result is quite stunning. Then, together with the artist, we created a pop-up in Paris with a concept store offering the brand-new, limited-edition Hennessy VS Cognac and a bar with an original cocktail menu and street food. Once we've worked with the artist, there's a logic to it, and it shows […] So that's how we work. There's the work created by the artist, and then we use different media. (Interviewee 2)

Adding an artistic dimension enables the brand to tailor experiences to each community, which magnifies the product and transforms it into an artwork, especially with rare editions. The partnership contracts signed with the NBA in 2020 and the boxing movie *Creed 3* illustrate this desire to bring Cognac closer to its target audience. Each collaboration has to offer unique experiences, exclusivity, and excellence to customers according to the values of the brand.

5.3 Value architecture: how artification impacts the organization

Our data indicates how artistic collaborations enhance internal organization, known as value architecture. At Hennessy, each Cognac type has a specialized team, fostering innovation, efficient decision-making, and end-to-end project management. These teams, often matrix-based, comprise professionals from development, marketing, and production, facilitating market understanding and consumer engagement. Subdivisions enable tailored strategies for each Cognac range, promoting effective market penetration and coherent partnerships, as per the artistic collaboration department (ACD). While formally part of the marketing department, the ACD operates independently, supporting product teams and managing artistic relations within allocated budgets. Based in both the Paris and Cognac offices, the ACD selects and oversees artistic projects, collaborating with technical services and suppliers to realize artified products. Functioning as a creative agency, the ACD prioritizes creativity and connecting with artists and galleries to fulfill Hennessy's project-specific needs:

> My first role is to make sure the marketing needs are in line with our artist's search. That the artist responds to the marketing needs and delivers an artwork. My artistic network allows me to be in contact with real artists.
>
> (Interviewee 1)

Concerning governance mechanisms, our research indicates a preference for fostering creativity and innovation, exemplified by LVMH's support for internal mobility among employees. For instance, Laurent Boillot, Hennessy's current president and CEO, transitioned to this role in 2020 after 18 years at Guerlain. Similarly, the former marketing director of Hennessy now holds a position at Guerlain. Such mobility encourages internal benchmarking and knowledge exchange. Another governance mechanism involves establishing a dedicated art department solely for artistic collaborations, fostering a human connection with artists.

The ACD creates trust through long-term connections, as each collaboration spans at least two years, with some extending even longer, especially for artists with multiple collaborations within the LVMH group. This underscores the Maison's strength in resource organization, particularly in human resources (HR). Artification enhances working conditions and fosters a quest for excellence, contributing to a positive atmosphere for employees. Interviewee 2 states:

> The artistic dimension is present in all our offices. For example, in Cognac offices, we have artworks on display...There's a real artistic dimension. We have a corner when you enter in where you discover the creative process around the house's artistic approach where you can see drawings made by the artists themselves. The Maison emphasizes what we do, and that's pleasant.

As a result, creativity thrives, with HR remaining central to the BM. Marketing activities benefit from iterative exchanges between the creative department and marketing teams. Long lead times for artistic projects, planned at least two years in advance, enable the creative department to select the "right artist" and allow for the creation of works that enhance bottle packaging or become stand-alone artworks capable of significantly increasing the value of a Cognac bottle. HR serves as a tangible resource, encompassing teams of artisans and technical experts who bring artistic ideas to life on an industrial scale. This reliability is noted by artists, enhancing their trust in the organization. When asked why artists collaborate with Hennessy, Interviewee 1 replied:

> We respect their work. When I ask Frank Gehry to collaborate on a Frank Gehry creation, I leave him completely free—under technical limits, of course, but what artists like is also that we have a stunning technical team, able to go beyond what, for others, would be technical limitations, that would make products unfeasible.

Such aspects make Hennessy popular in the artistic milieu. In such a context, the quest for excellence stimulates the artists' work. Hennessy has super technical teams who can pull off technical prowess that artists themselves can't do.

Finally, the artification sounds credible for Hennessy because artists consider the creative department legitimate. In the words of Interviewee 1, "We know how to talk to artists. I come from an artistic environment. I am privileged because I know how to talk to artists. I respect them." Such artistic dynamics sometimes give life to new activations that were not meant to be initially—a form of innovation allowed by artification. Thus, real knowledge of the art world and art networks, together with skills in the laws of the arts, legitimize the company in the eyes of artists and their managers.

Within the corporate culture, the classical values of luxury brands still guide Hennessy's marketing strategy. The culture of excellence manifests, for instance, in targeted marketing, which explains, together with its distribution network and the power of the LVMH conglomerate, why Hennessy is the most sold Cognac in the world.

Interviewee 2 elaborates, "We find the codes of luxury, and we're challenged every day on the side of excellence. The quest for excellence at Hennessy will never go away." Hennessy adapts its marketing strategy according to the countries in which it is sold. The ability to "find the right and true artist" (Interviewee 1) who appeals to communities for which the product is meant shows a marketing skill of understanding demand. It's also important to understand the longevity of the artification process.

Employee well-being is an integral part of the corporate values at Hennessy, fostered by the artistic and cultural activities embedded within the company. This emphasis on well-being is believed to be influenced by the brand's close ties to Black-American culture, particularly through the Hip-Hop and rap movements. This connection helps Hennessy avoid the artificial and elitist image associated with some luxury brands, presenting itself as more inclusive, modern, and cool. This approach resonates well with its primary market, particularly in the US. Interviewee 2 stated, "Today, it's true that artistic openness brings other profiles to work here....it's a bit like, you know, Cognac. It's a blend of eau-de-vies and, well, Hennessy. Today, it's a blend of personalities!"

While Cognac consumption is minimal in France, Hennessy strategically positions itself in China with a tradition-focused approach, leveraging French gastronomic culture to enhance brand awareness. This strategy appears to be highly valued within the company:

> Personalities drive the spirit of the house. In Cognac, you had to put on a good show, come in your costume. There was a real representation of luxury that had to be matched. Today, we have other personalities—US, UK, Chinese. Hennessy today is an assembly of personalities.
>
> (Interviewee 2)

The brand has been a pioneer in many ways, and this is also the case in activating artistic collaborations in the wine and spirits sector "before competitors did" (Interviewee 1). Another element of the corporate value relates to the LVMH's commitment "to ensure the development of each of its Maisons while respecting their identity and autonomy."[16]

The organization of activity is a fifth component of the value architecture. According to Interviewee 2, decentralized organizations can leave "Maisons both autonomous and responsive" and ensure that "rapid, effective and appropriate decisions can be made. This approach also sustains the motivation of our employees, encouraging them to show true entrepreneurial spirit." Organic growth is meant for the brands of the group and the employees, who are encouraged to excel and supported in their career growth. Vertical integration "fosters excellence both upstream and downstream, allowing control over every link in the value chain, from sourcing and production facilities to selective retailing."[17] Finally, sustaining *savoir faire*[18] drives the organization of the activities of LVMH brands to "preserve their distinctive identities and excellence... and ensure that craftsmanship and creative jobs are attractive to younger generations."

Table 7.1 summarizes the elements of value architecture to emphasize their power to explain artification as more than a marketing strategy.

Our elaboration from the value architecture definition given by Roy & Pellegrin (2024, p. 44).

5.4 Art and value capture: maximize profits with monitored investments

Two elements show how artification helps in maximizing profits. First, Hennessy can associate its brand with the most famous artists in the world. "We have the clout of our group with the budget to carry out our artistic creations" (Interviewee 1). Nevertheless, budget control exists to rationalize investments in artification. "We run five, six artistic collaborations in parallel at the same time. They result from arbitrations according to the

Table 7.1 Value architecture elements due to artification

Organizational structure -Organization of work	*Governance mechanisms*	*Corporate culture & values*	*Organization of activity*	*Organization of resources*
Quick realization from segmentation of product teams --- Internal Mobility which foster innovation	A unique operating model inside the group --- Internal mobility into LVMH favoring benchmarks --- Artistic Department for artification projects partially out of the business logic (long timeframe, no financial objectives)	Culture of excellence --- Pioneer and innovative --- Long-tradition and long-term relationships with communities of consumers --- Well-being of employees --- Cool luxury brand	Decentralized organization --- Organic growth --- Vertical Integration --- Sustaining *savoir-faire*	HR - Artistic department connoisseurs of the art world (tangible) --- Technical team for realizing the artwork (tangible) --- Reliable to the artists eyes (Intangible resource) --- Willingness from artists to work with the brand (consequence of the intangible and tangible resources)

budget allocated in previous years to one product and another" (Interviewee 1). For rare editions and masterpieces, sales prices skyrocket and are totally disconnected from the cost of production, similar to the art market. The rarity effect is due to the limited quantity produced. A Cognac bottle *XO 150e anniversaries,* designed by Franck Gehry, sold for €48,000. This strategy brings the value capture to its highest as artification appears to be able to shift industrial products—even luxurious, artisanal products—to artworks. This is hybridization.

Second, through more affordable editions, Hennessy enhances its brand equity and captures value by selling at a premium price because they are co-designed by artists famous in subcultures. From collaborations with contemporary artists ranging from rap music (Nas), fashion design (Dior Home Artistic Director Kim Jones), and paintings (for sponsoring the NBA off-court), artistic collaborations also maintain the uniqueness of brand value. In addition, artistic investments are under control. The ACD receives a budget for each product from its director (i.e., marketing director). Potential synergies with artists who already collaborated with LVMH possibly allow for the rationalization of investments in terms of saving costs related to searching for and negotiating with the artist and legal aspects concerning the use and reproduction of the offered works. Synergies at the group level are interesting in terms of artistic collaborations; however, "we will avoid working with artists who have already worked with other group brands in the wine and spirits segment, but we will consider collaborations with artists who have worked with our perfumery or fashion brands" (Interviewee 1) to maintain uniqueness.

In conclusion, artification is integral to maximizing margins and encouraging partnerships and collaborations rooted in artistic expression to expand brand gains.

6 Case study's contribution to BM innovation

This research pioneers the analysis of art world collaborations in BM innovation, exemplified by the Hennessy case, enriching literature on BM innovation within the concept of a luxury artified BM. Unlike CCI's digitalization-driven BM innovation (Landoni, Dell'era, Frattini, Petruzzelli, Verganti, & Manelli, 2020), we introduce a novel form rooted in artistic collaboration. Describing BM innovation through art, we elucidate how art transforms value creation, architecture, and capture within the BM (Table 7.2). Artification presents fresh avenues to enhance the value of traditional, artisanal, and high-quality products. However, old businesses devoted to production excellence and tradition may struggle to adapt to market shifts. The artification process, as seen in Hennessy's case, offers inspiration for brands seeking reinvention through artist involvement. Artistic collaborations ensure brand relevance across diverse markets, aligning with trends and popular culture. Moreover, artification enriches the brand's value proposition, enhancing consumer experiences. It also impacts value capture by managing investments for luxury segments against elevated art market prices.

Second, we highlight that artists may be central players in business ecosystems. The artification process shows the need for brands to adopt an eco-systemic perspective: the firm can no longer rely on its own resources and capabilities but can create value through relationships with other stakeholders. Value is co-created by firms in conjunction with external stakeholders and singularly with artists (Gummesson & Mele, 2010). Artists use their own resources to co-create value; these are then integrated with a wide range of resources owned by other members of the community, such as the reputation and capital of the brand and the technical know-how of engineers, craftsmen, and artisans like master blenders, in our case. The result is an ensemble of resources that can represent a *constellation value proposition*, where the company appears as the hub around which various stakeholders gravitate, connecting to create a collective value proposition. The brand accepts a loss of

Table 7.2 Comparison between Luxury BM and an artified luxury BM

Luxury BM	*Artified Luxury BM*
Value proposition	
• Excellence of the product • Exclusivity • Privilege • Artificial rarity	• Scarcity • Authenticity • Aesthetic experiences for customers • Relevance of the brand in each market • Luxury meet popular cultures
Value Architecture—Key resources	
• Organizations driven by family legacy • Observance of tradition and heritage • Adoption of luxury codes by employees	• Organizations driven by creativity and innovation • Melting pot of talent working for the brand • Improved well-being at work • Aesthetic experiences for employees
Value Architecture—Key processes	
• High-skilled artisans • International distribution • Communication adapted to each market	• High-skilled technical teams • Global distribution impacted by activations around artistic collaborations • Artistic collaborations adapted to each community
Value Capture	
• High-cost structure to produce the highest luxury segment • High margins allowed by the large volumes sold through affordable luxury	• High-investments monitored • High-cost structure balanced by artification value capture • Superior margins allowed by masterpieces sold as artworks, and • by popular products sold at a premium price because of artistic collaborations

control of the brand value proposition by giving artists the freedom to explore the brand's DNA. Here, the strength of the Hennessy brand, its heritage, and the size of the LVMH group facilitate the meeting of several stakeholders and encourage them to collaborate. The brand seems to play a facilitating role, bringing people together and encouraging the co-creation of shared value.

We contribute to the literature by highlighting the role of organizational capabilities in encouraging innovation in BMs. Artification allows brands to modernize their image, attract new and different talents, and avoid the rigid codes of traditional luxury, thus escaping the risk of *museification* (Antonaglia & Passebois-Ducros, 2020).

Finally, within the LVMH group, which includes Hennessy, we witness a form of open innovation. As defined by Chesbrough and Bogers (2014), open innovation involves purposefully managing knowledge flows across organizational boundaries for mutual benefit, using both pecuniary and non-pecuniary mechanisms aligned with the organization's BM. Luxury conglomerates embrace an open innovation approach by strategically managing knowledge within their companies. They achieve this through actions, such as inter-brand HR transfers fostering an outside-in, open innovation strategy. This strategy allows LVMH to tap into external resources within its communities. Moreover, the group encourages synergies with artists, collaborating across different segments, such as wine and fashion, thereby adhering to the principle of widely distributing useful knowledge, ensuring no single entity monopolizes it.

7 Conclusion

Hennessy has been a pioneer in the wine and spirits sector and has maintained its market leadership over the last decades. The brand has successfully met the challenges of globalization and diversification of consumers without losing its qualitative excellence or brand equity. Artification has contributed to making this game a genuine success by promoting BM innovations. Artification contributes to the profit maximization of the brand without dissolving the rarity and *not-for-all aura* of luxury. The analysis of the Hennessy case reveals significant findings in two main areas. It uncovers the evolution of the artification process within the company, illustrating how this process has led to innovative changes in the brand's value proposition, architecture, and capture. Artification at Hennessy unfolds in three key ways: through collaborations with artists, becoming a patron of the arts, and positioning the brand itself as artwork. These initiatives not only rejuvenate brand equity but also modernize traditional approaches, exemplified by iconic collaborations. These artistic collaborations redefine Hennessy's value proposition by infusing products with unique narratives and aesthetic appeal, enhancing their perceived value among consumers. Artification also influences Hennessy's internal organization, notably through value architecture. Segmented product teams facilitate quick decision-making and effective market penetration, while a dedicated artistic department autonomously manages collaborations, fostering creativity and innovation. Governance mechanisms prioritize creativity and internal mobility, encouraging excellence and reinforcing the brand's cultural and human values. This fosters a dynamic corporate culture focused on excellence, adaptability, and employee well-being, enhancing brand resonance and market competitiveness. Ultimately, the artification strategy not only elevates Hennessy's brand image and consumer appeal but also enriches its internal processes, reinforcing its position as a global leader in the luxury spirits market.

Given that artification in luxury is now widespread, further research should question what luxury brands can do to remain original and innovative and whether artistic collaborations are still an avenue for this aim. Also, researchers may be interested in whether it is possible for luxury artified brands to diversify to increase their rentability without trivializing their brand equity.

A limitation of our work could be associated with a form of coopetition observed during the field research, which was not thoroughly addressed and resulted from the open innovation within the companies of the group. To our knowledge, this type of coopetition has not been described in previous research and thus deserves further attention.

Notes

1 Source: Xerfi.
2 Source: Estimation from Bain & Compagnie with Altagamma, quoted in Xerfi.
3 Entretien CEO https://www.youtube.com/watch?v=7pbjbRLMOKw.
4 Financial report https://r.lvmh-static.com/uploads/2022/07/lvmh_interim-financial-report-2022.pdf.
5 Cougard, M. J. (2017). *Le casse-tête des producteurs face à l'engouement pour le cognac*. Les Echos, retrieved January 19th, 2023. https://www.lesechos.fr/2017/10/le-casse-tete-des-producteurs-face-a-lengouement-pour-le-cognac-184766.
6 Kwate, N. O. A. (2023). *Les Afro-Américains et le cognac: histoire d'un mythe romantique*. The Conversation, retrieved January 19th, 2023. https://theconversation.com/les-afro-americains-et-le-cognac-histoire-dun-mythe-romantique-209890.
7 Source: Sud Ouest in its recent report on the latest statistics from the Bureau national interprofessional du cognac (BNIC).
8 Source: LVMH Group's latest financial report, published on January 25 of 2024.
9 Source: According to the BNIC.
10 Source: LVMH Statista, 2022.
11 The black community was tied to Cognac long before. According to mainstream media and industry myth, the consumption of Cognac by African Americans dates back to either the first or second world war. Black-American soldiers, then sent to southwest France, fell as much in love with the liquor as they did with the country they considered decidedly less racist than their own. Food and beverage distributors have long sought to attract African Americans with advertising campaigns designed exclusively to capture these potential consumers at a time when market share was relatively low (Source: The Conversation, 2023).
12 https://press.hennessy.com/dame-jeanne/.
13 Source interview in https://www.terredevins.com/actualites/cognac-hennessy-la-maison-qui-aime-les-artistes.
14 Source interview in https://www.terredevins.com/actualites/cognac-hennessy-la-maison-qui-aime-les-artistes.
15 https://presse.hennessy.fr/hennessy-par-zhang-enli-2-2-2/.
16 Source: LVMH website.
17 Source: https://www.lvmh.com/group/about-lvmh/model-lvmh/.
18 Source: https://www.lvmh.com/group/about-lvmh/model-lvmh/.

References

Antonaglia, F., & Passebois-Ducros, J. (2020). Christian Dior: The Art of Haute Couture. In Massi M. & Turrini A. (Eds.), *The Artification of Luxury Fashion Brands: Synergies, Contaminations, and Hybridizations* (pp. 113–139). Cham, Switzerland: Palgrave Macmillan.

Baumgarth C. (2018). Brand management and the world of the arts: Collaboration, co- operation, co-creation, and inspiration. *Journal of Product and Brand Management*, *27*(3), 237–248.

Berthon, P., Pitt, L., Parent, M., & Berthon, J.P. (2009). Aesthetics and ephemerality: Observing and preserving the luxury brand. *California Management Review*, *52*(1), 45–66.

Bowman, C., & Ambrosini, V. (2000). Value creation versus value capture: Towards a coherent definition of value in strategy. *British Journal of Management*, *11*(1), 1–15.

Carlucci, D., & Schiuma, G. (2018). The power of the arts in business. *Journal of Business Research*, *85*, 342–347.

Casadesus-Masanell, R., & Ricart, J.E. (2010). From strategy to business models and onto tactics. *Long Range Planning*, *43*(2–3), 195–215.

Chesbrough, H. (2010). Business model innovation: Opportunities and barriers. *Long Range Planning*, *43*(2–3), 354–363.

Chevalier, M., & Mazzalovo, G. (2021). *Luxury Brand Management in Digital and Sustainable Times*. Hoboken, NJ: John Wiley & Sons.

Cervellon, M.C. (2013). Conspicuous conservation: Using semiotics to understand sustainable luxury. *International Journal of Market Research*, *55*(5), 695–717.

Demil, B., & Lecocq, X. (2010). Business model evolution: In search of dynamic consistency. *Long Range Planning*, *43*(2–3), 227–246.

Eckhardt, G.M., Belk, R.W., & Wilson, J.A. (2015). The rise of inconspicuous consumption. *Journal of Marketing Management*, *31*(7–8), 807–826.

Eisenhardt, K.M. (1989). Building theories from case study research. *Academy of Management Review*, *14*(4), 532–550.

Franco, S., Presenza, A., Messeni Petruzzelli, A., & Peruffo, E. (2022). Tradition-driven business models at luxury companies: Revealing value-creation and value-capture activities. *Journal of Knowledge Management*, *26*(11), 486–506.

Gummesson, E., & Mele, C. (2010). Marketing as value co-creation through network interaction and resource integration. *Journal of Business Market Management*, *4*, 181–198.

Griskevicius, V., Tybur, J.M., & Van den Bergh, B. (2010). Going green to be seen: Status, reputation, and conspicuous conservation. *Journal of Personality and Social Psychology*, *98*(3), 392.

Heinich, N., & Shapiro, R. (2012). *De l'artification: Enquêtes sur le passage à l'art*. Paris, France: Éditions de l'École des Hautes Études en Sciences Sociales.

Jelinek, J.-S. (2018). Art as strategic branding tool for luxury fashion brands. *Journal of Product & Brand Management*, 27, 294–307.

Kapferer, J.N. (2014). The artification of luxury: From artisans to artists. *Business Horizons*, *57*(3), 371–380.

Kapferer, J.N. (2020). *The Artification of Luxury Fashion Brands: Synergies, Contaminations, and Hybridizations*. New York: Springer Nature.

Landoni, P., Dell'era, C., Frattini, F., Petruzzelli, A.M., Verganti, R., & Manelli, L. (2020). Business model innovation in cultural and creative industries: Insights from three leading mobile gaming firms. *Technovation*, *92*, 102084.

Massi, M., & Turrini, A. (Eds.) (2020). When fashion meets art: The artification of luxury fashion brands. *The Artification of Luxury Fashion Brands: Synergies, Contaminations, and Hybridizations* (pp. 1–32). Cham, Switzerland: Palgrave Macmillan.

Osterwalder, A., & Pigneur, Y. (2010). *Business Model Generation: A Handbook for Visionaries, Game Changers, and Challengers* (vol. 1). Hoboken, NJ: John Wiley & Sons.

Passebois-Ducros J., Trinquecoste, J.-F., & Pichon, F. (2015). Stratégies d'artification dans le domaine du luxe: Le cas des vins de prestige. *Décisions Marketing*, *80*, 109–124.

Poisson-de Haro, S., Espejo, A., & Martí, I. (2022). Business model evolution and entrepreneurial adaptation of festivals: The case of Santiago a Mil. *International Journal of Arts Management*, *24*(2), 77–95.

Patrin-Leclère, V., Marti de Montety, C., & Berthelot-Guiet, K. (2014). *La fin de la publicité? Tours et contours de la dépublicitarisation*. Le Bord de l'eau. Bordeaux, France.

Roy, P., & Pellegrin-Boucher, E. (2024). Building a competitive business model: The case of Montparnasse Tower in Paris. *International Journal of Arts Management*, *26*(2), 43–54.

Schiuma, G. (2011). *The Value of Arts for Business*. Cambridge: Cambridge University Press.

Smiraglia, C. (2014). Artworks at work: The impacts of workplace art. *Journal of Workplace Learning*, *26*(5), 284–295.

Stake, R. (1994). Case studies. In D.N.K. Denzin & Y. Lincoln (Eds.), *Handbook of Qualitative Research* (pp. 236–247). Thousand Oaks, CA: Sage Publications.

Styhre, A., & Eriksson, M. (2008). Bring in the arts and get the creativity for free: A study of the artists in residence project. *Creativity and Innovation Management*, *17*(1), 47–57.

Teece, D.J. (2010). Business models, business strategy and innovation. *Long Range Planning*, *43*(2–3), 172–194.

Teece, D.J. (2018). Business models and dynamic capabilities. *Long Range Planning*, *51*(1), 40–49.

Venkatesh, A., & Meamber, L.A. (2008). The aesthetics of consumption and the consumer as an aesthetic subject. *Consumption, Markets and Culture*, *11*(1), 45–70.

Yin, R.K. (1984). *Case Study Research. Design and Methods* (1st ed.). Thousand Oaks, CA: Sage Publications.

8 Business model innovation in the film industry

Paulina Knobloch

1 Introduction

In times of streaming platforms, user-generated content, and the ubiquitous availability of moving content, the film industry faces major transformations. The industry has always evolved around technological change, for example, the invention of sound film, color film, and home video (Eliashberg, Elberse, and Leenders, 2006; Kehoe and Mateer, 2015). Current innovations, however, have much stronger and more direct consequences (Küng, 2008). The launch of online film distribution platforms in 2006, such as Apple's iTunes Store and Amazon Unbox, marks a turning point that widely altered the modus operandi of the film industry (De Vinck and Lindmark, 2014). Known as transactional video on demand (TVOD), these platforms provide films and series for purchase or rent on a pay-per-view basis. With Netflix entering the Scandinavian market in 2012, a second mode of digital distribution was introduced: subscription video on demand (SVOD) that offers a catalog of films and series on a subscription basis.

In contrast to the traditional film distribution chain, which relies on temporal and territorial exclusivity in pre-defined exhibition windows, for example, theatrical distribution, home entertainment, pay TV, and free TV, online distribution allows for cheaper sales directly to the audience. This circumvents traditional distribution windows, disintermediates the distribution chain, and challenges the role of the distributor. Many authors have described a shift from a supply-led to a demand-led market (Finney and Triana, 2015; Kehoe and Mateer, 2015). Instead of producing and distributing content in the traditional top-down format, existing players need to adjust their offerings more closely to the needs of the consumers (Kehoe and Mateer, 2015).

The wide-ranging changes require strategic action. As Finney states, "the 'traditional' models are starting to either struggle, fail to adapt, acquire businesses they don't understand, or go bankrupt" (Finney, 2014, p. 12) or in other words, existing models need to either "change or die" (Finney and Triana, 2015, p. 222). Astoundingly, very little knowledge exists about how this change looks like, since the film industry, especially outside Hollywood,

DOI: 10.4324/9781032714462-8

has received only very limited (but growing) attention from a management perspective (Küng, 2008).

To shed light on this under-explored topic and to better understand how film companies have reacted to a fundamentally changing industry a longitudinal, comparative case study will be conducted. On the basis of the two Nordic film studios SF Studios and Nordisk Film, it will be analyzed which parts of the business model (BM) have been most affected by innovation since the inception of online film distribution in 2006. The study will not only provide insights into current developments, trends, and challenges in the film industry but also contribute to the understanding of the film industry from a management perspective.

2 Theoretical background

2.1 *Business model innovation*

The BM of a firm is regarded as a strategic element to gain a competitive advantage. It can facilitate innovation but is also subject to innovation itself (Teece, 2010; Zott, Amit, and Massa, 2011). Therefore, the concept of business model innovation (BMI) was introduced which adopts a dynamic view on changes and adaptions to the BM (Saebi, Lien, and Foss, 2017). In their review of BMI research, Foss and Saebi define BMI as "designed, novel, non-trivial changes to the key elements of a firm's BM and/or the architecture linking these elements" (2017, p. 201).

Ramdani et al. (2019) identify four key areas for BMI with four components each (see Figure 8.1). This study will use this framework to identify changes in the business models of the two cases.

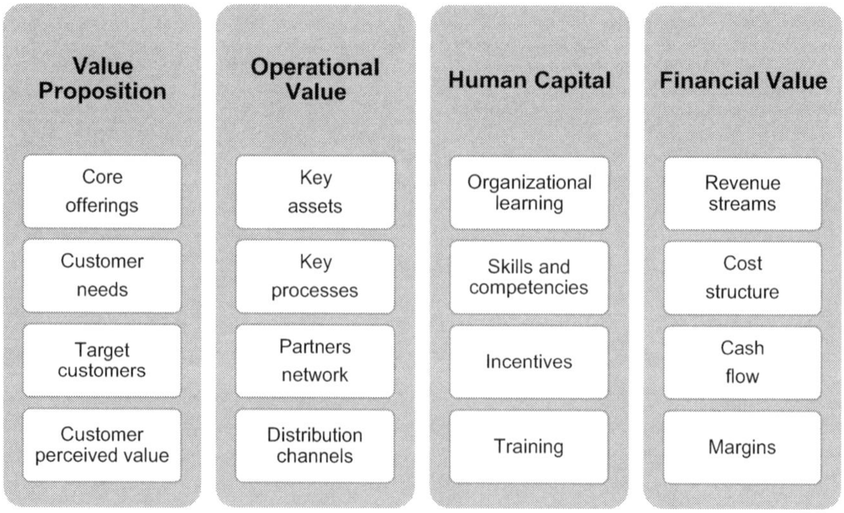

Figure 8.1 Areas for BMI according to Ramdani et al. (2019).

2.2 *Business model innovation in the film industry*

Scholars and practitioners agree that the recent changes in the film industry require strategic action, however, it is still unclear what this reaction should look like (Finney, 2014; Finney and Triana, 2015; von Rimscha, Wikström, and Naldi, 2014). Some authors see vertical integration as continuingly important in the film industry (Finney, 2014). Others regard vertical integration as obsolete and no longer profitable and instead propose fluid organizational forms and strategic alliances (Küng, 2008). What most authors agree on, however, is the importance of partners as an opportunity to gain new market knowledge and competencies (Finney, 2014; Küng, 2008).

Even though the industry dynamics are accompanied by a growing research interest in the film industry, studies looking specifically at BMI are still rare. Some studies analyze new business models but not necessarily BMI. Solidoro and Viscusi (2020), for instance, study the case of the Italian start-up "Movieday.it" which introduces the concept of cinema on demand. Ferrer-Roca (2014) analyzes the case of the "Make My Movie" project in New Zealand which presents a new way of funding independent film projects by relying on social media to fund, produce, and distribute films.

Other studies only focus on one specific area of the BM, for example, distribution channels or revenue streams. Hennig-Thurau et al. (2007) analyze how the traditional sequential distribution of movies can be optimized to increase revenues. They conclude that shorter exclusive cinema windows would be more profitable for the distributor. However, since this study was conducted in 2007, digital film distribution was not yet considered. Gaustad (2019) provides more recent numbers with his analysis of how the revenue streams of film producers in Norway changed between 2010 and 2016. He found that theatrical distribution gained relative importance to a 66% share of all revenues while DVD and BluRay sales decreased from 43% to 11%. Neither TVOD nor SVOD revenues reached the level of the former physical home entertainment market. TVOD only contributes to 13% of the total revenues, SVOD only to 2% despite a market share of 31% with regards to consumer spending. Gaustad, therefore, indicates that producers could profit from refraining from an SVOD release and relying more on higher-yielding theatrical and TVOD distribution.

Still others look at the industry as a whole but do not necessarily focus on BMI. The study of von Rimscha et al. (2014) provides an overview of the European film industry and outlines the challenges that film producers face. The authors find that film producers predict a decline in the cinema market, stagnation in the TV market, and growth potential in mobile and online distribution. With regard to BMI, the authors suggest that financial areas, such as revenue and cost structures, and partner networks will see the biggest changes, while the key activities, that is, the actual production, will be less prone to changes. However, the overview study provides no insights into what companies actually do in reaction to the industry changes.

In brief, while the research interest in the film industry from a management perspective is increasing, many questions remain unanswered. Most studies take small companies or start-ups as their subject, which means that little is known about incumbents and bigger companies such as independent studios.

3 Method

This study employs a comparative, longitudinal case study to analyze BMI in the Nordic film industry. Case studies are a common research tool in the social sciences, law, and economics to investigate phenomena in the present or recent past with a clear temporal and spatial boundary (Eisenhardt and Graebner, 2007). Since the research question addresses change processes, innovation, and transformation, a longitudinal case study is appropriate. The comparative character of the case study allows identifying differences, similarities, and patterns between the cases which enhances the robustness and generalizability of the case study (ibid.).

3.1 Case selection

This study focuses on the Nordic film industry and analyzes the cases of SF Studios and Nordisk Film between 2006 and 2021. The year 2006 has been set as the starting point of this study as it marks the beginning of online video distribution through platforms, such as iTunes and Amazon.

The companies SF Studios and Nordisk Film have been chosen since they are the major film studios in Scandinavia. For more than 100 years, the companies have produced and distributed films and drama series (Nordisk Film, n.d.; SF Studios, n.d.). Being successful in the market over such a long time indicates that BMI occurs in these companies.

3.2 Data acquisition

The study draws upon two methods for data acquisition. First, a historical analysis of news from the past was conducted. This method is often used in marketing, innovation, and organization theory research as it is suitable to study developments over time (Landoni et al., 2020). Since the data was produced at the time when the studied phenomenon took place, it provides a prospective look at the event that is not biased by recollecting memories from the past. However, the historical analysis also involves a certain degree of uncertainty due to the complex, diverse, and sometimes contradicting evidence (Golder and Tellis, 1993). Therefore, this study follows the control criteria proposed by Golder and Tellis (ibid): competence (using sources that were published at the time of the studied event), objectivity (using only sources from third parties that were not involved in the actual phenomenon), reliability (using respected periodicals), corroboration (using only information that is reported by multiple sources).

SF Studios	SF1	Member of management board
	SF2	Member of management board
	SF3	Manager in production
	SF4	Manager in acquisition
	SF5	Manager at SF Anytime
Nordisk Film	NF1	Member of management board
	NF2	Member of management board
	NF3	Manager in distribution

Figure 8.2 Interviewee overview.

The basis for the analysis was online news and articles sourced from the industry news pages Variety, Television Business International, and Nordisk Film & TV Fond. In order to find relevant articles, a keyword search of the company names was conducted through the search option of the online archives of the three industry news pages. The headings of the found articles were then checked to identify whether the articles actually dealt with the two case companies in question. As a second criterion, the articles had to be published after 1996 which marks ten years before the start of the studied period as a means to understand the status quo of the two companies by 2006. In total, 314 news pieces and articles were analyzed, 167 for SF Studios and 147 for Nordisk Film. Relevant information in the news items was compiled according to the following themes: general information about the company, strategy, financing, production, distribution, exhibition, sales, divisions/subsidiaries, expansion, and personnel.

As a second method for data acquisition, eight semi-structured interviews with managers of the two companies were conducted in March and April 2021. The 30-minute interviews included five executives from SF Studios and three from Nordisk Film (see Figure 8.2). The interviews consisted of four parts. First, the interviewees were asked to introduce themselves and their role at the company. The second part dealt with their view on industry changes in the period between 2006 and 2021. In the third part, they were asked to describe changes within their company in the same time period. The last section dealt with the interviewees' views on the future of the industry. The interviews were concluded with the option for the interviewees to add further remarks. The information brought up in the interviews was categorized according to the following areas: general information about the company, industry changes, changes within the company, BMI in general, the BM areas according to Figure 8.1, and outlook on the future.

Interviews are a common source for case studies as they provide primary insights into the case. The semi-structured character is suited as it opens the opportunity to ask in-depth follow-up questions. However, interviews are susceptible to subjectivity and personal bias as the interview subjects describe their retrospective and subjective view of the studied phenomenon (ibid.). Therefore, an integration of both sources, interviews and historical analysis, was used to provide a more holistic view of the case.

4 Case study

4.1 Empirical introduction

The film industry deals with the development, production, distribution, and exhibition of motion pictures. Only a very limited number of film companies, all of which in Hollywood, combine all parts of the value chain in a vertically integrated organization. These so-called major studios are responsible for a film from financing to distribution single-handedly. Examples are Universal Pictures, Disney Pictures, and Warner Bros. Pictures (Betzler and Leuschen, 2019; Finney, 2008; Küng, 2008; Ulin, 2019). Despite often being described as major producers, Ulin regards the major studios as "finance and distribution machines" (Ulin, 2019, p. 5) that produce movies simply to own the rights to sell them.

A vast majority of film companies, especially in Europe, belong to the independent sector which is characterized by a fragmented structure and a disintegrated value chain (Betzler and Leuschen, 2019; Kehoe and Mateer, 2015). Many small and mid-sized companies are specialized in one area and interact in complex networks (Landoni et al., 2020; Peltoniemi, 2015).

A special form of independents is the so-called independent studio. Companies, such as SF Studios in Sweden, Nordisk Film in Denmark, and StudioCanal in France have a high production output, broad distribution activities, and are more integrated than most independent players. Still, they do not have the power of US majors and rely heavily on their partner network (Ulin, 2019).

4.2 Film industry overview

At the beginning of the 21st century, film distribution in the Nordics followed a typical release pattern. Films, both local and international ones, were first released in theaters and a few months later for home entertainment. The biggest share of revenues originated from the DVD market on which the distributor had high margins. Lastly, the film was made available on pay and free TV.

In 2005 and 2006, the first online film distribution channels were launched with Apple's iTunes Store and Amazon Unbox which soon replaced physical distribution. DVD sales peaked in 2008 and have since then decreased rapidly.

In 2012, Netflix and HBO Nordic entered the Scandinavian market as the first SVOD players. Since then, the SVOD sector has grown steadily and SVOD platforms have become major players characterized by their immense demand for content.

4.3 *The case of SF studios*

4.3.1 *Background*

SF Studios was founded as Svensk Filmindustri[1] in 1919. It was a leading producer and distributor of early Swedish films in the silent era in the 1920s. During the 20th century, SF Studios was involved in several successful productions, including films by Ingmar Bergman and adaptions from Astrid Lindgren's children's books. In 1983, SF Studios was acquired by the media conglomerate Bonnier but continued to act under its own brand. In 1989, SF Studios expanded to Norway and ten years later to Denmark. In 2000 SF Studios expanded to Finland and had thereby established production and distribution activities in all Scandinavian countries.

Around the year 2006, the starting point of this study, SF Studios acted mainly as a distributor of local and international films in the Scandinavian market. Distribution made up about 90% of its activities while only 10% were connected to production as interviewee SF3 explained. SF1 described SF Studios as: "a distribution company that happened to make a little bit of production."

4.3.2 *Distribution*

SF Studios acts as a local distributor of international films and has distribution deals with international producers. In 2006, the distribution deals included films by the Hollywood producers Fox, New Line Cinema, and Spyglass Media Group, which is reported by four articles. SF1 described that the distribution used to focus on cinematic films and matched the traditional exhibition chain starting with a release to cinemas followed by other windows, such as home entertainment, pay TV, and free TV.

Until today, theatrical distribution plays an important role for SF Studios as it provides secure margins and a stake in the financial success of the films, as described by SF4. Over the years, SF Studios has successively extended the deals with more international studios. Since 2011, SF Studios has had a distribution deal with Warner Bros. for distribution in Denmark, Norway, and Finland. In 2019, the deal was extended to include the rights for Sweden as well as reported by three articles. In 2014, SF Studios made a theatrical distribution deal with French StudioCanal for all of StudioCanal's new releases which is described by four articles. Furthermore, SF Studios has distribution deals with the Swedish production companies Memfis Film, FLX, and STX Entertainment which is reported by three articles. By 2020, SF Studios has significantly deepened its existing relationships and extended its partner network with bigger players.

Besides theatrical distribution, the distribution of physical home entertainment, especially DVDs, used to be a secure revenue stream with comparatively high margins, which was explained by SF3 and SF5. The rapid decrease in DVD sales after 2008 was a major shake-up for SF Studios since an important distribution channel and revenue stream disappeared. According to SF5, about 50% of the turnover from DVD sales was lost in just a few years.

The emergence of TVOD provided a new revenue stream, however, it could not replace the revenues from DVDs since margins on TVOD are a lot lower, which was described by SF3. To reach profitability and increase revenues, the volume of distributed films had to be increased. This was stated by both SF4 and SF5.

Yet, digital distribution also offered an opportunity. Due to the digital infrastructure, TVOD can potentially have a wider reach with comparatively little effort and resources. Already in 2002, SF Studios' mother company Bonnier launched its own TVOD platform SF Anytime. According to SF2 and SF5, the platform is now the biggest TVOD service in Scandinavia and the Baltics while currently only employing 19 people. In 2016, SF Studios launched a second service, SF Anytime Kids, which is directed at children's and family content. SF2 described that SF Studios' TVOD platforms distribute the studio's own films and have deals for film input with major international producers. That way, SF Studios has expanded downstream closer to the end-user.

The rise of SVOD a few years after the launch of TVOD platforms had even more profound consequences for SF Studios. On the one hand, SVOD players can be seen as competitors for SF Studios' own VOD platforms and as challengers of its traditional distribution strategy, which was described by SF4 and SF5. On the other hand, SVOD represents a new potential distribution channel and source of revenue. Approximately five years after the drop in DVD sales, SVOD recouped and even exceeded the lost revenue stream, as described by SF3. However, as highlighted by SF4, SVOD as a distribution channel has some fundamentally different rules and requires new right bundles from the distributor to fit the concept. In the past, SF Studios served each exhibition window separately and dealt with various partners, for example, for theatrical release, pay TV, and free TV, sometimes even separately for several countries. Content sold to SVOD players often includes all rights for all territories. SF Studios is then no longer involved in the distribution and does not hold any rights for other markets or windows. To make profits from this new cash flow, the volume of films sold to SVOD players has to be increased.

4.3.3 Production

Film production in Scandinavia used to happen on a rather small scale with small budgets. As typical for the independent sector, the Scandinavian film production market consists of many small companies. Consequently, many players are involved in a project, including production and co-production companies, national and international TV networks, film funds, and distributors. The production of the film "Everything will be fine" from 2010 serves as an example of the complex partner network. The Danish, Swedish, and

French film was produced by Alphaville Pictures in co-production with SF Studios and four other film production companies. The film was co-financed by the Danish Radio (DR) and the Finnish Broadcasting Company YLE and received support from the Danish Film Institute and Nordisk Film & TV Fond. SF Studios handled the distribution in Denmark, while the rights for other countries were sold to local distributors.

With the financial power of SVOD players, these partnerships change. This was highlighted by both SF1 and SF3. Instead of many small partners, it is now enough for a producer to work with one SVOD player which provides enough money to finance a full project. The Netflix film "Red Dot" from 2021 can be seen as an example. As commissioned production, SF Studios is the only producer and Netflix owns the worldwide rights for distribution.

For SF Studios, cooperating with SVOD players is a means to build reliable and long-term partnerships. From the SVOD's side, strong partners that ensure a steady and continuing content supply are desirable. SF1 highlighted that SVOD platforms are looking for "selected relationships with a small number of players who they know and trust." With fast-increasing production output, well-developed production infrastructure, and operations in all Scandinavian countries, SF Studios is such a partner. Thus, while partnerships are still important for SF Studios, the value and number of the partners have changed from many small partners to selected, more powerful partners.

The cooperation with SVOD players has significant effects on the revenue structure. When SF Studios produces films for an SVOD player they receive a fixed but secure margin, however, they do not hold a stake in the upside of the project, as described by SF4. Thus, no matter the success of a film, SF Studios receives the same revenue. This means that film production is moving to become a volume business, where a high production output is necessary to make a profit as pointed out by SF4 and SF5.

With more and more SVOD players entering the market and existing ones extending their offerings, content is available over a wide variety of platforms. This influences the audience's viewing behavior and customer perceived value. SF3 described that with less content available a few years ago, each piece had a higher value and was more exclusive. Today, the value of each film has decreased, as has the willingness of the audience to pay for content. But while the amount of content is growing, the available information about each film is increasing as well, for example, reviews from critics and other viewers, ratings, and top lists. This helps the audience to make more well-founded decisions on what to watch which, in turn, means that the audience is a lot pickier and more oriented toward quality than before. Thus, while SVOD players generally value content that can be produced fast, the demand for quality content to stick out of the masses is increasing as well. High-quality content also presents a more secure revenue stream as the willingness of the audience to pay for such content is higher as noted by SF3.

On the content level, the death of the DVD and the rise of SVOD platforms have had another consequence. SF1 described that until the beginning of the 2010s, films were very strong and well-financed not the least through the sales of DVDs. When digital distribution, especially on SVOD, took over, the demand for serial content increased substantially. SVOD platforms but also traditional broadcasting channels started to express an interest in drama series. SF Studios has taken advantage of this shift and adjusted its value proposition. Since 2017, SF Studies has increased its production of drama series for free TV and SVOD outlets. The studio has, for example, produced the drama series "Hunters," "Alex," and "First Responders" for Viaplay and "Easy Money" for Netflix, which seven articles report about.

All the changes that SVOD brings along, for example, new distribution platforms, partners, and revenue streams, as well as a changed perceived value and a shift to serial storytelling, lead to an increased demand for content and more precisely big-budget, high-quality content. SF Studios reacted to this trend, by increasing its production capacities. Fifteen years ago, only 10% of its operations were connected to production. Today, the production side is as strong as distribution and is expected to gain even more importance in the next few years as SF3 predicted. SF1 stated that SF Studios now has five times the revenues and three times the staff in production compared to ten years ago. The growth of the production side was enhanced by acquiring stakes in other Scandinavian film production companies. In 2007, SF Studios bought Swedish producer and distributor Sonet Film (reported by two articles). In 2012, SF Studios acquired a majority share in the Norwegian production company Motion Blur, and in 2013, it acquired the Swedish production company Tre Vänner (each reported by five articles). In 2019, it acquired the Norwegian company Paradox (reported by two articles) which allowed full-scale production in Norway. In the same year, SF Studios also acquired a majority stake in the Swedish company FLX (reported by two articles).

4.3.4 *Internationalization*

In addition to increased production capacities in Scandinavia, SF Studios expanded its production operations beyond the Nordics and started producing English-language films for an international market. In 2014, SF Studios made a co-production deal for English-language productions with the French independent studio StudioCanal, which among others included the production of the drama series "The Lawyer," which is described by two articles.

In 2016, Svensk Filmindustri rebranded as SF Studios to make the company name more accessible internationally, remove the focus from the Swedish-ness of the studio, and position the company as an international player, as described by four articles. Furthermore, as six articles report, SF Studios opened an office in London in the same year to strengthen its international production, make use of the infrastructure and talent abroad, and open up for bigger budget productions.

4.4 *The case of Nordisk film*

4.4.1 *Background*

Nordisk Film was founded in Denmark in 1906 as a cinema operator as well as a production and distribution company of silent films. It is now the oldest still-running film studio in the world and has produced some of Denmark's most well-known films, including the "Olsen Gang" movies. In 1992, Nordisk Film was integrated into the Nordic media group Egmont. It has operations in Denmark, Norway, Sweden, and Finland.

By 2006, Nordisk Film was characterized by a fragmented business structure. It was active in the production and distribution of feature films as well as TV productions, cinema exhibitions, music production, and the distribution of PlayStation consoles and games in the Nordics, as two articles report. Shortly after, it sold its television division and its music company in order to streamline operations around movies and interactive games.

4.4.2 *Distribution*

As a cinema owner and film distributor, theatrical distribution plays an important part in Nordisk Film's operations. Despite new digital distribution channels, the cinema market is comparatively stable as NF3 highlighted. NF1 added that even though admissions to cinemas have gone down, the audience is willing to pay more for the experience which means that the overall revenues from theatrical distribution are unchanged. Digital technologies, such as digital film copies, make the delivery process to cinemas easier, faster, and more cost-efficient, which decreases the costs for theatrical distribution, as described by NF3. Nordisk Film has over the years expanded its cinema segment, for example, by acquiring Oslo Kino, the largest cinema chain in Norway in 2013, which is reported by two articles.

The home entertainment market, in contrast, has seen major changes on several levels. NF1 explained that distribution has shifted from physical to digital media. Sales of DVDs have decreased substantially but have not disappeared completely. Until today, some revenue is generated through DVDs.

With TVOD and SVOD, new distribution platforms become available. For a distributor like Nordisk Film, this means first and foremost more potential buyers of its content and thus, more potential revenue streams as NF1 and NF2 described. What is special about the distribution to SVOD platforms, as explained by NF1, is the fact that the distributor receives a fixed revenue but does not hold a stake in the upside of the film nor keep any rights for other release windows or markets. In turn, Nordisk Film is not involved in the potential risk of a film and receives the same revenue regardless of the financial success of the film. This is in contrast to its own films that Nordisk Film distributes through several channels. Here, Nordisk Films holds equity in the movie and profits from the financial upside but also runs greater risks.

Distribution now is much more focused on partners compared to 15 years ago and long-lasting partnerships are important as NF3 described. Nordisk Film has deepened existing partnerships, for example, with producers to secure a steady content flow for distribution. In 2007, Nordisk Film acquired a majority stake in the Finnish company Solar Films (reported by two articles), as well as a 50% share in Norwegian Maipo Films (reported by three articles) and Swedish S/S Fladen (reported by two articles). Nordisk Film took over the Nordic distribution and international sales for the films of these companies. In 2008, Nordisk Film acquired a 50% share in Danish film company Zentropa, which two articles describe.

Additionally, Nordisk Film has extended its partner network with players in the digital distribution businesses and even players outside the film industry. Partners today include, for example, telecom operators in Scandinavia, as well as multinational corporations, such as Apple and Amazon with their respective streaming services, as NF1 and NF3 explained.

With the ubiquitous availability of content through a wide variety of platforms, consumer expectations have risen. Both NF1 and NF3 noted that the audience expects fast access to content, low prices, and high technological quality. As NF3 described, Nordisk Film implemented a consumer insights team in 2011 to better understand consumer needs. By integrating user testing and user involvement in the distribution process, Nordisk Film is able to discover and address changes in consumer behavior and target the audience more specifically. In the words of NF3, the goal is to "target the right consumers at the right time with the right message" which means that Nordisk Film is more aware of what the audience wants. Started as a marketing tool, the consumer insights were soon channeled back to production and acquisition. That way, the acquisition of intellectual property (IP), for instance, is more oriented toward market demands. With that knowledge, Nordisk Film's distribution department has moved upstream in recent years. Instead of only picking up projects for distribution, Nordisk Film is interested in getting involved in projects at the development stage to have more control over the content that is being produced, which is reported by two articles. However, a certain risk is involved with this process. Several years can pass between the acquisition of the rights and the distribution of a film during which the market demands can change.

In general, the many options that are available to distribute a film nowadays have made Nordisk Film more conscious about the type of project and the best possible release strategy tailored to each project individually, which was expressed by NF1. This requires a higher degree of flexibility and has led to organizational changes at Nordisk Film. NF3 described that in the past, the distribution department was split up according to release windows and geographical markets. Country managers ran their segments independently with little exchange between the departments. Today, the organization is much more connected, which provides a more efficient way to distribute films through several windows. This allows for a more holistic approach and skill-sharing between employees.

4.4.3 *Production*

With a growing number of distribution platforms, the demand for content is rising. Nordisk Film has increased its production capacities and supply of content, mainly through the acquisition of stakes in local film production companies. As described in the distribution chapter, Nordisk Film has acquired stakes in the Finnish company Solar Films, Norwegian Maipo Films, Swedish S/S Fladen, and Danish Zentropa, among others. In addition to content flow for distribution, these partnerships are also an opportunity to get involved in more productions and co-productions in all Scandinavian countries, as reported by three articles.

In general, partners have become more important over the past years. Nordisk Film has extended and deepened relationships with local and international partners and uses a network of partners for sourcing IP and talent and to produce content, which was described by NF3.

With the emergence of SVOD in 2012, streaming platforms have become a new tier of partners with increasing importance as highlighted by NF1. SVOD players bring in new money and are a significant source of production financing. With their interest in a big catalog, the demand for content is high.

In order to attract consumers, content providers are interested in exclusive titles as NF1 explained. This means that besides a generally increasing demand for content, special focus is placed on high-end content. Nordisk Film has made use of this trend by increasing its high-end production output for streaming platforms but also for theatrical release. In 2015, for instance, Nordisk Film's Norwegian production arm started the production of the high-end feature film "The 12th Man" with a budget in the range of \$6–10 million, as reported by two articles. In the same year, Nordisk Film joined forces with the Swedish regional film fund Film i Väst, and Swedish public broadcaster Sveriges Television (SVT) to produce high-quality films in Sweden with budgets of \$4–6 million, which is about double the average Swedish production budget. This is reported by two articles. In addition to big-budget films, Nordisk has also moved into the production of drama series for SVOD platforms and broadcasters, as reported by two articles.

Big-budget and drama series productions have been facilitated by new technology, such as digital film cameras, advanced computer-generated imagery, and more powerful computers, that have simplified production processes and decreased production costs. This was brought up by NF1 and NF2. Compared to 2006, a film of the same standard and with the same technology can be produced for a much lower cost. At the same time, audience expectations regarding quality are rising, which means that production companies need to invest in new technology to keep up with the market demand.

While technology can be upscaled comparatively easily, the bottleneck of increasing production activities is creative talent, as NF1 described. Since the number of creative workers has not increased compared to 15 years ago, there is now a higher demand and more competition for talent. Consequently, the cost for talent has increased and creators hold more negotiating power and influence than in the past.

4.4.4 Expansion in neighboring industries

In addition to the activities in the motion picture industry, Nordisk Film has expanded in neighboring entertainment-related areas and invested in digital growth markets. As two articles report, Nordisk Film has been the official distribution partner of PlayStation in the Nordic and Baltic countries already since the 1990s and has therefore had a special relationship with gaming. NF2 explained that in 2016, a new gaming unit was created to produce games as well. Today, the division Nordisk Games owns nine independent game studios, including Avalanche Studios and StarStable, that create a wide range of games, ranging from blockbuster to indie and mobile games.

Nordisk Film has also expanded beyond moving content. NF2 described that in 2012, Nordisk Film acquired the event ticket provider Venuepoint which runs the online portal billetlugen.dk. However, in 2018, Nordisk Film retrieved from event ticketing and sold Venuepoint. Nordisk Film has also expanded into the e-commerce business by building a gift card company. In 2014, Nordisk Film acquired the Danish gift card provider gavekortet.dk, which later merged into a new business area called GoGift. What started as gift cards for experiences has now expanded into gift cards for a diverse selection of products and services.

5 Main results

The cases of SF Studios and Nordisk Film show that the companies have undergone fundamental transformations during the studied period.

In 2006, SF Studios was a distributor of theatrical films and adjacent windows in Scandinavia with just minor production activities. Over the studied period, theatrical distribution remained important and SF Studios has continuously extended its distribution deals with international and local producers. In the first few years of the studied period, SF Studios substantially increased its production output of local films which can be seen as the first stage of BMI after the emergence of TVOD. In 2014, when SVOD had settled on the market, the second phase of innovation was entered when SF Studios expanded beyond its core of local movies. It started the production of English-language titles and expanded internationally. Shortly after, the third stage of BMI started, when SF Studios moved into the production of serial content with several releases in 2017. Today, SF Studios is a distributor for theaters and digital channels as well as a producer of feature films and drama series in Scandinavia and internationally. SF4 described the company as a "Nordic content producer and distributor that works anyway with anyone."

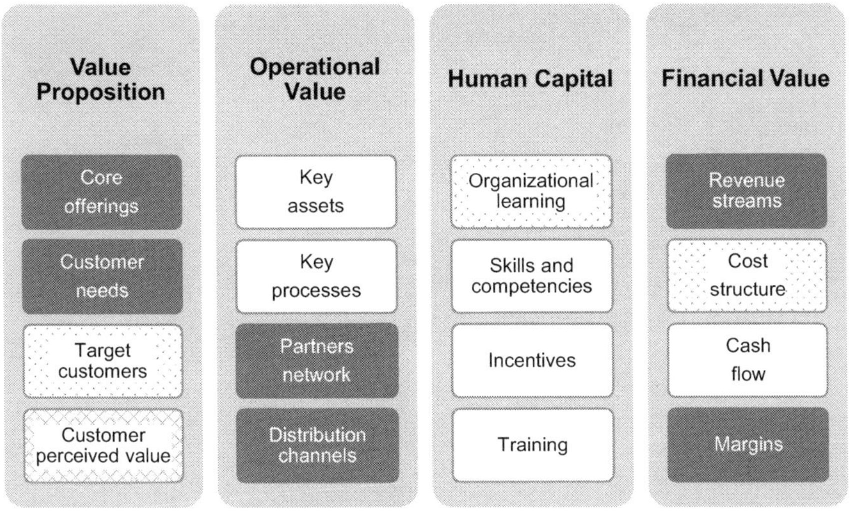

Figure 8.3 Changes to SF Studios' and Nordisk Film's business model: Grey boxes indicate that changes happen in both cases, checkered boxes represent changes that only happen in the case of SF Studio, while boxes marked with dots refer to the case of Nordisk Film. White boxes indicate that no changes have been identified in those areas in either of the two cases.

At the beginning of the studied period, Nordisk Film was active in the production and distribution of films and TV shows, as a distributor of PlayStation, and as a music producer. In 2006, it started streamlining its operations and focusing on local feature film production which can be seen as the first stage of BMI. The shift was accompanied by the introduction of a consumer insights team in 2011 to target the audience more specifically. In the second step since 2012, Nordisk Film opened up for new business areas again, started looking for digital growth contenders, and expanded into neighboring industries, most importantly gaming. Shortly after the emergence of SVOD, the third stage was entered when Nordisk Film started producing high-end feature films with its first production released in 2015. Around the same time, it moved into the production of drama series which marks the fourth phase of BMI. Today, Nordisk Film is a portfolio company in the entertainment business with its core in the production and distribution of films and series, or as NF2 put it: "an old movie studio that has managed to modernize and find new areas of revenue."

As both cases show, changes to the BM happen in several areas across all four dimensions of value proposition, operational value, human capital, and financial value. Figure 8.3 summarizes which BM areas are affected by changes. While the cases differ in detail, most overarching developments are shared between both companies. The cases indicate that distribution channels, revenue streams, margins, partner network, customer demands, and core offerings have been affected the most by BMI.

5.1 Distribution channels

Digital distribution has led to a rapid decrease in DVD distribution and a rise in TVOD and SVOD channels which results in two coexisting distribution strategies that the companies follow.

Until today, the traditional distribution and release strategy remains, with the only difference being that TVOD replaces the DVD. Films start their journey in cinemas, are then released on the (digital) home entertainment market, and finally on pay and free TV. Theatrical distribution still plays an important role, which can be seen in the responses of the two film studios. SF Studios extends its distribution deals with international producers, Nordisk Film increases its cinema ownership.

The second distribution option is a direct-to-SVOD release. This circumvents the traditional distribution chain with major effects on other BM areas, most importantly the revenue stream and margins. Since margins on digital distribution are lower than on DVD distribution, a higher volume is necessary to reach the same revenues. Additionally, new right bundles are required as SVOD players buy out the distributor and producer. Still, SVOD players have become an important new source of revenue, especially in the late 2010s when they started to source local content in Scandinavia.

With more options for distribution available, the distributor is able to adjust the release strategy of each film individually. However, this also requires more flexibility in the distribution process.

5.2 Partner network

Partnerships and alliances have become more relevant both in production and distribution. A trend is visible toward stronger and more powerful partners and long-term partnerships both within and beyond the film industry, including local and international film producers, TVOD and SVOD services, and access providers.

5.3 Customer needs

The shift toward online distribution has had big effects on the customer needs. TVOD has brought producers and distributors closer to the end-user and has made them more conscious of the customer needs. SVOD has led to a massive increase in content demand, which in turn has made the audience pickier and more quality-oriented.

5.4 Core offerings

The aforementioned transformations have prompted a major change in the core offerings. Both companies focus more on the production of their own content. At the beginning of the studied period, both companies strengthened their in-house production of local, that is, Nordic films. A shift occurred around the year 2014, when the studios expanded their offering beyond their core, however, in different directions. SF Studios moved into the production of English-language films for a global audience. Nordisk Film remained in the local language market but put much more focus on high-budget productions. Shortly after, in 2016 and 2017, both companies started to produce drama series.

While the studios have acted similarly regarding these changes, they differ in one major point. Throughout all the changes, SF Studios has stayed close to its original offering, namely motion pictures. Nordisk Film has expanded in neighboring industries, most importantly gaming. Thus, while both companies are actively searching for new markets and expanding their offerings to fit the new digital media landscape, they have different conceptions of what they are: SF Studios as a classical film studio that evolves with the digital market in the Nordics and beyond; Nordisk Film as a portfolio company in the Nordic entertainment business with its core in movies.

6 Discussion

The film industry has seen major changes in the last 15 years and as this study illustrates, film studios are in a permanent process of adapting and innovating their BM to fit their rapidly changing environment. Through a BM lens, this case study shows that Nordic film studios are open to new developments, partners, and techniques and are active in adapting their BM accordingly. Two developments stand out in this context.

First, SVOD players have become major partners for film studios, specifically in the second half of the 2010s when SVOD players started to show a stronger interest in local content. From the SVOD players' side, independent studios are regarded as reliable partners due to their high production output and strong position in the market, compared to smaller production companies. As a result, the structure of partnerships has changed, making multi-year alliances with big players more important compared to the predomination of flexible project-based partnerships between several small players in the past.

Second, film studios have increased their production output. Three phases can be differentiated in this process. In the first few years of the study, the companies focused on increasing the output of local films. While this changes the balance of the studios' core activities of production and distribution, it does not yet introduce any new offerings. This changed around 2014 when the studios' output was expanded by English-language productions and high-end Nordic feature films. English-language films are an opportunity to extend the potential audience geographically, while higher-budget films often provide more value to the viewers and are thus more attractive. In the second half of the 2010s, the third phase was entered, when both studios expanded their offerings by drama series. The similarities regarding the move to drama series are hardly surprising since the whole film industry, not just in Scandinavia, has seen an increasing demand for serial content from both SVOD players and traditional broadcasters.

Apart from adjusting the offering to the changing market demands, in-house production, in general, has two major merits. On the one hand, it allows studios to profit from higher margins on the distribution of their own content compared to third-party content. It also gives studios more control over what content is being produced instead of only picking up projects for distribution. Both production (i.e., what content is produced) and distribution (i.e., how, when, and where the content will be delivered) are now more targeted to the end-user putting the audience at the center of all activities. As described by Finney and Triana (2015) as well as Kehoe and Mateer (2015) among others, this can be seen as a shift from a supply-led to a demand-led market.

On the other hand, in-house production serves as a way to secure a steady content flow for distribution. More major studios are launching their own SVOD platforms, for example, Disney with Disney+, Warner Media with HBO Max, and Paramount with Paramount+. This jeopardizes the role of the local distributor as major international producers use their own outlets to release content. Increased in-house production and consequently a higher degree of vertical integration allow local distributors to acquire control over the content flow and become independent from third-party producers.

The trends of stronger alliances and increased vertical integration indicate that big players, both international organizations and local studios, grow and strengthen their position in the market. The European film industry, which is characterized by a fragmented structure, will undoubtedly be affected by these shifts. It remains unsolved in this study, however, what this means for the future and how network structures, collaborations, other companies, and the final products, that is, films and series, will be affected.

6.1 *Limitations and future research*

The case study did not include any data about the economic state of the two companies, for example, in terms of turnover or number of employees. Therefore, no conclusions about the financial success of the aforementioned changes to the BM can be drawn. Future research is needed to investigate, how the changes to the BM affect the profit of the companies. It would also be worthwhile to study smaller players in the film landscape, for example, independent producers. Being utterly different from the European studio in terms of size, value proposition, and degree of vertical integration indicates that they are affected differently by the industry trends.

7 Conclusion

Initiated through digital film distribution, the film industry has undergone severe transformations during the last 15 years. To stay competitive in a changing market, existing players need to adapt and innovate their business models.

Therefore, this study aimed to identify the areas of the business models of Nordic film studios that have changed the most since the launch of digital film distribution platforms in 2006. By analyzing the cases of SF Studios and Nordisk Film, it could be concluded that distribution channels, revenue streams, margins, partner network, customer needs, and core offerings have been most affected by innovation. The studios open up for online distribution channels, which generates a new source of revenue and new partnerships. The demand for content, especially high-quality content, is higher than ever, which led the film studios to increase their own production output. This allows them to get control over the content and, thus, become less dependent on other content suppliers while at the same time targeting the audience more directly.

With these findings, the study contributes to the understanding of the film industry from a management perspective. It has provided insights into BMI during the last 15 years and presented an overview of current trends and developments in the film industry which can be used to design the future. Most changes to the BM are connected to SVOD players, indicating that they will continue to play a major role in the industry. High content availability and a more quality-oriented audience suggest that content producers and distributors have to adapt to a demand-led market. Increased vertical integration of the Nordic studios and alliances between big players will impact the power structures of the formerly dispersed European film industry with yet unknown consequences, especially for smaller players.

Note

1 Svensk Filmindustri was rebranded as SF Studios in 2016. For easier understanding the term SF Studios will be used to describe the company even before 2016.

References

Betzler D, Leuschen L. 2019. *Digitized Value Chains in the Creative Industries: A Systematic Comparison of Swiss Game and Film Production*. Lisbon, Portugal: 14.

De Vinck S, Lindmark S. 2014. Innovation in the Film Sector: What Lessons from the Past Tell us about Hollywood's Digital Future – and What That Means for Europe. In *International Perspectives on Business Innovation and Disruption in the Creative Industries*. Edward Elgar Publishing: 105–127. Available at: http://www.elgaronline.com/view/9781783475339.00013.xml.

Eisenhardt KM, Graebner ME. 2007. Theory Building from Cases: Opportunities and Challenges. *Academy of Management Journal* 50(1): 25–32. Available at: http://journals.aom.org/doi/10.5465/amj.2007.24160888.

Eliashberg J, Elberse A, Leenders MAAM. 2006. The Motion Picture Industry: Critical Issues in Practice, Current Research, and New Research Directions. *Marketing Science* 25(6): 638–661. Available at: http://pubsonline.informs.org/doi/10.1287/mksc.1050.0177.

Ferrer-Roca N. 2014. Business Innovation in the Film Industry Value Chain: A New Zealand Case Study. In *International Perspectives on Business Innovation and Disruption in the Creative Industries*. Edward Elgar Publishing: 18–36. Available at: http://www.elgaronline.com/view/9781783475339.00008.xml.

Finney A. 2008. Learning from Sharks: Lessons on Managing Projects in the Independent Film Industry. *Long Range Planning* **41**: 9.

Finney A. 2014. Value Chain Restructuring in the Film Industry: The Case of the Independent Feature Film Sector. In *International Perspectives on Business Innovation and Disruption in the Creative Industries*. Edward Elgar Publishing: 3–17. Available at: http://www.elgaronline.com/view/9781783475339.00007.xml.

Finney A, Triana E. 2015. *The International Film Business: A Market Guide Beyond Hollywood*, 2nd ed. London; New York: Routledge, Taylor & Francis Group.

Foss NJ, Saebi T. 2017. Fifteen Years of Research on Business Model Innovation: How Far Have We Come, and Where Should We Go? *Journal of Management* **43**(1): 200–227. Available at: http://journals.sagepub.com/doi/10.1177/0149206316675927.

Gaustad T. 2019. How Streaming Services Make Cinema More Important: Lessons from Norway. *Nordic Journal of Media Studies* **1**: 67–84.

Golder P, Tellis G. 1993. Pioneer Advantage: Marketing Logic or Marketing Legend? *American Marketing Association* **30**(2): 158–170.

Hennig-Thurau T, Henning V, Sattler H, Eggers F, Houston MB. 2007. The Last Picture Show? Timing and Order of Movie Distribution Channels. *Journal of Marketing* **71**: 63–83.

Kehoe K, Mateer J. 2015. The Impact of Digital Technology on the Distribution Value Chain Model of Independent Feature Films in the UK. *International Journal on Media Management* **17**(2): 93–108.

Küng L. 2008. *Strategic Management in the Media: From Theory to Practice*. London; Thousand Oaks, CA: SAGE.

Landoni P et al. 2020. Business Model Innovation in Cultural and Creative Industries: Insights from Three Leading Mobile Gaming Firms. *Technovation* **92–93**. Available at: https://linkinghub.elsevier.com/retrieve/pii/S016649721730086X.

Nordisk Film. n.d. *About Nordisk Film*. Available at: https://www.nordiskfilm.com/about.

Peltoniemi M. 2015. Cultural Industries: Product-Market Characteristics, Management Challenges and Industry Dynamics: Cultural Industries. *International Journal of Management Reviews* **17**(1): 41–68. Available at: http://doi.wiley.com/10.1111/ijmr.12036.

Ramdani B, Binsaif A, Boukrami E. 2019. Business Model Innovation: A Review and Research Agenda. *New England Journal of Entrepreneurship* **22**(2): 89–108. Available at: https://www.emerald.com/insight/content/doi/10.1108/NEJE-06-2019-0030/full/html.

von Rimscha MB, Wikström P, Naldi L. 2014. European Audio-Visual Production Companies Adapting to Strategic Challenges. In *International Perspectives on Business Innovation and Disruption in the Creative Industries*. Edward Elgar Publishing: 66–87. Available at: http://www.elgaronline.com/view/9781783475339.00011.xml.

Saebi T, Lien L, Foss NJ. 2017. What Drives Business Model Adaptation? The Impact of Opportunities, Threats and Strategic Orientation. *Long Range Planning* **50**(5): 567–581. Available at: https://linkinghub.elsevier.com/retrieve/pii/S0024630116300590.

SF Studios. n.d. About us. Available at: https://sfstudios.se/about-sf-studios.

Solidoro A, Viscusi G. 2020. Digital Transformation and Business Model Innovation in the Film Industry: The Case of Movieday.it. In *Technology and Creativity: Production, Mediation and Evaluation in the Digital Age*. Palgrave Macmillan, 239–265. Available at: https://doi.org/10.1007/978-3-030-17566-5_10.

Teece DJ. 2010. Business Models, Business Strategy and Innovation. *Long Range Planning* 43(2–3): 172–194. Available at: https://linkinghub.elsevier.com/retrieve/pii/S002463010900051X.

Ulin J. 2019. *The Business of Media Distribution: Monetizing Film, TV, and Video Content in an Online World*, 3rd ed. American Film Market presents. Routledge: New York.

Zott C, Amit R, Massa L. 2011. The Business Model: Recent Developments and Future Research. *Journal of Management* 37(4): 1019–1042. Available at: http://journals.sagepub.com/doi/10.1177/0149206311406265.

9 Building an open business model between competitors

A case study from the architecture industry

Estelle Pellegrin-Boucher and Pierre Roy

1 Introduction

For the past two decades, cultural and creative industries (CCIs) have been undergoing profound transformations linked to developments in the economic landscape: acceleration of globalization, technological disruptions, digital impact, shifts in consumer behavior, and more. In response to these environmental changes, companies within CCIs are compelled to develop innovative, high-quality offerings that differentiate themselves from competitors (Gander & Rieple, 2004; Loots, Cnossen, & Van Witteloostuijn, 2018). Beyond their offerings, these companies are also required to rethink their organizational modes to thrive in an increasingly uncertain and competitive environment (Dikova, Van Witteloostuijn, & Parker, 2017). In this perspective, several companies choose to transform some or all of their business models (BMs), even opening them up to partners—customers, suppliers, etc.—to enhance competitiveness, innovation, and value creation (Zott & Amit, 2010; Spieth, Laudien, & Meissner, 2020).

An open BM can be defined as a BM that integrates one or more partners, such as customers, suppliers, or other external stakeholders (Chesbrough, 2007, 2010; Ritter & Lettl, 2018). Recent research shows that sharing resources and expertise within such structures generates strong innovation capability and creates more value (Zott & Amit, 2010; Braun, 2015; Spieth, Laudien, & Meissner, 2020). However, in the literature on strategic management, studies on open BMs primarily focus on innovation projects between non-competing partners. There is currently only one study on open BMs among competitors, but it mainly analyzes performance impacts and does not address operational methods (Ritala, Golnam, & Wegmann, 2013). Specifically, no research has been conducted so far on open models among competitors in CCIs, despite the increasing instances of cooperation among competitors in these sectors (Gundolf, Jaouen, & Gast, 2018; Pellegrin-Boucher & Roy, 2019).

This emerging research topic remains largely unexplored, especially regarding its mechanisms and strategic implications. Our research aims to contribute precisely to this body of knowledge by exploring the construction

DOI: 10.4324/9781032714462-9

and characteristics of an open BM among competitors within a cultural and creative enterprise. Recent profound changes and previous research have led us to select the architecture industry as particularly fertile ground for deepening our understanding of this research topic.

This chapter is structured around five parts. Firstly, we establish the theoretical framework of the research by defining the concept of an open BM and the stakes of opening it to competitors. The second part is dedicated to presenting and justifying our methodological choices. Given the novelty of the research object in the strategic management field, we decided to conduct a single and qualitative case study. The selection of a unique case related to our research object focused on the renovation project of the Montparnasse Tower in Paris. Thus, the third part is dedicated to the presentation of the architecture industry and the specific case of the Nouvelle AOM agency. The fourth part, focusing on the results, analyzes the characteristics and operation of a new architectural agency (Nouvelle AOM) resulting from the association of three competing agencies. Finally, the ultimate section is discussing the contribution of our research about open BMs, especially in the field of CCIs.

2 Theoretical background

2.1 The emergence of open BMs

A BM is a representation of how a company creates, delivers, and captures value (Chesbrough and Rosenbloom, 2002). The BM also specifies the key elements that enable a company to thrive by describing how it generates revenue, establishes partnerships, interacts with its customers, manages its resources, and positions itself in the market. In other words, the BM provides an overview of the strategic and economic logic that guides a company's activities, how it creates value, delivers it to its customers, and ensures its economic viability (Demil and Lecocq, 2010).

The literature in strategic management has identified three main dimensions of the BM. The first dimension is the value proposition, which corresponds to the various products and services offerings to the company's target customer segments through channels tailored to these offerings. This value proposition must differentiate itself from competitors' offerings (Chesbrough, 2010; Dahan et al., 2010). The second dimension is the value architecture, which corresponds to the organization of the company, including its organizational structure, governance type, mechanisms and management rules, culture and values, relationships with its partners, and its entire value chain (Johnson, Christensen, and Kagermann, 2008; Osterwalder and Pigneur, 2010). Finally, the third dimension, more financial, corresponds to value capture, also known as the economic equation, which refers to all costs and revenues generated by the organization (Chesbrough and Rosenbloom, 2002; Demil and Lecocq, 2010; Osterwalder and Pigneur, 2010; Teece, 2010).

Some recent research has emphasized the importance of developing innovative BMs because they offer numerous advantages. Innovative BMs allow companies to distinguish themselves from competitors with a new and distinctive value proposition in the market (Demil and Lecocq, 2010; Osterwalder and Pigneur, 2010; Bucherer, Eisert, and Gassmann, 2012). They also offer the opportunity to adapt more quickly to changes in the environment, thus ensuring their long-term relevance. Moreover, innovative BMs can lead to the discovery of new market opportunities, new customer segments, or new ways to meet consumer needs (Chesbrough, 2007; Bucherer et al., 2012). For example, some innovative BMs integrate processes and technologies that improve operational efficiency, resulting in reduced costs, better resource utilization, and overall optimization of operations (Teece, 2010). Finally, innovative BMs can also benefit stakeholders, such as customers, suppliers, employees, etc. Thus, the development of innovative BMs provides a powerful means for companies to remain competitive, create value, and adapt to rapidly changing environments, ensuring long-term sustainability (Demil and Lecocq, 2010; Bucherer et al., 2012).

The literature on innovative BMs has also emphasized the interest in open BMs and their innovation potential. An open BM can be defined as a collaborative BM integrating one or more partners, such as customers, suppliers, or any other external stakeholders (Chesbrough, 2007, 2010; Ritter and Lettl, 2018). The sharing of resources and expertise among partners within an open BM enables companies to be more innovative and create more value (Zott and Amit, 2010; Braun, 2015; Spieth, Laudien, and Meissner, 2020). For example, based on qualitative research in the automotive industry, Spieth et al. (2020) analyze how an open BM can be developed within the framework of strategic alliances between customer-supplier type partners. The researchers demonstrate that this type of BM improves industrial and logistical processes at the alliance level as well as at the level of each individual company. They thus highlight the positive effects of cooperation within an open BM, benefits that would accrue to all involved.

In recent years, research in strategic management on open BMs has developed and shows that open BM foster collaboration and innovation allowing companies to leverage external ideas and resources to develop new products and services (Chesbrough, 2010). These models promote shared value creation among various stakeholders, including customers, partners, leading to more robust and sustainable ecosystems. They offer greater flexibility and adaptability to market changes and technological advancements, as they rely on networks and collaborations rather than rigid internal structures (Saebi and Fos, 2015). Open BMs have also led to the emergence of new, innovative economic models, such as digital platforms, open markets, and innovation communities, disrupting many traditional sectors (Spieth and Meissner, 2018).

However, this approach primarily focuses on collaborations between non-competing companies. The studies and reflections on open innovation among competitors have been very rare. Moreover, there is a lack of research within the CCIs, despite the growing prevalence of cooperation among competitors in these sectors (Gundolf, Jaouen, and Gast, 2018; Pellegrin-Boucher and Roy, 2019). Furthermore, due to the highly dynamic and competitive nature of these environments, companies in these sectors are increasingly driven to develop innovative offerings that address consumer demands, even when the partners are also competitors (Gander and Rieple, 2004; Loots, Cnossen, and Van Witteloostuijn, 2018). Additionally, they are compelled to completely restructure their organizations (Dikova, Van Witteloostuijn, and Parker, 2017).

2.2 *Open BMs between competitors*

A growing number of studies indicate that in competitive and volatile environments, cooperative relationships between competitors, commonly referred to as coopetition strategies (Bengtsson and Kock, 2000), are increasingly acknowledged as effective methods to foster innovation and enhance performance. These strategies are characterized by the fact that the involved companies can both cooperate and compete with each other (Bengtsson and Kock, 2000; Gnyawali et al., 2016). They collaborate on certain activities or projects while remaining competitors on others, which allows for economies of scale, cost reduction, risk sharing, and exploration of new market opportunities (Czakon and Czernek, 2016; Ritala, 2012). Competing companies can, for example, join forces to develop new standards, share infrastructures, or create joint ventures to exploit business opportunities.

An increasing number of authors have also shown that this type of strategy promotes innovation through resource and expertise sharing (Bouncken and Fredrich, 2012; Park, Srivastava, and Gnyawali, 2014). These strategies are thus a source of performance, although they also generate tensions between partner companies due to the coexistence of a certain level of competition (Pellegrin-Boucher, Le Roy, and Gurău, 2013; Tidström, 2014). Companies must strike a delicate balance to avoid conflicts arising from competition while leveraging the benefits of cooperation. Cooperation among competitors is thus a complex strategy that requires skillful relationship management but offers significant benefits to companies when well managed.

In CCIs, some researchers have also shown in recent years that cooperative relationships between competitors are relevant strategies because they enable coping with environmental uncertainties and facilitate access to additional resources (Gundolf, Jaouen, and Gast, 2018; Pellegrin-Boucher and Roy, 2019). However, no research has yet studied the development or characteristics of open BMs among competitors. We have identified only one article on the subject that highlights the impacts on the performance of these open BMs (Ritala, Golnam, and Wegmann, 2013), but without examining their action mechanisms or organizational specifics.

Therefore, given the development and stakes of open BMs among competitors, our research question is as follows: how can cultural and creative enterprises construct a BM among competitors, and what are its main characteristics? In this investigation work, we rely on a unique case study conducted in the architecture industry: the renovation of the Montparnasse Tower in Paris. This renovation project is managed by three competing Parisian architectural firms that have created a specific open BM (Nouvelle AOM).

The next section describes our methodological choices for studying the characteristic elements and mechanisms of this type of BM.

3 Method: a qualitative case study

Our research aims to understand an emerging concept in the strategic management field: the construction of an open BM among competitors. In this regard, the choice to conduct a qualitative case study emerged as a suitable method in line with the recommendations of the literature (Eisenhardt, 1989; Yin, 2015). With this perspective in mind, we decided to explore the field of CCIs, and particularly the architecture industry, whose recent developments are directly linked to our research objective.

In accordance with the principles of qualitative case study research (Eisenhardt, 1989; Yin, 2015; Miles, Huberman, & Saldana, 2018), we collected primary and secondary data to develop an understanding of the case under study. The data collection period spanned from 2006 (the creation of the three individual agencies) to 2023.

Initially, we gathered secondary data to enhance our knowledge of the industry concerning key stakeholders, recent industry developments, the organization of the industry value chain, critical numerical data, the timeline of the tender process related to the renovation of the Montparnasse Tower, profiles of the three agencies at the core of our case study, etc. These secondary data were collected between 2018 and 2023 from various sources, such as the websites of the three agencies and Nouvelle AOM, interviews conducted by the partners in the press, public documents related to the tender process, statistical data on the French architecture industry, data published by the French architects' union, etc.

Subsequently, our research prompted the collection of primary empirical data to refine the understanding of the case and generate theoretical knowledge related to our research objective. Thus, thirteen semi-structured interviews were conducted between 2018 and 2022 with the partners of the architectural agencies affiliated with Nouvelle AOM (seven interviews) and various stakeholders involved in the project (six interviews: competing agencies, partners, industry experts). The collected data has been coded following the qualitative analysis principles (Miles, Huberman, & Saldana, 2018) and based on the themes and sub-themes at the core of the theoretical elements.

4 Case study presentation

4.1 *The architecture industry*

The architecture industry represents in France an approximated turnover of 54.8 billion euros (2020). The value chain of the architecture business can be divided into two separate activities. The first one is concerning the design of an architectural project. This activity implies artistic competences as well as knowledge concerning technical software and skills regarding various studies (technical, urban, economic, etc.). The second activity in the value chain concerns the construction part and supposes a coordination and control of the different stakeholders involved in this process.

Value creation is equally divided between these two activities. When it comes to the design and construction of big projects (i.e., an airport, a residential tower, a museum, etc.), architecture agencies are competing within a call for tender process. In this case, the client receives different propositions from agencies and selects the best one based on the project characteristics (its design, its cost, its risks, etc.).

Over the past two decades, the architecture industry has undergone numerous transformations impacting how architectural firms conceive and implement their strategies. Among these recent developments, one can mention the acceleration of globalization in the industry, the influence of dominant players and their brand strategy ("starchitects," such as Norman Foster, Jean Nouvel, Frank Gehry, etc.), the significant growth of sustainable materials and techniques, as well as the collaboration between competitors to enhance success in certain bids.

Regarding this last evolution, our previous work within the architecture industry led us to identify a major case of the creation of an agency among competitors within the framework of the tender (2017) for the renovation of the Montparnasse Tower in Paris. This 300-million-euro project garnered interest from numerous highly reputable architectural firms internationally but was won by the Nouvelle AOM agency, the result of a collaboration between three competing Parisian agencies. In our research, we thus selected the entity Nouvelle AOM as the unit of analysis to explore how three competing companies developed a BM among competitors to win a coveted bid and jointly lead the project. The following subsection revisits the key dates of the tender and the construction of the Nouvelle AOM BM between three competitors.

4.2 *The case of Nouvelle AOM*

In 2014, the city of Paris launched a program titled "Reinventing Paris" that aimed at modernizing the urban space of the French capital city. Among the major projects involved was the renovation of the 210-meter-tall Parisian skyscraper built in 1973: the Montparnasse Tower. In 2016, over 700 candidates responded to the tender for the renovation of this major and highly criticized building in the Parisian skyline. Among the candidates, seven agencies were selected for the final phase of the competition: Architecture Studio (France), Dominique Perrault Architecture (France), MAD Architects & DGLA (China), Nouvelle AOM (France), OMA (Netherlands), PLP Architecture (United Kingdom), and Studio Gang (United States).

In September 2017, the winner of the competition was announced: it was the project titled Nouvelle AOM born from the collaboration of three competing Parisian agencies founded in 2006: Franklin Azzi Architecture (40 employees), Chartier-Dalix Architectes (86 employees), and Hardel-Le Bihan Architectes (51 employees). Nouvelle AOM is a dedicated structure for the renovation project of the Montparnasse Tower, alongside the three independent agencies that retain their individual projects and activities. The renovation includes the addition of extra stories to the tower, a new envelope, the addition of green spaces and reprogramming of the activities located in the tower (a new hotel, some restaurants, shopping area, etc.). Among the reasons justifying the selection of the Nouvelle AOM project by the client are the combined size and complementary nature of the three agencies, the creative potential offered by this collaboration, and the innovative dimension of the project in terms of architecture.

Initially created in 2016 for the renovation project of the Montparnasse Tower, the Nouvelle AOM agency has since won other bids for architectural projects, alongside projects won individually by the three pre-existing and remaining agencies. Thus, the sustainability of this BM among competitors raises several questions related to our conceptual framework. Therefore, the next section is dedicated to a detailed analysis of this open BM between competitors in the architecture industry.

5 Results

5.1 Value proposition between competitors

The analysis of the empirical data collected first allowed us to understand how three competing architecture agencies developed and positioned the Nouvelle AOM BM alongside their respective BMs.

The creation of a dedicated entity positioned Nouvelle AOM as an independent structure targeting specific and innovative architectural projects. Concretely, Nouvelle AOM's value proposition was formalized and differentiated from that of existing agencies through an explicit and formalized agreement among the partners. Nouvelle AOM is intended to respond to calls for tenders that share similarities with the renovation project of the Montparnasse Tower: projects involving the renovation of existing buildings, the presence of a historical or emblematic character of the building, and a transformation in the building's use (e.g., transitioning from offices to residential).

This allowed the partners to clearly distinguish the tenders they collectively respond to (via Nouvelle AOM) from those they respond to individually (via their own agency). Interviews conducted with the partners illustrate that this was aimed from the outset of the project to reduce potential tensions arising from conflicts of interest. One partner mentions the concern to limit the emergence of potential tensions:

> We quickly understood that rules would be needed to manage all of this. And specially to see how Nouvelle AOM projects could coexist with our individual projects. Not to overshadow each other and not to put each other in difficulty. So, we decided to specify criteria on which we would respond together with Nouvelle AOM compared to projects we respond to solo.

This formal differentiation of Nouvelle AOM's value proposition appears as one of the factors justifying the sustainability of this BM and the additional projects won by the collective since four other tenders have been won by Nouvelle AOM in addition to the renovation of the Montparnasse Tower. One of the partners explains, "*We were able to quickly envision projects and a long-term vision, unlike other partnerships in the past, because we established a specific and distinct organization, vision, and offering for Nouvelle AOM compared to our respective businesses.*"

Furthermore, the establishment of the Nouvelle AOM BM has strengthened the innovative nature of the value proposition. Indeed, the collaboration between the three competing agencies has had positive effects on creativity and idea generation within the new BM. The pooling of skills and the synergies encountered have also benefited the three individual agencies, as mentioned by one of the partners:

> Since the development of Nouvelle AOM, we have worked on innovative projects that can boost the development of new skills, especially technical skills. For example, in terms of the materials we use, we have developed expertise in eco-responsible construction (...) the same goes for renovation techniques. We have gained skills for our offers making us the best in the sector.

5.2 *Value architecture between competitors*

Regarding the value architecture of Nouvelle AOM, our empirical data allows us to understand how the competing partners developed a distinct and independent BM from their individual ones.

This intention initially led to the creation of an independent legal entity in which the three individual agencies invested equally (33% each). Specific governance rules were also formalized regarding the criteria for responding to calls for tenders (joint response or solo response), along with a balanced and rotating annual presidency among the members of the three associated agencies. This helped to limit tensions and "preserve the egos" of the associated architects, as highlighted by one of them during an interview:

> From the outset, we thought about balancing the forces at play. We quickly agreed that there needed to be a rotating presidency to ensure clarity and to avoid wasting time on issues of pride in the operation of Nouvelle AOM (...) as the company is an SAS, there is a president and a CEO, so for the sake of fairness, the president changes every year, and each fiscal year we have a different president rotating among the three agencies. We have a principle of equivalence among the three agencies. And the CEO also changes, we try to have a president and a CEO from two different agencies. It has been like this since the beginning, and it happens naturally.

The treatment of empirical data also allows us to understand how the Nouvelle AOM BM operates organizationally and humanly. The partners decided from the preparation stage of the response to the Montparnasse Tower tender to create specific project offices and locate them in the tower itself. Thus, Nouvelle AOM was immediately an organization independent of the pre-existing individual agencies. This allowed the partners to separate activities conducted between competitors from those conducted individually. One partner explains:

> This was something that was considered very early on. From the outset, we needed to separate our joint activities from our individual ones. This ensured that we could both feel more confident and comfortable with collective projects and continue to invest freely in our individual activities or with other partners.

The creation of Nouvelle AOM therefore prompted the recruitment of around twenty human resources dedicated specifically to projects of this BM. A manager from the Nouvelle AOM agency, not from the three pre-existing agencies, was also recruited to ensure some neutrality in project and team management. The same goes for investment in dedicated material resources for Nouvelle AOM, not from the individual agencies. The partners met during this research emphasized the initial desire to develop new skills within Nouvelle AOM and to create a neutral and peaceful environment for employees.

Furthermore, the partners engaged in a reflection on the functioning of the Nouvelle AOM entity and its articulation with the constraints related to their individual agencies. Thus, the partners decided to establish rules for the distribution of work in terms of schedules. Two half-days per week (Monday and Friday mornings) are dedicated to advancing Nouvelle AOM BM projects. This rule forced the partners to be simultaneously present on-site bi-weekly and to separate their working time between individual projects and Nouvelle AOM projects.

Additionally, they exchange contacts and utilize services, such as communication agencies, construction firms, and IT equipment suppliers. However, they refrain from sharing customer information associated with specific agencies. The partners of the three agencies are all aware that it is necessary to share many resources, but that certain information must also be protected.

Finally, the establishment of the new BM led to the sharing and development of both tangible and intangible resources. The collaboration among the three partners within Nouvelle AOM facilitated investments in cutting-edge and expensive equipment, including a laser cutting machine, 3D modeling technology, and the BIM tool. Additionally, the partnership allowed for the accumulation of intangible assets, such as enhanced communication capabilities, encompassing the creation of a website, management of press relations, accumulation of industry know-how, and expansion of professional networks.

5.3 Value capture between competitors

The question of value capture within Nouvelle AOM also raised several issues for the associated architects, particularly concerning the rules for cost and revenue allocation. Concerned with maintaining a balance of power and limiting the risk of tensions, the associates opted for an equitable distribution key for costs and revenues. Indeed, the analysis of the empirical case shows that the associates chose to bear the costs and benefit from the revenues equally, at 33% for each individual agency involved in Nouvelle AOM. This rule of equitable distribution was decided and formalized from the outset in conjunction with the governance rules mentioned earlier.

The question of value capture was also impacted by the sustainability of the Nouvelle AOM BM. The success encountered with the Montparnasse Tower tender quickly prompted the associates to jointly respond to other tenders. Thus, four other architectural projects have been won to date by this BM among competitors, alongside the activities of each individual agency.

The other projects won have enabled the Nouvelle AOM BM to sustain its activity and revenue in the face of high costs and deadline extensions encountered on the Montparnasse Tower project. Several legal challenges and certain exogenous events (e.g., the Covid crisis) have delayed the project delivery from 2024 to 2028.

Moreover, regarding revenues and costs, several points merit attention. Initially, revenues and costs generated by Nouvelle AOM were divided according to an egalitarian distribution formula formalized from the outset. This principle applied equally to other tenders secured by Nouvelle AOM. Secondly, the reputation of Nouvelle AOM contributed to the enhancement of revenue generated by individual agencies.

Table 9.1 Summary of the Nouvelle AOM open BM

BM dimensions		*Nouvelle AOM open BM between competitors*
Value proposition	Customer segments	Allocation of customer segments and projects between Nouvelle AOM and the three individual agencies
	Offer	Specialization of the Nouvelle AOM offering in certain types of architectural projects (renovation of buildings with a historical or emblematic character)
	Value creation	Enhanced innovation capacity through collaboration among the partners, resulting in higher-quality architectural projects that combine the expertise of the three agencies
Value architecture	Legal structure	Creation of an independent entity specifically dedicated to collective projects between competitors
	Governance	Development of a formal charter specifying rules for responding to calls for tender and governance (rotating presidency)
	Culture and values	Closer ties between the three agencies within the Nouvelle AOM, facilitated by inter-individual links and cultural and generational proximity
	Work organization	Recruitment of a new team dedicated to the Nouvelle AOM collective, with a manager from outside one of the three agencies to ensure neutrality. Sequencing of the week for associates (two half-days a week devoted to the Nouvelle AOM and the rest to their individual agencies)
	Material resources	Creation of a new workspace dedicated to the Nouvelle AOM group Acquisition of new resources specific to Nouvelle AOM (e.g., laser cutting equipment)
	Intangible resources	Joint acquisition of software, transfer and sharing of technical know-how. Creation of a dedicated joint website and development of a communication strategy
	Knowledge	Transferring and sharing knowledge about Nouvelle AOM projects (customers, calls for tender, etc.) and developing new knowledge. Protection of knowledge and data on individual agency projects
	Key partners	Pooling of contacts and services (communication agencies, construction companies and IT equipment suppliers) Non-sharing of customer information linked to individual agencies

(*Continued*)

Table 9.1 (Continued)

BM dimensions		*Nouvelle AOM open BM between competitors*
Value capture	Revenues	Revenue generated by Nouvelle AOM and shared based on an egalitarian distribution key formalized at the outset. Revenue generated by individual agencies favored by the reputation of Nouvelle AOM
	Costs	Costs generated by Nouvelle AOM projects and allocated based on a formalized egalitarian distribution key at the outset

From a strategic perspective, the sustainability of the BM among competitors appears relatively innovative compared to the more common practice of a temporary association among competitors for a single project, particularly in the architecture sector. One of the associates mentions this strategic intention to continue the BM among competitors in the long term:

> When Nouvelle AOM won the tender for the renovation of the Montparnasse Tower, we quickly realized that there would be other projects: our idea was innovative, different from what was being done in architecture. We were more creative, so it motivated us to go further together and win other tenders.

Table 9.1 provides a comprehensive overview of the key components comprising the BM of Nouvelle AOM in its competitive landscape. This synthesis encapsulates the fundamental aspects and strategies employed by Nouvelle AOM to develop and implement an open BM between competitors. It offers a consolidated view of the structural framework, operational processes, and strategic initiatives that characterize Nouvelle AOM's approach.

6 Research contribution

6.1 Theoretical contribution about open BM between competitors

The case study of Nouvelle AOM contributes to enrich the existing and growing literature about open BMs (Spieth et al, 2020; Teece 2010; Zott and Amitt, 2010; Braun, 2015). In particular, it explores the main characteristics of a BM between competitors, which represents a theoretical gap in the existing literature. Research focused on this topic is indeed almost non-existent even as cases of collaboration between competitors are multiplying in all sectors (Ritala, Golnam, and Wegmann, 2013), particularly in the CCIs (Dikova et al., 2017; Gundolf et al., 2018; Pellegrin-Boucher and Roy 2019).

Our research first shows that in the context of an open BM between competitors, the value proposition must differ from those of individual BMs. A differentiated value proposition makes it possible to develop innovative offers, seize new market opportunities, and diversify its resources and skills without competing with individual companies. It is also about differentiating customer segments in order to avoid excessive competition and tension within the open BM. The strategic issue that lies behind this idea is the long-term coexistence of both individual BMs and an open BM developed by competitors.

Secondly, the case study highlights some of the specificities concerning value architecture of a BM between competitors. Data analysis shows that it is in the interest of companies to set up a legal structure dedicated to the BM between competitors with a new organization, a specific work team, new resources, and formalized governance rules. The choice of a new manager, recruited specifically to manage the new BM within dedicated premises, also facilitates the establishment of a neutral leadership and climate. Balanced governance with fair rules and a rotating presidency ensures a good distribution of powers. The proximity of socio-cultural and generational profiles of partners also facilitates the construction and management of the BM between competitors. Concerning the resources and skills of the BM (Demil and Lecocq, 2010; Ritter and Lettl, 2018), our research shows that the pooling of these resources and skills benefits not only the BM between competitors but also individual BMs in the way that it increases their capacity for innovation. However, in the context of a BM between competitors, it is necessary to protect information about individual projects and customer data associated with individual projects conducted by independent BMs.

Finally, regarding the value capture of an open BM between competitors, our results show that they can benefit from an equitable distribution of revenues and costs, provided that these distribution rules have been formalized upstream. Our research also highlights that the creation of a BM between competitors allows to generate new revenues for the open BM but also for individual companies' BMs. The companies engaged into the open BM benefit from the notoriety acquired by such a BM as well as the sharing of resources and skills that lead to a greater capacity for innovation and creativity. Table 9.2 summarizes the main dimensions of an open BM between competitors.

6.2 *Managerial implications for architecture and CCIs*

From a managerial perspective, our research shows that architecture agencies can benefit from creating an open BM with competitors. This strategy appears as highly relevant for reaching new customer segments, improving a market visibility, accessing new resources, developing new skills, and increasing an innovative capacity (Dahan et al., 2010; Demil and Lecocq, 2010; Teece, 2010). The case study also highlights an increase in product and service innovations (new, more innovative, and sustainable

Table 9.2 Managing an open BM between competitors

BM dimensions		*Application to an open BM between competitors*
Value proposition	Customer segments	Targeting dedicated market segments for the individual BMs and the open BM between competitors
	Offer	Differentiating the offer between individual BMs and the open BM between competitors Benefiting from the increased innovative capacity Communicating about the added value for clients
	Value creation	Enlarging the value creation through open BM between competitors
Value architecture	Legal structure	Creating a dedicated legal structure for the open BM between competitors (benefits include autonomy, reduced tensions, management of knowledge sharing/protection)
	Governance	Balanced governance between competitors through the rotating presidency of the open BM between competitors
	Culture and values	Socio-cultural proximity between partners facilitates creation and coordination of the open BM between competitors
	Work organisation	Creating a specific work team for the open BM between competitors, aside from the work teams of individual BMs
	Material and non-material resources	Sharing resources between competitors in the open BM benefits individual BMs
	Knowledge	Sharing knowledge between competitors and creating new knowledge within the open BM between competitors Protecting specific knowledge associated with individual projects
	Key partners	Sharing contacts concerning partners (e.g., suppliers) for the projects managed withing the open BM between competitors
Value capture	Revenues	Equal and formalized distribution of revenues between competitors within the open BM Taking benefits from additional revenues due to the positive impact of open BM between competitors on individual BMs
	Costs	Equal and formalized share of costs associated with projects managed through the open BM between competitors

offers corresponding to customer expectations), processes (new construction techniques, development of communication strategies that have not yet been developed), and organizational innovation (new organization and specific governance) that benefits all companies and projects carried out both jointly and individually.

The development of a BM between competitors thus accelerates the growth of individual companies that benefit from easier access to new skills and resources. The experience, market visibility, and notoriety provided by the open BM between competitors also allow each company to attract new customers and undertake innovative individual projects. Following the recent evolutions of the architecture industry, such a strategy appears as a successful way to remain competitive in a more aggressive and international environment. Architecture agencies that are able to simultaneously manage their own individual BM and an open BM with competitors may become more competitive and more attractive for clients. Our research contributed to the identification of some key success factors (see Table 9.2) for architecture agencies that could be interested in developing an open BM with some of their competitors.

Beyond the specific case of the architecture industry, our results can also be discussed in other CCIs. Indeed, our findings emphasize the importance of studying and developing strategies between competitors in CCIs, in accordance with what had already been suggested by some researchers (Gundolf et al., 2018; Pellegrin-Boucher and Roy, 2019). Indeed, several CCIs share similarities with the architecture industry in terms of the level of competition, the development of dominant international players, the specific role played by innovation or the increasing environmental issues to name a few. These evolutions suggest that individual companies can sometimes face bigger challenges in terms of development and innovation compared to what it used to be in the past.

Therefore, cooperation with competitors within an open BM appears as a solution for remaining competitive and guaranteeing the access to resources and clients. Parallels can be made with what can be observed in the edition industry where individual and competitive bookstores can share online platforms to reach online customers. We can also think about cooperation between competitive motion pictures and/or television studios for a specific film production that requires a combination of complementary resources. Open BMs between competitors have also been observed in the video games industry where innovation plays a key role in the success of a product and can lead competitors to jointly develop a new game. Conducting some empirical investigation in these other CCIs could be a stimulating way of testing and enriching the observations made in the architecture industry in our research.

7 Conclusion

The aim of this research was to highlight new forms of open BMs that are little studied in the strategic management literature. The case study of the Montparnasse Tower renovation project enabled us to explore how three competing architectural firms constructed an open BM between competitors and what its characteristics are.

We also show that the development of this type of BM gives the firms concerned access to new resources and new capacities for innovation, which accelerates their growth. These results enrich our knowledge of open BMs (Teece, 2010; Zott and Amit, 2010; Ritter and Lettl, 2018;), but also deepen our research into innovation and growth strategies in the CCIs (Gander, 2004; Dikova et al, 2017; Loots et al, 2018; Donelli et al, 2021; Poisson-de Haro et al, 2022).

These industries represent dynamic sectors that evolve rapidly in changing and uncertain environments. Innovation strategies in these industries are therefore of particular importance to remain competitive, stimulate growth and meet changing consumer expectations. In particular, the integration of partners within open BMs can stimulate innovation and creativity and generate synergies that benefit everyone and give them a competitive advantage.

Beyond the architecture industry, our research highlights that companies belonging to the CCIs could benefit from the construction of an open BM between competitors. It would therefore be interesting to extend this research by exploring similar strategies put in place in other sectors, such as the film industry, where competing production studios develop films and series, or the video games industry, where competing publishers co-develop new offerings.

A better understanding of open BMs between competitors would be extremely useful both for researchers and for the managers of cultural and creative businesses, who must constantly push back the boundaries of innovation in order to prosper in a constantly changing environment.

References

Bengtsson, Maria, et Sören Kock. 2000. "'Coopetition' in Business Networks—to Cooperate et Compete Simultaneously." *Industrial Marketing Management* 29, no. 5: 411–426.

Bouncken, Ricarda B., et Viktor Fredrich. 2012. "Coopetition: Performance Implications and Management Antecedents." *International Journal of Innovation Management* 16, no. 5: 1250028.

Braun, Andreas. 2015. "Linking Business Model and Open Innovation - Success and Failure of Collaborations." *International Journal of Entrepreneurship and Innovation Management* 19, no. 1/2: 59–76.

Bucherer, Eva, Uli Eisert, et Oliver Gassmann. 2012. "Towards Systematic Business Model Innovation: Lessons from Product Innovation Management." *Creativity and Innovation Management* 21, no. 2: 183–198.

Chesbrough, Henry. 2007. "Business Model Innovation: It's Not Just about Technology Anymore." *Strategy & Leadership* 35, no. 6: 12–17.

Chesbrough, Henry. 2010. "Business Model Innovation: Opportunities and Barriers." *Long Range Planning* 43, no. 2–3: 354–363.

Chesbrough, Henry, et Richard S. Rosenbloom. 2002. "The Role of the Business Model in Capturing Value from Innovation: Evidence from Xerox Corporation's Technology Spin-Off Companies." *Industrial and Corporate Change* 11, no. 3: 529–555.

Czakon, Wojciech, et Katarzyna Czernek. 2016. “The Role of Trust-Building Mechanisms in Entering into Network Coopetition: The Case of Tourism Networks in Poland.” *Industrial Marketing Management* 57: 64–74.

Dahan, Nicolas M., Jonathan P. Doh, Jennifer Oetzel, et Michael Yaziji. 2010. “Corporate-NGO Collaboration: Co-creating New Business Models for Developing Markets.” *Long Range Planning* 43, no. 2–3: 326–342.

Demil, Benoît, et Xavier Lecocq. 2010. “Business Model Evolution: In Search of Dynamic Consistency.” *Long Range Planning* 43, no. 2–3: 227–246.

Dikova, Dessislava, Arjen Van Witteloostuijn, et Simon Parker. 2017. “Capability, Environment and Internationalization Fit, and Financial and Marketing Performance of MNEs’ Foreign Subsidiaries.” *Cross Cultural & Strategic Management* 24, no. 3: 405–435.

Donelli, Chiara C., Simone Fanelli, et Antonello Zangrandi. 2021. “Inside and Outside the Boardroom: Collaborative Practices in the Performing Arts Sector.” *International Journal of Arts Management* 24, no. 1: 48–62.

Eisenhardt, Kathleen M. 1989. “Building Theories from Case Study Research.” *Academy of Management Review* 14, no. 4: 532–550.

Gander, Jonathan, et Alison Rieple. 2004. “How Relevant is Transaction Cost Economics to Inter-Firm Relationships in the Music Industry?” *Journal of Cultural Economics* 28, no. 1: 57–79.

Gnyawali, Devi R., et Byung-Jin Park. 2009. “Co-opetition and Technological Innovation in Small and Medium-Sized Enterprises: A Multilevel Conceptual Model.” *Journal of Small Business Management* 47, no. 3: 308–330.

Gundolf, Katherine, Annabelle Jaouen, et Johanna Gast. 2018. “Motives for Strategic Alliances in Cultural and Creative Industries.” *Creativity and Innovation Management* 27, no. 2: 148–160.

Laermans, Rudi. 2012. “‘Being in Common’: Theorizing Artistic Collaboration.” *Performance Research* 17, no. 6: 94–102.

Loots, Ellen, Boukje Cnossen, et Arjen Van Witteloostuijn. 2018. “Compete or Cooperate in the Creative Industries? A Quasi-experimental Study with Dutch Cultural and Creative Entrepreneurs.” *International Journal of Arts Management* 20, no. 2: 20–31.

Miles, Matthew B., Michael Huberman, et Johnny Saldana. 2018. *Qualitative Data Analysis: A Methods Sourcebook*. Thousand Oaks, CA: Sage Publications.

Mina, Andrea, Elif Bascavusoglu-Moreau, et Alan Hughes. 2014. “Open Service Innovation and the Firm’s Search for External Knowledge.” *Research Policy* 43, no. 5: 853–866.

Osterwalder, Alexander, et Yves Pigneur. 2010. *Business Model Generation: A Handbook for Visionaries, Game Changers, and Challengers*. New York, NY: Wiley.

Pellegrin-Boucher, Estelle, Frédéric Le Roy, et Călin Gurău. 2013. “Coopetitive Strategies in the ICT Sector: Typology and Stability.” *Technology Analysis & Strategic Management* 25, no. 1: 71–89.

Pellegrin-Boucher, Estelle, et Pierre Roy. 2019. “Dynamique de la Coopétition Commerciale avec Appels D’offres: Le Cas des Cabinets D’architectes.” *Management International* 23, no. 2: 115–126.

Poisson-de Haro, Serge, Alvaro Espejo, and Ignasi Martí. 2022. “Business Model Evolution and Entrepreneurial Adaptation of Festivals: The Case of Santiago a Mil.” *International Journal of Arts Management* 24, no. 2: 77–95.

Porter, Michael E. 1996. “What Is Strategy?” *Harvard Business Review* 74, no. 6: 61–78.

Ritala, Paavo, Arash Golnam, et Alain Wegmann. 2013. "Coopetition-based Business Models: The Case of Amazon.com." *Industrial Marketing Management* 43, no. 2: 236–249.

Ritter, Thomas, et Christopher Lettl. 2018. "The Wider Implications of Business-model Research." *Long Range Planning* 51, no. 1: 1–8.

Spieth, Patrick, Sven M. Laudien, et Svenja Meissner. 2020. "Business Model Innovation in Strategic Alliances: A Multi-layer Perspective." *R&D Management* 51, no. 1: 24–39.

Teece, David J. 2010. "Business Models, Business Strategy and Innovation." *Long Range Planning* 43, no. 2–3: 172–194.

Tidström, Annika. 2014. "Managing Tensions in Coopetition." *Industrial Marketing Management* 43, no. 2: 261–271.

Wright, Stephen. 2004. "The Delicate Essence of Artistic Collaboration." *Third Text* 18, no. 6: 533–545.

Yin, Robert K. 2015. *Qualitative Research from Start to Finish*. New York, NY: Guilford Publications.

Zott, Christoph, and Raphael Amit. 2010. "Business Model Design: An Activity System Perspective." *Long Range Planning* 43, no. 2–3: 216–226.

Index

Made in the USA
Monee, IL
12 November 2026

a056f6f2-e341-4ef4-a5c3-33d19c790445R02